T0304052

ROUTLEDGE LIBRARY EDITIONS: INDUSTRIAL RELATIONS

Volume 15

IMPROVING INDUSTRIAL RELATIONS

IMPROVING INDUSTRIAL RELATIONS

The Advisory Role of ACAS

ERIC ARMSTRONG
AND
ROSEMARY LUCAS

Routledge
Taylor & Francis Group

LONDON AND NEW YORK

First published in 1985 by Croom Helm

This edition first published in 2025
by Routledge
4 Park Square, Milton Park, Abingdon, Oxon OX14 4RN

and by Routledge
605 Third Avenue, New York, NY 10158

Routledge is an imprint of the Taylor & Francis Group, an informa business

British Library Cataloguing in Publication Data
A catalogue record for this book is available from the British Library

ISBN: 978-1-032-81770-5 (Set)
ISBN: 978-1-032-84796-2 (Volume 15) (hbk)
ISBN: 978-1-032-84855-6 (Volume 15) (pbk)
ISBN: 978-1-003-51532-6 (Volume 15) (ebk)

DOI: 10.4324/9781003515326

Publisher's Note
The publisher has gone to great lengths to ensure the quality of this reprint but points out that some imperfections in the original copies may be apparent.

Disclaimer
The publisher has made every effort to trace copyright holders and would welcome correspondence from those they have been unable to trace.

Improving Industrial Relations

The Advisory Role of ACAS

Eric Armstrong and Rosemary Lucas

CROOM HELM
London • Sydney • Dover, New Hampshire

©1985 E.G.A. Armstrong and R.E. Lucas
Croom Helm Ltd, Provident House, Burrell Row,
Beckenham, Kent BR3 1AT

Croom Helm Australia Pty Ltd, First Floor,
139 King Street, Sydney, NSW 2001, Australia

British Library Cataloguing in Publication Data

Armstrong, Eric
  Improving industrial relations: the advisory
  role of ACAS.
  1. Advisory, Concilliation and Arbitration
  Service — History
  I. Title II. Lucas, Rosemary
  354.410083'2   HD5545

  ISBN 0-7099-0554-8

Croom Helm, 51 Washington Street, Dover,
New Hampshire 03820, USA

Library of Congress Cataloging in Publication Data

Armstrong, E. G. A. (Eric George Abbott)
  Improving Industrial Relations.

  Includes Index.
  1. Great Britain. Advisory Conciliation and
Arbitration Service — History. 2. Industrial Relations
— Great Britain — History. I. Lucas, Rosemary.
II. Title.
HD5545.A6A76   1985   331'.0941   85-6638
ISBN 0-7099-0554-8

Printed and bound in Great Britain by
Biddles Ltd, Guildford and King's Lynn

CONTENTS

TABLES AND FIGURES

Tables

Figures

ACKNOWLEDGEMENTS

We wish to thank the following for permission to
quote copyright material:

Industrial Relations Research and Publications Unit,
University of Nottingham, 'The advisory function of
ACAS: a preliminary appraisal of the advisory visit'
by Armstrong and Lucas in Industrial Relations
Journal Spring 1984 and 'The lessons of the
Commission on Industrial Relations' attempts to
reform workplace industrial relations' by John
Purcell in Industrial Relations Journal, Summer
1979.

HMSO, with the permission of the Controller

Ministry of Labour and National Service, Industrial
Relations Handbook 1953, reprinted 1955. Ministry
of Labour, Industrial Relations Handbook 1961,
reprinted 1964. Report of Royal Commission on
Trade Unions' and Employers' Associations 1965-
1968, Cmnd.3623, June 1968. White Paper, In Place
of Strife - A Policy for Industrial Relations
Cmnd.3888, Jan.1969. ACAS First Annual Report 1975.

MCB University Press 'What is Good Industrial
Relations?' by John R. Dobson, Employee Relations,
4, 2, 1982. and 'The Advisory Function of ACAS -
A Preliminary Appraisal of In-depth Work' by
Armstrong and Lucas, Personnel Review, No.4 1983.

LIST OF ABBREVIATIONS

ACAS	Advisory Conciliation and Arbitration Service
CAS	Conciliation and Advisory Service
CBI	Confederation of British Industry
CIR	Commission on Industrial Relations
EPA 75	Employment Protection Act 1975
GFTU	General Federation of Trade Unions
HEO	Higher Executive Officer
IRO	Industrial Relations Officer
MPS	Manpower and Productivity Service
PASIRO	Period Appointment Senior Industrial Relations Officer
PIRO	Principal Industrial Relations Officer
SEO	Senior Executive Officer
SIRO	Senior Industrial Relations Officer
SMA	Senior Manpower Adviser
TUC	Trades Union Congress

PREFACE

"How far that little candle throws his beams!
So shines a good deed in a naughty world"
                Shakespeare: Merchant of Venice

        The primary purpose of this book is to present
and discuss the findings of research into the
advisory function of the Advisory, Conciliation and
Arbitration Service (ACAS). ACAS is probably more
widely known for its attempts to resolve industrial
disputes, usually through conciliation, than for
its endeavours, by advisory means, to improve industrial relations by, for example, reforming procedures and payment systems. And yet roughly four
times as many man-hours are devoted to advisory
work as to collective conciliation work. Such a
ratio suggests that not only might there be interesting things to discover about the ways in which
ACAS advisers carry out their duties but, more
importantly, a need to find out whether the advice
given is valued by those who receive it. It was
from such basic assumptions that the research was
undertaken.
        During 1982 and 1983 more than half of the
total 100 or so advisory staff were interviewed
and evaluative evidence was gathered from all
nine ACAS regions, by questionnaire, from 548
ACAS clients. That sizeable sample of 460 company
and 88 local trade union responses was supplemented
by questionnaire responses from 80 institutions
intimately involved in or closely concerned with
industrial relations. These institutions included
employers' associations, national trade unions,
management consultants, personnel management and
industrial relations training bodies. In this way,
a multi-perspective view of the ACAS advisory role
has been developed. It is submitted that such a

view is important, even essential, to the formation of a balanced judgement about the value of ACAS advisory work.

In all its operational modes of advising, conciliating in individual and collective differences and providing arbitration services, ACAS has a statutory duty, under the Employment Protection Act 1975, to improve industrial relations. Prima facie that is a formidable assignment and it is notable that a good industrial relations system is not defined by statute. Even so, improvement of industrial relations implies changes to the status quo. Such changes could be evaluated, for example, against any particular government's conception of good industrial relations, an influential model, or models, of a good industrial relations system formulated by industrial relations scholarship, an ACAS model of good industrial relations, the client's perception of what is good for him, his company, his trade union membership. But whose view should prevail if there was shown to be a marked lack of congruity between perceptions? Should the individual adviser, often working alone, mould his advice in conformity with any 'authorised' model of good industrial relations when his pragmatic experience tells him that this particular client will not accept the reforms required by the model?

In a mixed but essentially market economy it seems tenable to claim, certainly as a starting point, that the consumer of the advisory 'product', ie the client company or trade union is perhaps best placed to evaluate the worth of the particular ACAS advisory intervention. To claim otherwise is to assert that someone other than the adviser and the advised, ie some non-participant third party, knows better. This again raises the problems mentioned above.

On balance, it seemed better not to place our enquiries within an elaborate conceptual framework or with a view to testing some hypothesis related to good and bad industrial relations. Within the resources available, we were concerned to gather, in systematic fashion, as much information and comment as possible about the ACAS advisory role from those involved in or closely concerned with its operation. This is not to say that the questions we put were uninformed by theory and ideology – it could hardly be otherwise – but they were designed, in what we hope was their concern for objectivity, to encourage a good response rate from potential respondents. We believe, from the

evidence that will follow, that such a response rate
has been achieved.

By adopting this pragmatic approach and concentrating on the aggregation and analysis of evidence
gained directly from those involved in the advisory
transaction, it is hoped that any debate about particular features of advisory work will become a
better informed debate and less vulnerable to influential but possibly misguided preconceptions. One
such debatable feature concerns the issue of payment for advice. A strong abstract argument can
be advanced to support the idea that ACAS, like
commercial consultants, should be able to charge
for advisory work undertaken. For this to be done,
a change to the Employment Protection Act 1975 would
be necessary as ACAS is required under that Act to
give advice 'without charge'. While such a change
could cause technical difficulties, eg setting the
level of fees - and uncertainty, eg concerning the
organisational relationship between a paid advisory
service and a free conciliation service, the practical problems could conceivably be resolved.
Greater difficulties and much more uncertainty
surround the making of a judgement about the extent
to which payment, at any level, might affect the
employers' and trade unions' perceptions of ACAS
impartiality. As will be seen in Chapter One, the
restoration of employer and trade union confidence
in impartial conciliation and arbitration procedures
played the key part in the creation of ACAS. The
'free v fee' advice issue is a complex one and is
therefore discussed in some detail in Chapter Eight.
That discussion, and any discussions that might
follow from it, have the benefit of more than 500
client opinions, and those of other interested parties, to questions associated with the issue. That
is part of what was meant earlier by - a better
informed debate.

The payment question, although important, forms
but one of a number of issues that need to be taken
into account when trying to establish a properly
rounded assessment of the contribution the advisory
service makes to the achievement of the overall task
placed, by statute upon ACAS - that of improving
industrial relations. These issues which include -
the operational effectiveness of the advisory
function, the role of the ACAS Council, the development of an advisory policy, are discussed in the
later chapters. So too is that overall objective
of - improving industrial relations - which in
itself is a question begging term. But in terms of

what our sizeable sample of ACAS clients, companies and trade unions alike perceive to be improvement, there is clear substantial evidence that in many specific situations an improvement to industrial relations has resulted from advisory work. What that might signify in relation to what needs to be done, on some authoritative and widely acceptable reading of industrial relations generally, we would hesitate to say. But we would submit, without hesitation, that the advisory service emerges with appreciable credit from the investigation undertaken. In essence, that is the judgement of the clients and interested parties and that surely is what matters most of all.

In providing the information and evidence on which the above conclusion is based, a large number of people, some known and many unknown, have helped the researchers. We extend our warm appreciation to all concerned. Many individuals completed questionnaires in an impressively conscientious manner. Particular thanks are due to them. With ACAS Council approval generous access facilities were extended to us to interview advisers - and other staff, at all levels and in all regions. We thank all concerned for their unfailingly courteous co-operation.

An especial mention must be made of one person. Particularly warm thanks are extended to Mrs. Joyce Lea, our typist who with speed, accuracy and great good humour prepared both the typescript and the subsequent camera ready type for this book.

Chapter One

THE DEVELOPMENT OF THE ADVISORY FUNCTION

To understand the present nature of the ACAS
advisory function, it is necessary to give some
account of the way in which State provision of
advice on industrial relations has developed.
Unless this is done, it could wrongly be assumed
that the concern of governments to 'improve'
industrial relations by advisory means only began
with the formation of ACAS in 1974. In fact, the
ACAS advisory service represents important modifications to what has gone before rather than a
radical innovation or complete re-design of past
practice. The same holds true of the associated
conciliation and arbitration services. The historical outline which follows is of necessity short
but it does indicate the more important advisory
developments. It also identifies some of the more
important issues, for example, the uncertain
boundaries of the subject called industrial relations, which will be discussed in later chapters.
     As intimated above, the formation of ACAS in
1974 constituted the latest in a long line of
government decisions to accept some measure of
responsibility for the provision of conciliation,
arbitration and advisory services to those
involved in industrial relations. However, it
needs to be recognised that government concern to
provide assistance with the resolution of
industrial disputes has a much longer history than
the formal undertaking by government to provide
advice about industrial relations. The 1896
Conciliation Act empowered the Board of Trade to
inquire into the causes and circumstances of a
dispute, to conciliate, and, at the request of
both parties, to arbitrate. Such powers were later
transferred to the Ministry of Labour and that
Ministry's successors including the Department of

The Development of the Advisory Function

Employment. While the dispute resolution service
was strengthened in 1919 by the Industrial Courts
Act, industrial relations advice was not provided
by a government department on any formal basis or
significant scale until after 1945. During the
Second World War interest in the personnel management function had been stimulated by government
welfare and training measures. This interest had
been particularly marked in aircraft factories and
in 1945 specialist personnel staff were transferred
from the Ministry of Aircraft Production to the
Ministry of Labour and National Service to form
the Personnel Management Advisory Service. A few
years later the Ministry's Industrial Relations
Handbook stated that:

> The purpose of this Advisory Service is to
> stimulate the development of good personnel
> management by helping employers to formulate
> their personnel policy and to establish such
> organisation, or adopt such practical
> techniques, as are necessary to implement
> their policy. The advisers are available
> also to assist managements and personnel
> officers in the solution of personnel
> problems... 1)

The 1961 edition of the 'Ministry' Handbook
described the adviser's role slightly differently.

> In 1945 the Ministry of Labour set up a
> Personnel Management Advisory Service, the
> purpose of which was to assist in the
> improvement of relationships and manpower
> efficiency in industry by providing advice
> and information to employers on personnel
> management 2)

Parallel with this development had been the
formation of a small, separate but related advisory
service within the Ministry. The work of the
industrial relations officers concerned consisted
of 'advising on negotiating machinery and arbitration facilities and attempting conciliation in
cases of trade disputes.' 3)
In 1961 the personnel management and conciliation related advisory streams were merged to form
the Industrial Relations Service. A general
responsibility for providing advice and conciliation was placed on the new service. This remit
continued until 1968 when under a Labour Govern-

2

ment, much occupied with issues of industrial
productivity and efficiency, a Manpower and
Productivity Service (MPS) was established. At
regional level the staff and functions of the
Industrial Relations Service were taken over by
MPS which was charged with promoting efficiency at
the level of the individual firm. The number of
civil service advisers was increased and efficiency
experts were recruited from industry on a short-
term contract basis. Although the efficiency
objectives were revised in 1971 improved manpower
efficiency remained a major aim of the Service. In
March 1972 the Service was renamed the Conciliation
and Advisory Service (CAS) and its duties redefined
to harmonise with the Industrial Relations Code
of Practice. This code of practice prepared
by the Department of Employment, was concerned with the promotion of good industrial relations and constituted a fairly comprehensive
attempt by the State to give advice about industrial relations in published and authoritative form.
4) The Industrial Relations Act 1971 also established new individual employment rights relating to
unfair dismissal and thereby necessitated the
provision of additional and distinctive 5) conciliation resources for CAS.

Independence

In 1974 CAS became ACAS not because of changes to
the advisory function but as a result of a Labour
Government's determination to restore the confidence of employers and trade unions in the independent approach adopted by conciliation and arbitration services provided by the State. Employers
and trade unions had recently maintained that
restrictive incomes policies had inhibited conciliators and arbitrators from resolving disputes
and differences on their merits. Confidence in
the impartiality of the conciliation and arbitration service of the Department of Employment had
consequently been undermined. The Government
therefore detached the advisory, conciliation and
arbitration functions from the Department of
Employment and transferred them to a newly created
institution at first called the Conciliation and
Arbitration Service and re-titled (January 1975)
The Advisory, Conciliation and Arbitration Service
(ACAS) in order to reflect the complete range of
the Service's work. In a letter (8 August 1974)
to the Service's first chairman, the Secretary of

3

State for Employment, Mr Michael Foot stated:

> It is of course essential...that...the Service
> should be, and be seen to be, independent and
> so attract and retain the co-operation and
> support of all sectors of employment. So far
> as the Government is concerned, it will not
> seek to interfere in the activities of the
> Service. 6)

On 1 January 1976 ACAS became a statutory body
under the Employment Protection Act, 1975 which
made plain the independence to which Mr Foot had
referred.

> The functions of the Service and of its officers
> and servants shall be performed on behalf of
> the Crown, but (apart from accountability for
> accounts) the Service shall not be subject to
> directions of any kind from any Minister of
> the Crown as to the manner in which it is to
> exercise any of its functions under any
> enactment. 7)

That central support for independence is
buttressed in other ways. Oversight of the
Service's operation is the responsibility of a
Council consisting of representatives of employers
and trade unions, and a group of independent people
including the Chairman. A wide measure of ACAS
managerial discretion is exercised concerning the
circumstances and timing of interventions into
industrial relations problems and issues. This
is consistent with the manner of operation
referred to in statute. Nevertheless, the con-
stitutionally established independence requires
qualification and to be placed in a subtler
context. ACAS is funded by the State, the scale
and status of its manpower resources are monitored
and influenced by the Department of Employment
and the Secretary of State, after consultation with
interested parties, appoints the members of Council.
Even so, the volume of conciliation and arbitration
work undertaken by ACAS (cf. ACAS Annual Reports)
suggests that confidence in the independence of
the dispute resolution services has been restored
and maintained. An appreciable amount of advisory
work has also been carried out. The extent to
which this may be due to the perceived independence
of the new Service is not self-evident and is one
of the questions addressed in this book.

The Development of the Advisory Function

The basic remit given to ACAS in regard to advisory work was made plain by the Employment Protection Act 1975. Section 4(1) provides that:

The Service shall, if it thinks fit, on request or otherwise, provide, without charge, to employers, employers' associations, workers and trade unions such advice as it thinks appropriate on any matter concerned with industrial relations or employment policies, including the following -

There follows a list of specific industrial relations topics such as - procedures for avoiding and settling disputes and workers' grievances; payment systems, including job evaluation and equal pay. The nature of these and related advisory duties, for example, to issue Codes of Practice, will be explored later.

The creation of an independent advisory service is clearly one salient feature of the history of that service. Other historical developments and features of consequence are now briefly discussed.

As indicated above, State assistance with conflict resolution had been in operation for some fifty years before the advisory function was established. This suggests that a succession of governments had set greater store by the patching up of quarrels than endeavouring to remedy perceived or suspected industrial relations deficiencies. Apart from the largely ill-fated attempts of the Commission on Industrial Relations (CIR) 8) to reform troublesome aspects of industrial relations much the same situation has obtained since the creation of the advisory service in 1945. Post-war governments, of all political persuasions, have tended to regard industrial conflict with disfavour. It was, for example, a Labour Government that introduced in 1969 a White Paper with the revealing title of In Place of Strife. Whatever reasons a government may have for tackling a particular strike or the strike 'problem', there are certain factors, in addition to the obvious ones of economic and political damage, which may help to explain why a higher priority has been given to dispute settlement (principally through conciliation) than advisory work. These factors might be labelled visibility and measurement.

The Development of the Advisory Function

Visibility and Measurement

The employment relationship is premised on the
basic assumption that people go to work not in
order to strike or be locked out - but to work.
A strike or lockout, whether held to be justified
or not, is regarded as a breakdown in normal
employment relationships and therefore at some
point - 'something ought to be done about it'.
Because industrial action does constitute a breakdown in relationships it tends to be reported,
even publicised, dependent on the scale of the
industrial action. In short, the disruption can
become highly visible and may well damage the
interests of parties not directly involved in the
dispute. Such observable conditions lend themselves to attempted conciliation by an independent
party. In contrast, an employer and his workforce
who enjoy amicable relationships may long have
accepted a payment system tacitly acknowledged to
be highly inefficient and possibly damaging to
future commercial and employment prospects. Conceivably, this form of industrial relations
inefficiency could be as harmful to the interested
parties as some instances of industrial action but
it may well remain invisible to the advisory
service because no signal is received from the
problem situation.
    Of the four main methods - conciliation,
mediation, arbitration, inquiry - available to
the State for resolving disputes, conciliation is
the method most extensively used. This is because
the solution, if there is one to the dispute,
results essentially from the work and interaction
of the parties themselves with the conciliator
serving as a vital catalyst in the social processes
involved. To put the issue of solution, and
therefore of achievement, starkly, conciliation
succeeds if it brings about a resumption of normal
working relationships - under whatever terms. In
1982 ACAS completed 1634 conciliation cases. In
342 of these cases conciliation was unsuccessful
but in the remaining 1292 cases conciliation
resulted in 'a settlement or progress towards a
settlement'. 9) In 79% of cases therefore conciliation could be held to be successful. This
constitutes an important measure of the effectiveness of conciliation work. Additional but more
subjective and piecemeal measures can be devised,
for example, the estimated savings achieved by an
earlier, conciliated return to work in a strike

6

situation than would have been the case had conciliation not been attempted. No such measures
are available for advisory work. Recommendations,
for example, concerning pay structure reform, may
take time to implement. Assessing the effects of
the implementation may require an additional period
of time and entail recognition of new factors that
have entered the original situation. It is highly
unlikely that advisory work can ever be associated
with the visible kind of success that may accompany
the conciliated settlement of a major dispute.

There is another difficulty associated with the
measurement of the effectiveness of advice. This
also can best be illustrated by comparison with
the conciliation function. A conciliated settlement is considered a success because the dispute is
over and the industrial relations situation, on a
peace restored measure, is improved. If advice is
offered in situation A and is acted upon we have
situation B. But how can it be known whether
industrial relations in situation B are better
than those in situation A? The 'simple' test of
the ending of a dispute is not available. The
Employment Protection Act, 1975 gives no definition
of good industrial relations although it charges
ACAS with the general duty of 'promoting the
improvement of industrial relations'. 10) While
the reluctance of legislators to define good
industrial relations is perhaps understandable
the adviser, often working alone has to judge how
best to measure what he first finds in a 'problem'
situation against some measure or model of good
or at least better industrial relations. We shall
return to this theme later.

From the foregoing, it would seem inherent in
the differing nature of the processes of conciliation and advising that there will remain a
greater public awareness of the conciliation 11)
function of ACAS than of its advisory function.
And yet the ratio of advisory to collective
conciliation manpower resources is of the order
of 4 : 1. This points up the need to look at the
advisory service with some care.

Moving on from issues of visibility and
measurement, the historical development of the
terms of reference for the advisory function repays
attention. Two questions in particular require
consideration. At whom is the advice to be
directed? What should be the subject matter of
the advice?

The Development of the Advisory Function

Terms of Reference

It will have been noticed that the quotations describing the early activities of the advisory service referred to 'helping employers', 'to assist managements and personnel officers', 'providing advice and information to employers on personnel management'. The subsequent advisory work undertaken by MPS and later by CAS was directed essentially at the individual firm, and by implication at management, with efficiency objectives very much in mind. The other advisory activity of this period was described as 'advising on negotiating machinery and arbitration facilities'. While such work would obviously entail discussions with trade unions, and while the personnel management/efficiency advisory function would also necessitate some involvement with workpeople and their representatives, the essential remit of the advisory service reflected a <u>formal</u> emphasis on a unilateral approach to the improvement of industrial relations by working primarily with and through management. The advisory remit of ACAS is formulated quite differently and demonstrates what might be termed an open and formally announced bilateral approach to advisory work. Statute provides that advice shall be given to 'employers, employers' associations, workers and trade unions'. 12)

In terms of advisory <u>availability</u> therefore, ACAS is required to be even handed. Commonsense suggests that the use made of that availability by employers and unions/workpeople is likely to be uneven and to fluctuate over time. This issue will also be discussed later and has been commented on in earlier work. 13) The important present point is that employers and employed have been given equal status as potential clients of the advisory service, a situation that did not obtain before the creation of ACAS.

During a period spanning nearly forty years it would be surprising if changes to the subject matter of advice included in the service's terms of reference had not been experienced. In broad terms however, these changes tend to be ones of emphasis rather than topic. Reference has already been made to the linking of personnel management policies and practices with manpower efficiency in the first years of the advisory service. The efficiency objective was given particular emphasis when the Manpower and

8

The Development of the Advisory Function

Productivity Service was formed in 1968. This
expanded service sought 'to promote industrial,
commercial and administrative efficiency generally
within the economy by means of action at the level
of the individual firm'. 14) To this rather
ambitious end not only were work study specialists
recruited but accountants as well. This expansion
of objectives from manpower efficiency to general
business efficiency caused a certain amount of
disquiet and:

> When the work of the Service was reviewed in
> May 1971 the Secretary of State announced
> that it would in future concentrate on work
> related to the manpower and industrial
> relations functions of the Department. In
> addition to conciliation in industrial
> disputes the Service would continue to
> provide advice to industry on such matters
> as the efficient use of manpower, labour
> productivity, labour turnover and absenteeism,
> payment systems and personnel practices. It
> would not concern itself with questions of
> general efficiency outside these fields
> except to the extent necessary to carry out
> its main tasks. 15)

This reduction of emphasis on efficiency
objectives was to continue. Under Section 1 of the
Employment Protection Act, 1975, ACAS as an entity
is 'charged with the general duty of promoting the
improvement of industrial relations, and in
particular of encouraging the extension of
collective bargaining and the development and,
where necessary, reform of collective bargaining
machinery'. Under Section 4 of the same Act, as
has been pointed out earlier, the advisory arm
of ACAS can give advice 'on any matter concerned
with industrial relations or employment policies...'
A list of eleven broad topics follows. Neither
the 'general' nor the 'particular' duty refers to
general business efficiency or specific manpower
efficiency. The same holds true regarding the
topics listed under Section 4. Terms such as
'productivity' or 'labour productivity' do not
appear. In short, no explicit reference is made
to efficiency considerations or objectives.
However, among the eleven topics given as examples,
there appear '(i) manpower planning, labour
turnover and absenteeism'. All three terms
obviously carry strong connotations of the desir-

ability of improving manpower efficiency.

In short, whereas general efficiency and later manpower efficiency used to be specific objectives, this is no longer the case. Such objectives, if there at all, are now implicit. Whether this change of emphasis has made any real difference to the effectiveness of the advisory work carried out must, in the absence of past research into the matter, remain a moot point. In any event, the tangible changes resulting from the changes of emphasis in the wording on efficiency may be more shadow than substance. Much depends on how the duty to 'improve industrial relations' is inter-preted and made operational by ACAS. 'Bad' industrial relations are not usually associated with business efficiency. If the bad relations become less bad or improve to 'good', business efficiency may well improve. Furthermore, ACAS can advise 'on any matter concerned with industrial relations or employment policies...'(emphasis added). Neither 'any matter' nor 'industrial relations' are defined in the statute. Prima facie therefore, ample scope exists for marking out the boundaries and content of the subject of industrial relations in a flexible rather than a tightly drawn manner. This discretion is further strengthened by the statutory choice afforded to the Service to give 'such advice as it thinks appropriate'. The weight given to efficiency or other matters 'concerned with industrial relations' is therefore much more likely to be situation specific than of general application. This point will also be elaborated at a later stage.

NOTES AND REFERENCES

1. Ministry of Labour and National Service, Industrial Relations Handbook 1953, reprinted 1955, HMSO,p.113.
2. Ministry of Labour, Industrial Relations Handbook 1961, HMSO,p.129.
3. Ibid.,p.129.
4. The Code while not directly enforceable could be taken into account in court and Industrial Tribunal proceedings.
5. An ACAS convention, reflected in the Service's annual reports, makes a distinction between individual and collective conciliation. Collective conciliation denotes the long established practice of attempting to resolve industrial disputes. Individual conciliation is of much more

recent origin and relates to the exercise, by
individuals, of individual employment rights
established by statute. The expansion of such
rights in the past twenty years has necessitated
the appointment of specialist Conciliation Officers-
Industrial Tribunals (COITS).

6. Quoted in ACAS First Annual Report 1975,
p.42.

7. Employment Protection Act 1975, Schedule 1,
para.11.

8. J. Purcell, Good Industrial Relations;
theory and practice, Macmillan, 1981.

9. cf ACAS Annual Report 1982, p.61.

10. Section 1, Employment Protection Act 1975.

11. Arbitration is not considered here partly
because it is far less extensively used than
conciliation but more particularly because it is
carried out by non-ACAS personnel i.e. by
persons who themselves are independent of ACAS.

12. Section 4, Employment Protection Act 1975.

13. Eric Armstrong and Rosemary Lucas, 'The
advisory function of ACAS: a preliminary appraisal
of the advisory visit', Industrial Relations
Journal, Spring 1984, vol.15, no.1 pp.17-28.
E.G.A. Armstrong/R.E. Lucas, 'The advisory
function of ACAS: a preliminary appraisal of
in-depth work', Personnel Review, vol.12, no.4
(1983), pp.26-36.

14. Department of Employment, Conciliation
and Advisory Service Handbook, July 1972, p.5.

15. Conciliation and Advisory Service Handbook,
p.5.

Chapter Two

THE VOLUME OF ADVISORY WORK

Any discussion concerning the value of ACAS
advisory work entails the use of both quantitative and qualitative measurements. In the
attempted evaluation process two central
questions need to be addressed. How much work
was done? What good did it do? Obviously it is
far easier to answer the first than the second
question. The volume of ACAS advisory work can
be quantified readily enough in a number of
objective ways. Assessing the quality and
effectiveness of the advice given is quite
another matter requiring subjective judgements and
decisions about who the judges should be. While
the main purpose of this book is to present
evidence and discuss issues associated with
advisory quality and effectiveness, it remains
necessary to present salient statistics about
the volume of advisory work carried out by ACAS
since its establishment in 1974. Such is the
purpose of Chapter Two.
    Before the statistics are presented and
discussed some preliminary explanations and comments
may be helpful.
    i) With few modifications the methods of
compiling the statistics, and their forms of
presentation in the ACAS Annual Reports, have
remained the same since the formation of ACAS in
1974. A basic continuity of data analysis has
thus been maintained. (The major modification
occurred in 1983 as the result of the revision of
the Standard Industrial Classification. Because
of this revision the industry group table for 1983
cannot be compared directly with industry group
tables for previous years. 1983 industry group
figures have therefore been omitted from
Tables 2.5 and 2.6.)

The Volume of Advisory Work

      ii) In its classification of different types
of advisory work ACAS makes a broad distinction
between Short-Term Work and In-Depth Work. Short-
term work consists of advisory enquiries and
advisory visits. Advisory enquiries are usually
dealt with in the regional offices of ACAS, by
telephone, letter or private interview. While
the volume of these enquiries is not tabulated
in the statistical appendices of the ACAS annual
reports, the numbers of enquiries handled are
given in the text of the reports - and the numbers
are considerable. For example, the 1982 Report
(p.44) referred to 'some 284,000 enquiries' for
that year. Advisory visits are of two types -
requested (the majority) and non-requested. The
latter, sometimes called development visits,
enable the adviser to inform potential clients of
the nature of the advisory service and to increase
his own awareness of the state of industrial
relations in the area in which he operates. A
requested advisory visit typically accounts for
a day's work and could consist of helping a small
company with the overhaul of its grievance/
disciplinary procedures. The statistical
appendices of the annual reports give the totals
of all visits and not separate totals for the two
types.
      Turning to in-depth work:

      For statistical purposes exercises taking more
      than a single visit are classified as
      projects (a series of linked visits), surveys
      (continuous ACAS involvement, usually over a
      week or more, to conduct a diagnostic analysis),
      or extended training exercises (assistance
      with industrial relations training designed
      especially for the organisation). 1)

      The average number of man-days required for a
typical piece of in-depth work is about twelve.
The work might well comprise assistance with the
reform of a payment system.
      iii) The tables in the annual reports give the
totals of pieces of advisory work carried out by
category eg. projects, visits. But - and it is a
significant but - there is no indication either by
category, or in the aggregate, of the man-days
taken up by advisory work. The tables therefore
reveal no time value for advisory work although
ACAS, for its own manpower resource management purposes, compiles such information in a detailed way.

The Volume of Advisory Work

Information about relative as distinct from
actual time spent on advisory work is, however,
given in other parts of the annual reports.
Starting with the 1978 Annual Report a series of
annual pie-charts demonstrates the distribution
of time, on a percentage basis, between all the
advisory activities. (Details are given below.)
While this method reveals some interesting shifts
in the time distribution among the various advisory
activities, there remains no systematic published
data on, for example, the average time of a
project, of a survey, of a visit - or the distribution of activities within a series of time
consumption ranges. The tables which give totals
of the different types of advisory work carried
out are therefore relatively unsophisticated. 2)
        iv) The last point is underlined by the fact
that each type of advisory work is related at any
one time to only one of the four following
variables - subject (of advice), industry group,
size of organisation and ACAS region. The reasons
for choosing these particular variables are not
stated in the annual reports but it seems
reasonable enough to identify and quantify work
undertaken by reference to its subject matter and
industrial sector location. Relating types of
advisory work to the size of the organisation
(by number of employees) provides useful clues to
the acceptability of the ACAS advisory role in a
wide range of differently sized organisations.
The value of openly relating type of advisory work
to ACAS region is less clear. Taken in isolation
such a table invites inter-regional comparisons
which could be misleading. For example, why did
Region A carry out more surveys than Region C but
fewer than Region B? The tempting answer is
that Region A performed better than Region C but
not as well as Region B. The tempting answer
could be the correct answer but alternatively it
could be wildly inaccurate because no two regions
are identical in character. Their industrial
structures will differ as will the nature and
extent of trade union activity, the levels of
unemployment and economic prosperity. Any or all
of these factors could influence the amount and
type of advisory work undertaken. For these
reasons it would be rash to claim that there is a
benchmark region which can fairly serve for the
measurement of individual regional performance.
This is not to imply that inter-regional comparisons should not be made by the management of the

advisory service with a view to maintaining/raising
levels of performance. Such comparisons are in
fact made but from a much larger and far more
complex data bank than the regional table in the
annual report.

v) It cannot be assumed that the tables given
below necessarily reflect a fully representative
sample of the remedial work necessary to improve
British industrial relations. It has to be
remembered that the nature and size of the advisory
service is fundamentally demand related, ie
determined by the number of clients seeking advice.
While the demand can be stimulated to some extent
by increasing the awareness of potential clients
of the advisory role through development visits
and various forms of publicity, the bulk of ACAS
advisory work results from direct requests from
companies and trade unions. It is worth bearing
in mind, for example, that ACAS has not so far
been requested to give advice on some of the major
industrial relations problems of recent times, eg.
the determination of pay in the public sector
generally and in particular in those areas of
public employment where some of the greatest
difficulties have arisen - the civil service,
water supply, steel, coal-mining, the National
Health Service.

It is time now to turn to the statistics
which illustrate, in a variety of ways, both
the volume of advisory work and its changing
patterns since 1974 when ACAS was formed. The
tables are compiled entirely from ACAS annual
reports. Except where otherwise stated the
explanatory comments are those of the authors.

The overall volume of advisory work

While a detailed explanation of the volume
variations shown by Table 2.1 is beyond the scope
of this Chapter, some relevant comments may be
ventured. Given what was said earlier, the volume
of work can obviously be affected by the demand
for it. The volume can also be affected by the
supply side of the advisory activity, ie by the
number of advisers available. Both demand and
supply factors have been materially (but not
exclusively) affected by government interventions
in industrial relations and manpower policies:

The new employment legislation had a major
influence on the volume and pattern of

Table 2.1: Volume of Advisory Work, 1974-1983

		1974 Sept-Dec	1975	1976	1977	1978	1979	1980	1981	1982	1983	Totals
IN DEPTH WORK	Surveys	50	112	82	85	84	128	143	114	123	135	1,056
	Projects	15	96	126	174	242	254	290	309	359	437	2,302
	ETEs*					39	75	43	45	33	46	281
	JWPs+										99	99
SHORT TERM WORK	Visits	1,938	7,277	8,901	8,792	10,390	12,602	15,222	12,484	10,841	10,892	99,339

*Extended Training Exercises   +Joint Working Parties, separately categorised in 1983

The Volume of Advisory Work

advisory work in 1976. The Equal Pay and Sex
Discrimination Acts and the Trade Union and
Labour Relations Act 1974 were in force at
the beginning of 1976. During the year most
of the provisions of the Employment Protection
Act (1975) came into effect. 3)

As in 1976, employment legislation was a major
influence on advisory work. (1977 Annual
Report) 4)

Pointing to the fall in the number of surveys
compared to 1980, the 1981 Annual Report commented:

This fall was partly due to a reduction in
resources available for advisory work... 5)

The reduction referred to has to be placed in
a wider context of a government plan to reduce the
size of the Civil Service which requires
reductions in the staff of ACAS. 6)

Relative distribution of advisory activity - by type

Table 2.1 reveals the considerable difference that
exists, on a simple 1:1 count basis, between the
volume of in-depth work and the volume of advisory
visits. If the total of pieces of in-depth work
is expressed as a percentage of the total of all
pieces of advisory work carried out, then on a
yearly basis the in-depth percentages have been as
follows:

1975	1976	1977	1978	1979	1980	1981	1982	1983
2.8	2.3	2.9	3.4	3.5	3.0	3.6	4.5	6.2

This suggests a rising trend in the demand for
in-depth work. While this change must obviously
reflect, to some degree, changes in the patterns
of client demand for advisory help, there is reason
to believe, as later evidence will indicate, that a
change in ACAS policy itself has had some influence
on the trend. Latterly ACAS has been concerned to
bring about a different balance between in-depth
work and advisory visits in favour of a higher
proportion of in-depth work being carried out. The
first clear indication of proportion, based on a
time spent factor, was given in the 1978 Annual
Report where a pie chart 7) showed the distribution
of time between the different advisory activities.

The Volume of Advisory Work

While no percentages were given, the pie-chart indicated that advisory visits accounted for about
two thirds of the total time, in the year, spent
on advisory work. From 1979 onwards percentages
were given for the different portions of the pie-
charts. Table 2.2 presents these percentages.

Table 2.2 Percentages of time spent on different
types of advisory work as a proportion of all
advisory work 1979-1983

| | Advisory Visits | In-depth work | | | Indoor enquiries* | Talks, Seminars etc |
		Projects	Surveys	ETEs		
1979	46	8	19	2	17	8
1980	52	9	17	1	13	8
1981	47	10	21	1	14	7
1982	47	13	21	1	12	6
1983	37	20+	22	2	12	6

*Dealt with within the ACAS office concerned
+Includes JWPs, 1983. 1% on information collection

While the time span concerned is perhaps too
short to allow of firm conclusions, it is worth
while pointing out the changing ratio of in-depth
work to visits in terms of proportionate time
spent on the respective activities. The ratio
derives from the figures in Table 2.2.

	In depth		Visits			
1979	29	:	46	or	1 : 1.6
1980	27	:	52	or	1 : 1.9
1981	32	:	47	or	1 : 1.5
1982	35	:	47	or	1 : 1.3
1983	44	:	37	or	1 : 0.8

Except in 1980, and with a possible 'over-
compensation' in 1983, a steady movement towards
a closer alignment of the respective time consump-
tions of visits and in-depth work appears to have
taken place. This movement is highly pertinent to
the discussion on an ACAS policy issue of where
advisory time is better spent - on advisory visits
or project and survey work.

The Volume of Advisory Work

The 'exceptional' ratio for 1980 can largely
be explained by the highest number of visits, by
far, having been carried out during this year,
some 21 per cent above the next highest total in
1979, cf Table 2.1. An important part of the 1980
deviation from the trend referred to would appear
to lie with the:

> increase in the percentage of visits on which
> the rights of individual employees was
> discussed...a movement reflecting the changes
> in legislation introduced in the Employment
> Act 1980. 8)

In 1979 'rights of individual employees', as
a subject of advice had featured in 3,965 visits.
The corresponding figure for 1980 was 5,361. 9)
Having given some indication of the changing
volume of the different categories of advisory
help and the distribution, by time, of advisory
resource between such categories, it would seem
appropriate to turn next to the subjects that
engaged advisory time, and their quantitative
significance.

The subject matter of advice

Presentation of the statistics is affected by
changes to ACAS subject headings in 1979. These
were associated with earlier changes to employment legislation. Nevertheless, it is possible
to present tables, built up from the annual reports,
which cover 1978-1983 in respect both of advisory
visits and of in-depth work.
In considering Table 2.3 it is essential to
keep in mind that whenever an advisory visit is
made, the likelihood is that more than one
industrial relations subject (as classified in ACAS
reports) will be discussed. Similarly when a piece
of in-depth work is carried out (Table 2.4) it is
probable that an adviser will be dealing with more
than one subject. ACAS collects and tabulates its
subject statistics on this multi-subject, per
operation, basis.
Although some conjecture is inevitably entailed,
a number of reasonable inferences, of a broad
nature, can be drawn from Table 2.3. Procedural
matters (subject 2) seem consistently central to
discussions between advisers and their clients.
The peak frequency (1980) is conceivably linked with
the many redundancies brought about by the recession.

Table 2.3: Advisory visits analysed by subject 1978-1983 (Percentage of all visits in which the subject featured)

Subject	1978	1979	1980	1981	1982	1983
1. Recognition, negotiating procedures, local plant bargaining arrangements	25.5	30.8	28.2	24.9	24.9	24.1
2. Grievance, disciplinary, disputes and redundancy procedures	48.1	52.6	56.3	51.5	50.2	51.1
3. Safety committees/representatives	5.6	6.5	3.5	1.9	1.8	1.9
4. Consultation, employee representation and participation	10.1	16.7	16.2	15.7	15.6	16.3
5. Communications	5.8	10.4	10.8	12.2	11.5	14.1
6. Rights of individual employees	60.9	31.5	35.2	32.0	33.9	35.7
7. Equal pay, sex discrimination and race relations	2.2	3.5	1.8	0.9	0.8	8.3
8. Management organisation and structure	5.4	14.1	14.0	12.7	12.3	12.2
9. Labour turnover, absenteeism and timekeeping	9.4	20.2	18.8	20.8	19.6	11.7
10. Recruitment and selection procedures	3.6	8.7	6.1	3.7	3.4	4.2
11. Manpower planning	1.3	3.0	3.5	2.8	2.4	2.8
12. Induction and training	3.6	6.7	5.9	9.4	5.0	5.5
13. Payment matters and payment systems	13.6	20.3	21.8	19.4	21.3	22.7
14. Job analysis, job description and job evaluation	5.0	7.7	6.2	4.6	4.0	6.5
15. Work study	1.4	2.0	1.8	2.0	1.3	1.9
16. Hours of work, shift working and flexible working hours	1.8	4.3	4.6	4.7	6.4	5.6
17. Job satisfaction	0.7	0.5	0.5	0.3	0.3	0.6
18. Others	4.4	5.5	7.2	7.5	13.3	8.3
Number of visits undertaken	10,390	12,602	15,222	12,484	10,841	10,892

The highest frequency for any subject occurred in 1978 and appears against subject 6 - rights of individual employees. This suggests concern among numerous, and probably small employers, to understand and come to terms with complex new employment legislation. After 1978 the need for advisory help on this topic presumably declined but remained significant and consistently the second most frequently discussed subject. (There is an obvious link between 'rights' and 'procedures') New employment legislation prompted the introduction of a new subject (at 11.5 per cent) in 1983 - Self certification and ESSP (Employers Statutory Sick Pay - not shown in Table 2.3) and was also probably responsible for the sharp rise in 1983 in the percentage for subject 7 - new equal pay regulations being published during the year.

Collective bargaining arrangements, or attempts to bring them about (subject 1) remained significant and relatively stable throughout the six year period. From 1979 onwards, stability is observable at a notably higher level than 1978, until 1983, in subject 9 - labour turnover, absenteeism and timekeeping. It may be that as the recession deepened more help was sought by employers to bring about a more efficient use of the labour force. The same tentative explanation may hold true for the appreciable rise, again from 1979 onwards, in the frequency of mention of subject 13 - payment matters and payment systems. 1979 also marks a virtual doubling in the interest shown in subject 5 - communications - and a marked increase in the related subject (4) of consultation, employee representation and participation. Both increases and the continuance of the higher level of interest in these topics may be indicative of a need employers have felt to disseminate 'bad news' clearly and effectively if appropriate action was to be taken to ensure economic survival.

Three subjects that might be considered to be more the concern of personnel management than of industrial relations attract modest if consistent attention. These are recruitment and selection procedures (10), manpower planning (11) and induction and training (12). Their inclusion helps to remind us that the statutory duty placed on ACAS is to give advice on industrial relations 'employment policies'. The extent to which the subjects listed in Table 2.3 constitute the total elements of industrial relations and employment policy could be debated - at length. The appropriateness of the identification of the seventeen specific subjects also raises questions. The seventeen subjects themselves are obviously more than seventeen. Subject 2, for instance, refers to grievance, disciplinary, disputes and redundancy procedures. Each one of the four procedures probably merits a subject classification in its own right especially when compared, for example, to work study (15) or job satisfaction (17) the latter not having even reached 1.0 percent in Table 2.3. Table 2.4 reinforces some of these points.

From Table 2.4 it will be seen that procedural reform constitutes the staple diet of in-depth work. This closely parallels the advisory visits experience. As in the case of advisory visits, 1978 appears to form the high water mark of in-depth concern with the rights of individual employees. Thereafter this subject becomes far less prominent in projects and surveys than in advisory visits. This suggests that many issues associated with employment rights, often probably technical in character, do not require the more detailed study and analysis of in-depth work. The more searching work does appear to be called for, as could be expected, in regard to pay structure/ system reform - subjects 13 and 14, subject 13 providing the second highest frequencies of the Table. The rise in the work study figures for 1981 and 1982 is of related interest and lends support to the view advanced earlier that the recession has necessitated or enabled an overhaul of payment systems to be carried out on a wider scale.

The recession with its commonly attendant shift in the balance of power between employers and trade unions may also account for the marked falling away of in-depth work in the collective bargaining arena - subject 1. Even so, consultation (subject 4) and communications (subject 5) have remained significant but these subjects do not automatically entail a trade union presence. The point made above about communicating bad news also comes to mind. In practical work consultation and communication can be commonly linked with subject 8 - management organisation and structure where 'business' appears to have remained reasonably steady.

The demand for personnel management type assistance - subjects 10,11,12 - if modest, also appears fairly regular but generally not as high as the concern with manpower efficiency - subject 9,

22

Table 2.4: In-depth work analysed by subject 1978-1983 (Percentage of all pieces of work in which the subject featured)

Subject	1978	1979	1980	1981	1982	1983
1. Recognition, negotiating procedures, local plant bargaining arrangements	22.5	15.8	14.5	8.3	7.2	8.2
2. Grievance, disciplinary, disputes and redundancy procedures	44.1	44.0	37.0	40.4	46.2	48.0
3. Safety committees/representatives	-	1.1	0.8	1.3	0.6	1.7
4. Consultation, employee representation and participation	16.4	9.8	8.6	5.6	4.5	4.5
5. Communications	16.2	8.8	8.0	7.7	6.8	7.5
6. Rights of individual employees	36.7	15.3	9.7	8.8	8.3	11.7
7. Equal pay, sex discrimination and race relations	5.5	2.8	1.1	1.5	0.2	0.4
8. Management organisation and structure	7.7	7.4	6.5	6.0	4.1	4.6
9. Labour turnover, absenteeism and timekeeping	5.5	12.3	13.2	7.7	9.9	4.9
10. Recruitment and selection procedures	1.1	5.7	3.6	3.2	2.1	1.4
11. Manpower planning	1.1	0.2	1.5	0.9	1.6	1.4
12. Induction and training	2.5	6.6	4.8	7.9	4.3	4.2
13. Payment matters and payment systems	17.3	15.1	19.5	18.4	21.7	18.5
14. Job analysis, job description and job evaluation	5.2	12.5	14.7	12.0	7.0	10.9
15. Work study	1.1	0.9	0.2	3.2	3.5	2.4
16. Hours of work, shift working and flexible working hours	0.5	1.3	1.3	1.5	1.4	1.3
17. Job satisfaction	-	0.2	-	0.2	0.4	-
18. Others	0.8	4.2	2.3	11.3	16.7	10.2
No. of pieces of in-depth work undertaken	365	457	476	468	515	717

labour turnover etc. Subjects which consistently
appear to attract very little demand for in-depth
advisory assistance are broadly the same as low
demand subjects for advisory visits namely - 3,
safety committees/representatives; 7, equal pay,
sex discrimination and race relations; 11, manpower
planning; 15, work study; 16, hours of work, shift
working and flexible working hours; 17, job satisfaction. The specific reasons why these subjects
attract low frequencies are not readily apparent.
Two possible general reasons can readily be
imagined. The subjects concerned are those which
clients or potential clients do not regard as
causing particular problems - or they could be held
to be inappropriate for third party assistance.
Obviously some combination of the two general
reasons could exist. This kind of speculation leads
to the far more central issue of whether any optimum
relationship can theoretically exist between the
deployment of the ACAS advisory resource and the
subjects of the industrial relations system held to
be, on some view, most in need of reform. This
issue begs many questions, some of which will be
raised and discussed later in the book.

Having set out certain dimensions for the
subject matter of the advice given, the location
of that advice can be indicated in three ways.
The ACAS Annual Reports locate the advice recipients, by reference (separately but not in
combination) to industry group, size of organisation and ACAS region. Table 2.5 depicts, on a
percentage basis, the distribution of advisory
visits between industry groups. Table 2.6 does
the same for in-depth work. The industry groups
are the twenty-seven orders listed in the Standard
Industrial Classification 1968. 10) As mentioned
above, because of a revised SIC, industry group
figures for 1983 have been omitted from Tables 2.5
and 2.6.

Location of advisory work by industry group

Given its size, heterogeneity and strong traditions
of industrial relations, it was perhaps to be
expected that Mechanical engineering would feature
prominently in both industry group tables. What
is surprising, at first sight, is the prominence,
particularly in the later years, of Miscellaneous
services as a client. Miscellaneous services
includes cinemas, theatres, radio, sport,
gambling, hotels, restaurants, cafes, pubs and

Table 2.5: Advisory visits analysed by Industry Group - in percentage terms

Industry Group	1975	1976	1977	1978	1979	1980	1981	1982
Agriculture, forestry fishing	0.7	0.6	0.9	0.9	0.7	0.5	0.5	0.6
Mining and quarrying	1.1	1.2	1.1	0.7	0.5	0.6	0.5	0.6
Food, drink and tobacco	8.4	7.7	7.2	6.7	7.3	7.2	7.1	7.1
Coal and petroleum products	0.4	0.5	0.5	0.4	0.3	0.3	0.3	0.3
Chemicals and allied industries	5.0	4.2	4.0	3.8	3.8	3.9	3.3	3.7
Metal manufacture	4.4	2.9	2.4	2.8	4.5	2.9	2.5	2.9
Mechanical engineering	12.1	11.3	10.7	10.5	8.9	8.8	8.7	8.6
Instrument engineering	2.1	1.6	1.6	1.3	1.2	1.1	1.2	1.2
Electrical engineering	6.2	4.5	4.6	4.4	5.2	4.7	4.8	5.0
Shipbuilding and marine engineering	0.7	0.8	1.0	0.6	0.5	0.5	0.4	0.4
Vehicles	2.9	2.5	2.5	2.2	2.8	2.7	2.5	2.4
Metal goods not elsewhere specified	5.3	4.9	5.0	4.3	5.0	5.5	5.1	4.8
Textiles	5.6	4.5	4.5	4.1	4.5	4.3	3.6	3.9
Leather, leather goods and fur	0.5	0.7	0.6	0.8	0.5	0.7	0.5	0.7
Clothing and footwear	4.6	4.5	4.4	3.7	4.2	5.0	3.8	3.6
Bricks, pottery, glass, cement, etc	3.0	2.5	1.9	2.1	2.2	2.3	2.1	2.1
Timber, furniture, etc	2.2	3.0	3.4	3.1	2.5	2.8	2.3	2.9
Paper, printing and publishing	3.8	3.7	3.3	3.2	2.7	3.6	3.9	3.7
Other manufacturing industries	5.2	4.7	4.6	4.3	4.2	4.2	4.1	3.8
Construction	3.7	5.1	5.2	4.8	4.3	4.3	4.3	4.1
Gas, electricity and water	0.5	0.3	0.4	0.3	0.5	0.4	0.3	0.3
Transport and communication	2.9	3.0	3.6	3.7	3.4	4.3	3.7	3.9
Distributive trades	6.9	8.9	9.5	9.5	8.4	8.9	9.9	10.1
Insurance, banking, finance and business services	1.3	1.8	2.1	1.8	2.2	1.8	2.5	2.3
Professional and scientific services	3.1	3.6	4.2	4.5	4.4	3.7	5.2	4.4
Miscellaneous services	4.8	7.9	8.1	12.6	11.9	11.1	12.9	13.2
Public administration and defence	2.6	3.1	2.7	2.9	3.5	3.9	4.0	3.4
Total No of visits	7,277	8,901	8,792	10,390	12,602	15,222	12,484	10,841

Table 2.6: In-depth work analysed by Industry Group - in percentage terms

Industry Group	1975	1976	1977	1978	1979	1980	1981	1982
Agriculture, forestry, fishing	0.5	1.0	1.5	0.8	0.4	-	0.4	0.4
Mining and quarrying	-	-	0.4	0.3	0.2	0.8	0.2	0.2
Food, drink and tobacco	6.7	9.6	12.4	5.5	9.0	12.2	11.5	9.3
Coal and petroleum products	-	-	0.4	-	-	0.2	0.6	0.2
Chemicals and allied industries	5.8	3.4	3.9	5.5	2.0	4.6	3.6	2.3
Metal manufacture	7.2	4.8	4.2	3.3	3.5	4.0	3.4	1.9
Mechanical engineering	9.6	9.6	10.0	10.4	7.6	6.3	7.5	8.2
Instrument engineering	0.5	1.0	1.9	1.6	1.5	2.1	0.2	0.8
Electrical engineering	8.2	3.9	0.2	2.2	3.5	6.1	5.6	5.4
Shipbuilding and marine engineering	-	1.9	0.8	2.2	0.2	0.2	0.6	0.8
Vehicles	2.9	3.4	1.5	1.9	3.7	2.5	3.4	1.0
Metal goods not elsewhere specified	5.8	8.6	6.2	5.2	5.7	6.1	6.2	5.2
Textiles	6.7	5.7	5.8	5.5	5.7	5.7	2.8	4.7
Leather, leather goods and fur	1.0	1.4	-	0.3	0.7	-	1.1	0.6
Clothing and footwear	8.2	4.8	5.8	5.5	5.0	5.7	5.8	5.0
Bricks, pottery, glass, cement etc	3.3	3.9	1.9	4.4	2.2	2.3	2.8	3.1
Timber, furniture etc	3.8	2.9	3.5	3.3	4.4	3.1	2.1	3.5
Paper, printing and publishing	3.8	3.4	3.1	3.3	3.3	1.9	2.6	2.1
Other manufacturing industries	5.8	6.2	4.2	7.4	4.8	4.0	5.3	5.6
Construction	1.0	1.4	2.3	5.5	2.2	1.5	1.1	2.3
Gas, electricity and water	-	-	-	0.3	-	0.2	0.4	0.2
Transport and communication	1.4	2.9	3.5	3.8	3.5	3.6	2.8	2.7
Distributive trades	8.2	8.1	9.3	5.7	9.4	6.7	7.3	11.4
Insurance, banking, finance and business services	0.5	1.0	1.5	1.6	1.8	1.5	1.5	1.9
Professional and scientific services	1.9	3.4	2.3	5.2	8.5	5.0	6.8	6.0
Miscellaneous services	6.7	3.4	3.5	7.1	8.1	9.9	11.8	12.9
Public administration and defence	0.5	4.3	3.9	2.2	3.1	3.8	2.6	2.3
Total No of pieces of in-depth work	208	208	259	365	457	476	468	515

clubs, hairdressing, motor repairs and garages. The growth of advisory work in such sectors may reflect the growth in the service industries generally. The expansion of existing firms and the entry of new ones, with possibly little industrial relations expertise, may well have increased the demand for advisory aid. Similar remarks may also be relevant to the Distributive Trades. The not insignificant level of in-depth work in Professional and scientific services may owe something to the inclusion in this industry group of the National Health Service where it is known that ACAS advisers have done appreciable work at local level. Another notable 'consumer' is Food, drink and tobacco where again size and heterogeneity may help to explain the higher percentages.

Of equal, possibly more interest are the industry groups where the level of demand for advisory work is low or non-existent. It is to be expected that the many small and scattered units of employment that constitute Agriculture, forestry and fishing would not generate much demand for advice. But what of Vehicles? Here is an 'industry' with large concentrations of labour and a highly publicised and well documented history of turbulent industrial relations. Quite apart from the possible involvement of the fire-fighting conciliation and arbitration services of ACAS, it could reasonably be supposed that ample scope existed within the industry, which includes aircraft manufacture, for fire prevention ACAS advisory work to be undertaken. And yet the percentage figures in Table 2.6 for Vehicles represent for the eight years shown a total of only 74 or roughly 9 a year pieces of in-depth work. It may be that the companies and the trade unions concerned consciously prefer to achieve change by their own joint efforts only calling on ACAS conciliatory help, and not always then, when negotiations break down and disputes result. While this is a speculation some inferential evidence in its support can be advanced.

ACAS annual reports include tables of completed conciliation cases arising from collective industrial disputes. The total of such conciliation cases for the same eight year period referred to above for Vehicles was 793, a yearly average of 99. A ratio of 99 : 9 or 11 : 1 between fire-fighting and fire-prevention activity may or may not be typical of other industry groups' experience. (Such ratios could readily be determined). But the ratio does suggest, in this instance, a greater readiness to

seek ACAS conciliation help to get the assembly line
moving again, than to seek ACAS advisory help to
probe to the underlying as distinct from immediate
reasons for the assembly line being stopped in the
first place.
    Moving on to other industries of low demand for
advisory assistance it will have been noted (cf
Table 2.6) that in two of the eight years no in-
depth work was carried out in Mining and quarrying.
In the other six years one piece of in-depth work
was carried out each year except in 1980 when the
total was four. Similarly in Gas, electricity and
water no in-depth work was carried out in four
years and for the other four years the total was
five. Again we need to enter the realm of conjecture to seek an explanation for the figures. It
may be that these industries really do not need
advice although it remains difficult to believe
that ACAS advisers would be unable to make any recommendations aimed at improvement in a state of
affairs if invited to look at the affairs in
question. Another possibility is that management
and trade unions in these major public sector
industries consider that their jointly devised procedural and institutional arrangements are so well
developed that there is no role for the ACAS
adviser. So far as substantive matters such as pay
are concerned, the key factor, in the parties'
perception, remains the government of the day in
whatever role it chooses to play at the time of
pay bargaining. Whatever the role chosen, ACAS
advice, supposing it to be requested, would be
unlikely to influence that role in any significant
way.
    Turning to the second aspect of the location
of advice, Table 2.7 is pertinent to a policy issue
of concern to ACAS - the effectiveness of advice
given in relationship to the size of the organiza-
tion, by labour force, where the advice is given.
In other words, where is the ACAS adviser most
effectively deployed, in the small, medium, large
sized firms? Table 2.7 does not seek to answer
that question but charts what has taken place.
Some evidence relevant to the question just posed
will be given in a later chapter.

Location of advisory work by size of organisation

Perhaps what emerges most clearly and most importantly from Table 2.7 is the fact that the advisory
role is acceptable to organisations in all the size

Table 2.7: Advisory work by size of organisation – percentage distribution

Advisory Visits

Size of organisation (No. of employees)	1975	1976	1977	1978	1979	1980	1981	1982	1983
1 to 49	14.3	20.4	25.2	27.5	22.2	20.7	23.2	23.9	24.0
50 to 99	} 38.7	} 39.9	} 38.0	} 36.8	13.2	16.1	13.6	13.6	13.6
100 to 199					14.4	16.5	15.0	15.6	14.8
200 to 299					9.8	10.2	10.5	10.0	10.4
300 to 499	14.5	11.8	12.6	10.7	12.8	11.8	11.9	11.6	10.7
500 to 1,499	18.9	15.7	12.6	12.9	14.9	12.9	12.4	13.2	13.2
1,500 and over	13.6	12.2	11.6	9.3	10.2	9.0	10.5	8.7	9.4
Trade unions			NA	1.5	1.8	1.9	1.4	1.9	2.3
Employers associations			NA	1.3	0.7	0.9	1.5	1.5	1.6
Others									–
Total No of Visits	7,277	8,901	8,792	10,390	12,602	15,222	12,484	10,841	10,892

In-depth Work (Surveys, projects and extended training exercises)

Size of organisation (No. of employees)	1975	1976	1977	1978	1979	1980	1981	1982	1983
1 to 49	6.7	3.8	8.9	17.8	15.3	10.3	13.2	21.1	23.5
50 to 99	} 45.7	} 44.7	} 45.6	} 47.4	12.9	15.5	13.7	19.2	18.8
100 to 199					16.6	18.1	16.9	17.9	13.9
200 to 299					9.4	11.4	12.2	10.5	13.7
300 to 499	16.3	15.4	13.5	11.2	15.5	14.5	13.5	11.3	9.8
500 to 1,499	20.7	18.3	16.6	12.3	16.6	17.0	15.6	10.9	12.4
1,500 and over	10.6	17.8	15.4	10.7	12.7	12.6	13.7	9.1	7.7
Trade unions			NA	0.3	–	0.2	–	–	0.1
Employers associations			NA	0.3	0.2	0.2	0.6	–	0.1
Others					0.7	0.2	0.6		
Total No – pieces of in-depth work	208	208	259	365	457	476	468	515	717

NA = not available

29

divisions indicated. (As specialist industrial relations organisations formed to represent the interests of their respective memberships, employers' associations and trade unions need to be considered separately.) Whether the percentage distributions across the different size-bands are 'right' against any set criteria raises the question of what those criteria should be and could lead to unproductive discussion given that, as previously stated, advisory work is essentially demand related. For example, from what has been learned from the research, it is extremely unlikely that a request for advice would be refused by ACAS solely on the grounds that the request came from a particular size of organisation and that particular size was thought, for whatever reasons, not to merit assistance. In each of the nine years shown in Table 2.7, the percentage figures in each size band are such as to indicate that a significant proportion of the total advisory work load is carried out in each of the organisational size categories.

While Table 2.7 shows that the majority of assignments, visits and in-depth, are carried out in the smaller organisations (1-299) this may be no more than a reasonable reflection of the general distribution of 'smaller' and 'larger' organisations in the economy. Seeking to prove or disprove such a possibility hardly matters because of the client demand reason already given. Such demand is hardly likely to match some notional representative sampling by different size groups. It also seems plausible that the yearly variations observable in each size category in Table 2.7 are due far more to the natural dynamism of industrial relations than to any other reason such as a conscious ACAS attempt to alter the nature of client demand.

The same claim may have somewhat less strength when the regional location of advice is considered. This is because regional directors have work-load targets which may or may not be attained. As stated earlier, it is no part of this chapter to be drawn into discussion about comparative regional performance. A table showing 9 years' work on a regional basis has not therefore been compiled. Such a table could invite performance comparisons from inadequate data when what is needed is an illustration of the different activity levels region by region. Table 2.8 therefore reproduces Table 18 from the 1982 ACAS Annual Report which gives recent figures of volume.

The Volume of Advisory Work

Location of advisory work by ACAS region

While summarising only two years'work Table 2.8
still prompts various questions about the differences between regions, by type of activity - and
variations in volume one year compared with the
other. For instance, Wales had, in both years, by
far the fewest number of visits and yet in 1981
more surveys were carried out in Wales than in
London where overall, on the figures, a greater
volume of advisory activity is conducted than in
Wales. Why should the activity patterns of the
two regions differ so? Why, over the two years
should the North West and Yorkshire and Humberside
regions have carried out 38 of the total 78 extended training exercises for the nine regions?
Answers to these and many similar questions could
be interesting in themselves but again they really
belong to a discussion on inter-regional performance, which we do not examine, rather than to
this chapter concerned as it is to provide some
basic dimensions of the volume of advisory work.
    Before moving on to discuss the advisers and
their managers whose combined efforts produce the
volume of work just examined, it is necessary to
mention a fairly recent advisory development which
has come to assume a quantitative as well as a
qualitative significance. The different broad
types of in-depth work have already been briefly
described (see p.13). The 1981 ACAS Annual Report
devoted a whole chapter (Chapter 6) to an account of
the Joint Working Party as a particular form of in-
depth work. Very briefly a joint working party is
an attempt, in appropriate circumstances, at joint
problem solving with ACAS advisory assistance. By
joint is meant teams of management and employee
representatives. The advisory assistance can take
a variety of forms including chairmanship of the
joint working party. 'The aim is to foster as far
as possible a rational team approach to the solving
of problems which yields results compatible with
the objectives of both parties.' 11) The ACAS role
typically goes beyond the making of recommendations
to assistance with the implementation of change:

        Sometimes a JWP may have a precise objective,
        e.g., to introduce a particular method of
        job evaluation. In other cases JWPs may be
        used as a joint problem-solving mechanism or
        to review industrial relations practices and
        procedures in a situation where no apparent

Table 2.8: Advisory work analysed by ACAS Region

	1981				1982			
	Surveys	Advisory projects	Extended training exercises	Advisory visits	Surveys	Advisory projects	Extended training exercises	Advisory visits
London	13	46	5	2,020	17	32	2	1,458
Midlands	17	56	-	1,672	27	50	1	1,867
Northern	14	31	3	1,328	12	52	3	1,030
North West	17	42	11	1,953	8	56	9	1,753
Scotland	11	42	2	1,061	10	46	3	736
South East	8	26	8	1,360	12	22	2	1,036
South West	3	26	5	1,050	8	23	4	1,192
Wales	15	8	2	596	12	34	-	438
Yorkshire and Humberside	16	32	9	1,444	17	44	9	1,331
Total	114	309	45	12,484	123	359	33	10,841

conflict exists but constructive co-operation would be beneficial to the future success of the organisation. 12)

The scale of ACAS advisory operations now having been outlined it is appropriate to examine and discuss the nature of the advisory manpower resource and its management. This will be done in the next chapter.

NOTES AND REFERENCES

1. ACAS Annual Report 1982, p.46.
2. Lacking computer facilities ACAS is not well placed to provide more sophisticated analyses.
3. ACAS Annual Report 1976, p.25.
4. ACAS Annual Report 1977, p.23.
5. ACAS Annual Report 1981, p.36.
6. cf ACAS Annual Reports 1981, p.12. and 1982, p.18.
7. ACAS Annual Report 1978, p.32.
8. ACAS Annual Report 1980, p.36.
9. Ibid, p.119.
10. Central Statistical Office, Standard Industrial Classification Revised 1968, HMSO, Second impression, 1975.
11. ACAS Annual Report 1981, p.56.
12. ACAS Annual Report 1982, p.46.

Chapter Three

THE ORGANISATION OF THE ADVISORY FUNCTION

To understand the organisational structure and
operational processes of the ACAS advisory role,
two points in particular need to be kept constantly
in mind. <u>The basic unit of operation remains the
region.</u> (For ease of presentation Scotland and
Wales will be classified as regions along with the
current seven English regions). <u>The basic mode of
operation remains essentially one of self-management
by the individual adviser.</u> While both statements
require, and will receive, elaboration and qualification, it is important to high-light their significance at the outset of this chapter. For both
statements the verb 'remains' was chosen deliberately partly to suggest that ACAS inherited an
organisational structure and style of operation and
partly to indicate that although changes have been
made since 1974, these have not been of a fundamental nature.

The ACAS Region

While it is unnecessary to trace the history of the
how, when and why Britain was divided by government
departments for administrative purposes, some
illustrations of industrial relations regional
change are useful. In 1956 those seeking help from
the Personnel Management Advisory Service of the
Ministry of Labour and National Service could do so
from any of eleven regions. In 1974 'the regional
organisation of ACAS was formed by taking over the
regional conciliation and advisory staff of the
Department of Employment. The offices in Scotland,
Wales and the six offices in the English regions
are each headed by a director who is supported by
experienced Staff'. 1) Appendix G of the 1975
ACAS Annual Report provided the following map of

The Organisation of the Advisory Function

the regions.

Figure 3.1: Map showing ACAS regions (1975)

The Organisation of the Advisory Function

> On 2 October 1978 the South East Region of the
> Service was split into two regions, one cov-
> ering the area of Greater London, the other
> the remaining counties of the former region. 2)

The employment population and concentration
represented by Greater London would seem to
warrant a separate region but as reference to the
map will show, the South East region remains a
very large geographical area.

The effective deployment of advisers within
regions is obviously of concern to all regional
directors and, as will be shown later, the geogra-
phy and employment distribution of a region will
help materially to determine the management structure of the region. That management structure is,
of course, not only concerned with advisory work
in its various forms, but with the provision of
conciliation services, both individual and collective, and with the servicing of arbitration hearings.
The 'demand' from the environment, for advisory,
conciliation and arbitration assistance is unlikely
to be made in constantly uniform proportions and
this argues the need for the development of a
flexible and adaptable manpower resource within a
region. The map above suggests that there is no
typical region and this argues the further need for
a large measure of regional autonomy so that the
regional director, with his senior colleagues, can
decide how best to match the manpower resource to
the changing demands made upon it by the region's
unique character. Practical considerations of this
nature make for a tradition of regional autonomy,
a tradition which remains powerful to this day.
But whatever the actual or perceived level of regional autonomy, there remain the issues of regional
accountability to higher authority and the provision of broadly consistent advice by a national
service. These issues will be explored later but
the following excerpt from a CAS internal document
illustrates the point and the thoughts expressed
remain relevant to 1984 advisory concerns.

> It was agreed that Headquarters would draw up
> general principles for guidance for SMAs
> (Senior Manpower Advisers) on the deployment
> of these (advisory) resources. It would be
> wrong to impose a rigid pattern of working
> regardless of real differences between regions.
> At the same time the CAS is a single service
> and there should be a common approach.

The Organisation of the Advisory Function

Since that view was formulated the Department
of Employment CAS has become the independent ACAS
with a tri-partite governing Council and statutory
duties to improve industrial relations. Such
changes would seem to reinforce the desirability
of a common approach to advisory work.

Given what has been said about regional autonomy, it is open to a regional director to organise
his advisory manpower resource on either a generalist or specialist basis. The personnel concerned
could work as full-time advisers or full-time
collective conciliators ie as 'specialists' or
combine advisory and collective conciliation activities in varying proportions - as 'generalists'.
(Some advisers may also undertake individual conciliation duties). There are genuinely held and
subtle differences of opinion among ACAS staff
about the respective merits of the generalist and
specialist approach to ACAS work and internal discussion papers have been written on the subject.
Some of the key points from that debate will be
presented in subsequent chapters which deal with a
variety of the more complex advisory issues. Quite
apart from the 'abstract' pros and cons of the
debate, it has to be remembered that the individuals
concerned have strengths and weaknesses, varying
degrees of experience, and personal preferences
regarding the work they do. From interviews conducted we know that some advisers do not wish to
undertake collective conciliation. The converse
also holds. Other individuals enjoy a mixture of
both types of work. Some directors place particular value on their staff gaining a wide range of
experience. Others see merit in staff becoming
functional experts. At the end of the day geo-
graphy, client demand and staffing levels may play
a major part in deciding whether an individual
should be a specialist or a generalist. It may not
be cost effective to send both a specialist adviser
and a specialist collective conciliator from a
regional office to a far distant, small industrial
community in the region. A generalist, as a member
of out-stationed staff and living nearer to the
community in question, may well provide a less
costly but equally effective service. To the
client/s concerned, the distinctions between generalist and specialist are likely to be far less
important (even if known) than receiving help from
'that chap from ACAS'.

For present purposes, it is not necessary to
identify each region in terms of generalist

or specialist, the formative factors promoting such
distinctions having been indicated. But it is
important to point out that some regions are sub-
divided into geographical sectors. The North West
region provides one example with north, south and
west sectors. The regional office is in Manchester
but for the west sector a Merseyside office is
located in Liverpool. Similar terminology is employed for the three sectors of the Midlands region
which has a regional office in Birmingham and an
office in Nottingham serving as an operational base
for the East Midlands. The division into sectors
does not, of course, remove the need for choices
to be made about generalist and specialist operating
methods.

   Although there is no standard regional organisation chart, each regional director devising both
the actual structure and its diagrammatic representation, all the regional charts use common terminology in relation to the staff employed. The
numbers in the different civil service grades 3)
understandably differ between regions but as far
as advisory work is concerned, four grades in
ascending order of status are involved - Industrial
Relations Officer, IRO (Higher Executive Officer
Grade); Senior Industrial Relations Officer, SIRO
(Senior Executive Officer Grade); Principal Industrial Relations Officer, PIRO (Principal Officer
Grade); Director (Senior Principal Officer Grade).
Day-to-day advisory work is carried out by IROs and
SIROs. The PIROs are essentially co-ordinators and
managers. In the North West region each of the
three sectors mentioned above is managed by a PIRO
who is responsible for the operation of conciliation
(individual and collective) and advisory services in
his sector. In contrast, and to point up some of
the differences mentioned earlier, in the London
region one of three PIROs was responsible (1982)
for collective conciliation, staffing and administrative matters for the whole region, while the other
two PIROs had a sector of the region each and responsibilities for advisory work and individual conciliation in their respective sectors.

   From what has just been described it might be
supposed that each of the nine regions had an establishment of three PIROs. This is by no means the
case. The allocation to Wales for example is one,
to the South West one, to Yorkshire and Humberside,
two. The numbers of staff and their distribution
between grades is a matter of regular monitoring by
ACAS management and of periodic examination by

Department of Employment manpower survey teams.

As was stated above, the day-to-day advisory work is carried out by IROs and SIROs. There is an additional, if small advisory resource which reflects a decision taken when ACAS was newly formed. 'The need to have some staff with recent industrial experience has been recognised' 4) - and acted upon by the recruitment of, for example, work study/payment systems experts. The practice of buying in expertise and relevant industrial experience continues, the advisers concerned being employed on short-term contracts of two years with a possible maximum extension of an additional three years. Such personnel are known as period appointment advisers being usually appointed at the Senior Executive Officer level and styled PASIROs. Their numbers are limited by agreements, with civil service trade unions, which apply to external appointments, and although a few PASIROs, in the past, have been assimilated into the permanent civil service this is not now the practice. The role of PASIROs and their effectiveness raises many interesting points of discussion especially if the question is posed - 'well, what qualifies civil servants to advise people in industry about industrial relations?' The question is pertinent because PASIROs apart, the advisers whose work is being described, discussed and evaluated in this book, are career civil servants and only a few among them have experienced non civil service employment. This issue of what might be termed 'advisory credibility' joins the number of other issues already identified for later discussion. Returning to the PASIROs, it could be expected that one or two would be operating in each region at any one time. It would be usual for their expertise to be made available to the whole of a region rather than to a particular sector of it.

In looking at the basic features of the advisory resource, it is important not to overlook the support advisers receive from internal administrative, clerical, typing, information and library services. Such services are naturally shared with conciliators and staff involved in arbitration work. It will be recalled that a great deal of advisory work in the form of transmitting information is carried out at the enquiry points at regional offices (see p.13). Much of that work falls to clerical officers and executive officers and consists largely of answering

telephone enquiries about an extensive range of
industrial relations and employment matters. 5)
To list the formal hierarchy of civil service
grades already mentioned, together with those at
head office as yet unmentioned, could conjure up
an impression of ACAS constituting a large and cum-
bersome bureaucracy. The impression would be false.
The highest total of all ACAS staff employed was
reached in 1977 and 1978 when in both years the
figure was 819. 6) Of the 819 in 1978, 159 were
head office staff. 7) Affected by government economy measures the total staff in December 1983
numbered 628 including head office staff. Presenting such figures naturally leads to the question of
the size of the advisory resource with whose work
this book is principally concerned. It is not
possible to arrive at precise numbers because, as
already pointed out, it is quite common for advisers to combine advisory work with other duties
such as conciliation. Calculations have therefore
to be made on a full-time adviser equivalent basis
and it is from such a basis that ACAS have supplied
the figures which appear in Table 3.1.

Table 3.1: No. of advisers (expressed as full-time
equivalents)

Year	No.	Year	No.
1974	58	1979	147
1975	61	1980	150
1976	65	1981	131
1977	98	1982	125
1978	122	1983	129

Although explanations can be offered for the
year on year variations in the numbers of advisers,
it seems more profitable to point out that for the
years with which our research was primarily concerned, 1982 and 1983, an average of only 14 advisers
per region were carrying out visits and in-depth
work. Such numbers, even allowing for support
services, would seem sufficiently modest to absolve
the advisory function from the cliche accusation of
constituting a 'swollen bureaucracy'. However, the
extent to which 120 or so advisers can actually
improve industrial relations is quite a different
matter offering legitimate scope for independent
inquiry.
Before discussing the main characteristics and
operating procedures of the 120 or so men and women

who comprise the advisory field staff, it would
seem appropriate to complete the description of the
formal structure of ACAS. This entails a review
of the Head Office role of ACAS and its relationship with the regions.

ACAS Head Office

The first (1975) Annual Report of ACAS showed at
Appendix F the Organisation of ACAS at December
1975. This is reproduced below.
    Possibly because of the frequency of changes
known to have occurred, organisation charts have
not appeared in subsequent annual reports. However,
the following chart will serve as a basis for
explanation and commentary.
    It will be noted from the 1975 chart that reg-
ional directors reported to the ACAS Secretary. It
will also be seen that Director, Branch 3 had
responsibilities for Individual Conciliation,
Advisory and Industrial Relations Information
Services. (The Directors of Branches 1 to 5 inclusive, the Director Administrative Branch and Chief
Information Officer were, as might be imagined,
head office jobs). By 1982 a number of important
organisational changes had taken place. There was
no longer a post of Secretary to ACAS. The chairman of ACAS, now Mr. Pat Lowry, also served as the
Chief Executive of the service. The post of Chief
Conciliation Officer remained as before. Answer-
able to him was a director responsible for the
Conciliation (Collective) and Arbitration Branch.
The Advisory and Individual Conciliation Branch
continued to be headed by a director. These two
directors share a responsibility for the development and implementation of the functional aspects
of the Service's work throughout the country. In
place of Branches 4 and 5, Administration and
Chief Information Officer there appeared a
Resources and General Policy Branch - with a direct-
or in charge. This branch covered an administration division, a general policy division, and an
information division - including press relations.
    For the management of resources the regional
director is accountable, through the Director of
Resources and General Policy, to the Chief Executive. The regional director is directly accountable
to the two functional head office directors for the
implementation of functional policies. The three
head office directors together with the Chief
Conciliation Officer and the Chief Executive act as

The Organisation of the Advisory Function

Figure 3.2: Organisation of ACAS at December 1975

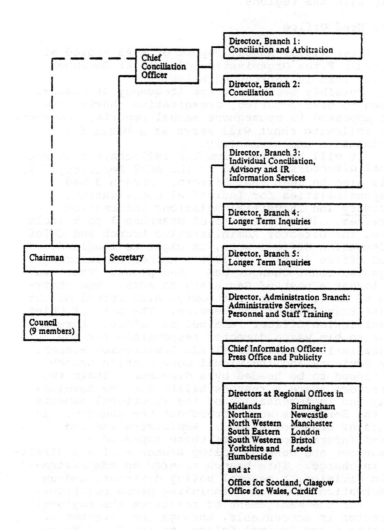

Chief Conciliation Officer	Director, Branch 1: Conciliation and Arbitration
	Director, Branch 2: Conciliation

Director, Branch 3: Individual Conciliation, Advisory and IR Information Services

Director, Branch 4: Longer Term Inquiries

Director, Branch 5: Longer Term Inquiries

Director, Administration Branch: Administrative Services, Personnel and Staff Training

Chief Information Officer: Press Office and Publicity

Directors at Regional Offices in

Midlands	Birmingham
Northern	Newcastle
North Western	Manchester
South Eastern	London
South Western	Bristol
Yorkshire and Humberside	Leeds

and at

Office for Scotland, Glasgow
Office for Wales, Cardiff

Chairman — Secretary

Council (9 members)

the top management team which seeks to bring regional activity into reasonable congruity with central-
ly agreed policy objectives. To that end, regular
dialogue takes place between head office and regional senior management.

The link between the regional director and the
Advisory and Individual Conciliation Branch consists of a discussion process whereby advisory targets for a region can be jointly set by head office
and the region - and modified in the light of justifiable circumstances. It is obvious that with an
advisory service that is largely client demand related, precise objectives and workloads cannot be
set for a region. Nevertheless, it is possible to
decide for example, that X per cent rather than Y
per cent of development visits in a region should
be made to firms in category size C. Similarly,
regional directors are encouraged to try and bring
about a higher proportion of joint working parties
in the in-depth work undertaken. The reasons why
head office should seek to bring about changes in
the mix of advisory activities are bound up with
policy decisions, the taking of which is a formal
Council responsibility. More will be said on this
point later.

During 1982 the head office Advisory and Individual Conciliation Branch consisted of three sections. Each had a measure of responsibility for
different aspects of advisory work. In a limited
number of cases and especially where large companies with establishments in different ACAS regions
were concerned, the responsibility for conducting
or co-ordinating an in-depth project would be taken
by the appropriate head office section. Another
section was responsible, among other matters, for
the collection, analysis and dissemination of a
vast amount of industrial relations intelligence.
The Industrial Relations Information Service - IRIS,
as it is usually designated - is available to
regional and head office staff. This advisory
section also prepares the published ACAS advisory
literature and manages the ACAS library. The third
section and the one most closely associated with
advisory work in the field was the concern of a -
Manager, Advisory Services. The responsibilities
associated with this post included - assistance with
the formation of advisory policy, the preparation
of papers to Council on aspects of advisory work,
monthly report on advisory work for Council, guidance and instructions to regional operational staff,
monitoring and appraisal of regional advisory work,

scrutiny and control of documentation submitted by regions on current advisory work, issue of operational memoranda, compilation of advisory work statistics.

The terminology employed in this 'job description' sheds light on the subtle task of achieving the right creative tension between regional autonomy and what was indicated earlier as being a need for 'a common approach' in 'a single service'. The latest attempt at 'a common approach' in regard to policy objectives was taken in 1979 with the endorsement by Council of 'operational guidelines' to be followed by regional directors and their staffs. Since then revised guidelines have been issued each year. Those for 1982 are given below:

ADVISORY WORK - OPERATIONAL GUIDELINES FOR 1982

1. To involve both management and employee representatives wherever practicable in ACAS work.

2. To use advisory contacts, especially visits, to promote consideration of <u>Improving Industrial Relations</u>* and encourage systematic examination of practices and procedures.

3. To offer help in identified organisations or industries where industrial relations problems exist or are apprehended and where the independence of ACAS has particular advantages.

4. To maximise the amount of in-depth work undertaken.

5. To undertake an agreed programme of contacts at regular intervals according to size of establishment to ensure that an adviser is known to most employers and full-time trade union officers in a region.

6. To establish contact with every significant employer and full-time trade union officer in localities where special employment factors exist.

7. To deal with enquiries and supply advice by the most appropriate means and to use such contacts to widen knowledge of advisory services.

8. To manage regional resources to improve the scope and quality of advice given and assess effectiveness by systematic follow up of completed work.

9. To develop a store of knowledge of good industrial relations practices and to ensure that this is made generally available both within the Service and outside.

* An ACAS leaflet of that title.

44

The Organisation of the Advisory Function

In themselves the guidelines may not seem very
remarkable. Their bland formulation may well invite attack from acerbic and radically inclined
academics. But it has to be remembered that the
formulation has to be acceptable to influential
management and trade union members of the Council
and the three independents who are usually - academics. The guidelines also need to be viable in
operational terms. It would not be feasible as a
policy or operational objective to include a guideline which said for example - 'improve industrial
relations in Fleet Street by any or all advisory
means'. Even so, as part of the guidance package
endorsed by Council, regional directors are expected to pay particular attention to identified
industries and localities within their own regions.
The selection criteria for 'priority industries'
and 'priority localities' include - a known history
of industrial relations difficulties, an industrial
area badly affected by the recession, an enterprise
zone where new or inexperienced employers moving
into the locality may welcome guidance on personnel
management matters.
    But the guidelines remain guidelines and do not
constitute strict instructions for precise operations. While allowing for the uncertain and fluct-
uating demand factor, the regional director is
expected to deploy his advisory resource in a
manner consistent with the guidelines. This seems
to represent an attempt to give considered direction to aspects of advisory work rather than to control, in a tight-reined manner, the advisory
function from head office. From the total interview
evidence, advisers appeared to welcome the guideline policy and did not regard it as a threatening
development. Criticisms were reserved for particular guidelines especially some of the earlier
choices which were held to be irrelevant to local
experience.
    The organisation structure of ACAS now having
been outlined and commented upon, it is appropriate
to turn to the operating procedures adopted by ACAS
in so far as they concern the advisory function.

Procedures and processes

As advisers are civil servants, commonly with past
experience in government departments, usually the
Department of Employment, they are well versed in
the arts of form design and completion. Awareness
of hierarchies and their differential significance,

45

and observance of orderly procedures are as second
nature to them. While it is not necessary to item-
ise all the documentation that comes an adviser's
way it is useful to draw attention to some of the
paperwork and the procedures of which it forms a
part.
     Head office provides an intermittent flow of
operational memoranda on advisory work to the
regions. Some of the memoranda are necessitated
by new legislation bearing on the employment relationship. A consistent service wide response is
obviously desirable when clients seek advice about
topics as tangential as the Patents Act 1977 and
its effect on the ownership of an invention made by
an employee; or as sensitive as the closed shop.
Advisers need to be au fait with the procedures
to be followed for liaising with, for example, the
Health and Safety Executive, the Equal Opportunities
Commission, the Commission for Racial Equality.
Other memoranda will relate to internal matters such
as the training of advisers or to the reporting of
regional advisory activities. The last type of
memorandum provides a clear picture of how the service seeks to build up a detailed and accurate
account of the advisory work that is being undertaken.
     The key document from which data is aggregated
and analysed for various management purposes is the
work diary. The diary is completed by individual
advisers and conciliators alike and covers a week's
work on a daily basis. The basic unit of measurement is a man-day and this can be divided into
units of 1/8th. It thus becomes readily possible
to calculate, for example, the number of man-days
taken up by a particular survey or project. Reasonably detailed guidance is given on the activities
that should be considered to be part of a project -
eg any special reading involved, preliminary visits,
time occupied by a feasibility study and follow-
up visits to the client after the formal conclusion
of the work. Similar guidance is given concerning
types of advisory activity. The process may sound
fussy but concern about efficiency would be a
fairer assessment because, to quote from an operational memo:

     In common with other public services, ACAS has
     a responsibility to try and ensure that it
     provides value for money...

     A significant contribution to the value for

money objective can result from efficient operating
procedures. An adviser therefore cannot decide on
his own account that a particular piece of in-depth
work should be undertaken. Keenness to do the work
is not anough. Cost effectiveness plays its part.
The adviser must formally seek his PIRO's permission or even regional director's, to carry out the
in-depth work. Such arrangements may seem to run
counter to the basic self-management character of
the adviser's job mentioned earlier, but this is
not really the case. The decision whether or not
to carry out a particular piece of in-depth work
remains a management decision. But if such work
is accepted then only the adviser/s at the company
location where, for example, job evaluation is being
introduced, can decide how best to manage the day-
to-day advisory inter-action with the client. At
particular times, senior colleagues including the
PIRO or even regional director may become involved
in the operational aspects of the in-depth work.
But, for the most part, the adviser remains responsible for the management of how the work task is
performed. As the man, or woman, on the spot where
the advice is being proffered, he is best placed
to make decisions about the many detailed operational points that arise, not least those concerning
who can be seen when. Such outwardly mundane but
often critical timing factors have to be placed
within the total work programme of the adviser.

Requests for visits, usually from companies,
form a regular part of the adviser's work. But
such requests do not come at regularly spaced intervals or necessarily from clients who are convenient-
ly located near to one-another, to the adviser's
office or home. The adviser will also be expected
to make a number of development visits, possibly,
as it turns out, to companies which have had no
previous contact of any kind with ACAS. Such companies, though polite, may well be puzzled by this
sudden (to them) overture by ACAS to discuss the
advisory role with them. In fixing any appointment
for any purpose the bias is inevitably in the
direction of the client's or potential client's
time preferences. An adviser himself needs time
in the office, as well as in the field, to read, to
complete his paperwork, write reports, discuss
matters with his colleagues. It needs only a little
imagination to envisage the complexities that can
help to shape the portfolio of the individual adviser's weekly activities. The nature of the job
requires that a wide measure of operational discre-

tion, of self-management, is allowed the adviser.

Another aspect of self-management derives from the fact that an adviser does much of his work alone. This is particularly true of visits. In-depth work will usually be conducted by a SIRO who may well have an IRO to help him. But even within a team of two or more and although liaising with colleagues, the individual adviser will often work alone on certain aspects of the assignment. Samples of employees may be interviewed by an adviser, discussions may be held by him with management and trade union representatives, separately and together. The advice is implanted in situations of variable but appreciable social complexity.

It is the adviser himself who must make what he can of the effectiveness of his personal performance - another aspect, and an important one, of self-management. He completes forms concerning different stages of the in-depth work, he drafts reports for clients. Forms and draft reports are read by the adviser's managers. Improvements to the report may be made, suggestions for operational improvement implemented. On the appropriate form an adviser sets down a cameo description of what took place at each advisory visit, request and development. He attempts a measure of evaluation of what was achieved by the visit. But visit or project the adviser remains essentially in a role in which he shapes what he does and how he does it in a very personal manner. Very often only he is there, on the client's premises, to judge how best to act, to react in the changing social circumstances that arise. 'But you weren't there, you don't know what it was like', can be the fair, if not necessarily fully justified, retort of the adviser to external criticism. (Much the same holds true, of course, of the negotiator, the conciliator, the arbitrator).

Given what was said earlier however, the nature of self-management has changed since ACAS was formed. The adviser enjoys less scope than formerly to determine his personal portfolio of activities. The development of guidelines tends to channel some of his work in certain directions - to particular localities, industries, sizes of organisation. He is encouraged to play his part in bringing about a higher proportion of in-depth work and to promote the concept and hopefully practice of joint working parties. The common reaction of advisers to these changes appears to be one of cautious approval - approval for the general idea of objectives and a sense of

direction - caution regarding the choice of objectives and setting of appropriate work load targets
for specific activities. As experienced advisers
see it, the wrong choices and the wrong emphases
could unwittingly nudge personnel into playing 'a
numbers game' in striving for target attainment and
potentially erode the freedom of the adviser in the
field to determine the most effective mix of advisory activities based on intimate local knowledge.
By 'numbers game' is meant distortions to classification and reporting systems that emerge to try and
meet numerical targets set for particular types of
activity, especially where such targets are thought
to be unrealistic by those to whom they are given.
The difficulties of achieving a sensible balance
between head office policy requirements and local
autonomy are openly acknowledged by all concerned.
Efforts to find that balance continue and they will
of course be materially influenced by the dynamics
of the industrial relations system itself.

The personal performance aspect of the self-
management character of the adviser's job has also
come under closer scrutiny in recent times. In
1978 it was decided to increase the managerial
strength of the advisory service and additional
PIROs were appointed in the regions. PIROs naturally form views about the abilities of the advisers
they directly manage, as do regional directors. But
an adviser who, for example, is a good report writer
cannot automatically be assumed to be a good adviser - or vice versa. Opinions concerning advisory
effectiveness can be volunteered by or sought from
clients and recently the attempt has begun to
collect information in a more systematic way from
clients after a piece of in-depth work has been
completed. Such 'follow-up' visits are carried out
by the advisers originally involved in the project
and although the intention is to evaluate what has
been achieved, rather than to evaluate the advisers
as individuals, the follow-up process cannot be
free of the drawbacks associated with self-evalua-
tion. To ask other advisers to do such follow-up
work could be wasteful, the problems tackled having
in effect to be studied twice, invite charges of
inspection by one's peers and strain relationships
between colleagues, some of whom will be competit-
ors in the promotion race. Our own, independent,
research into evaluation focussed upon the work
done and not the individuals who had carried it out.
We saw it as no part of our responsibility to affect
the careers of individuals.

The Organisation of the Advisory Function

This section on procedures and processes would not be complete without reference to what is probably the most important process which binds together the structure and procedures to create the organism called the advisory service. The process is simply that of talking. Discussion takes place at every level and between every level of the ACAS organisation. This is not to say that the ACAS chairman exchanges views with every clerical assistant but ample scope does exist for the transmission of information and opinions in both vertical and lateral directions. The methods employed are formal and informal.

Council meets each month. Reports are received from functional heads, including the director of the advisory service. The manager, advisory services, will be in attendance at Council meetings. Although the advisory report is unlikely to prompt as much discussion as the Chief Conciliation Officer's report on major disputes and attempts at their settlement, there is good reason to believe that Council members have become increasingly interested in advisory work. Regular conferences (seven/eight a year) of regional directors are also held chaired by the ACAS chairman. Functional heads make 'state of play' presentations regarding the functions for which they are responsible. Papers on particular features of industrial relations may be presented and discussed. Draft ideas on advisory guidelines for the following year may be considered. Following a regional directors' conference it is usual for a regional director to report back to his own staff about what has been taking place and what is planned.

Regional directors recognise the need to keep in close touch with their own staff. This reading of the management situation is consistent with our own research finding, from many interviews, that advisers identify primarily with their own geographical 'patch' and with their immediate superiors of SIRO (if an IRO), PIRO and director. For field advisers, head office personnel and their functions are remote and somewhat impersonal. For advisers, authority is embodied in their regional director and not the head of the advisory service although they acknowledge that the regional director's approach to advisory work is influenced by head office policies. Directors are well aware of these factors and tend to hold regular formal meetings with their senior staff and less frequent ones with larger numbers of their total work force. PIROs too convene meetings with their staff.

50

The Organisation of the Advisory Function

All of what has just been described is extensively supplemented by informal meetings which,
with relatively small numbers of staff involved,
can be fairly easily arranged. This tends to make
for a flexible local organisation which can adapt
quite quickly to the changing nature and level of
demand for advice from the environment. From close
observation of operating procedures in all nine
regions we would maintain that the adaptability of
the service is materially assisted by the absence
both of 'stuffiness' and the 'pulling of rank' by
those concerned. But those who do the adapting
also need other qualities to be able to give advice
on how to improve industrial relations. It is time
to give a broad brush portrait of the advisers.

The advisers

As our research was primarily concerned with the
evaluation of ACAS advisory work, it seemed sensible
to gather as much information as research resources
would allow, both from ACAS clients and from the
ACAS personnel who gave advice to clients. Analysis
of the information gathered from clients is carried
out in Chapters Four and Five. A brief description,
not of a stereotype adviser, but of the main characteristics of the advisory manpower resource now
follows. The description, and associated commentary, is based on interviews with 71 advisers and
adviser/managers - with just under half of the total
advisory field force in effect.

PASIROs apart, many advisers have reached their
IRO and SIRO positions by similar routes. Many,
particularly the older ones, were educated at gram-
mar schools gaining 'school cert' or, in the case of
younger personnel, 'O' levels. A few have university degrees. Typically an adviser will have entered the civil service directly from school, or after
national service, and joined the Ministry of Labour
as a clerical officer. Commonly there will have
followed years of experience in employment exchanges,
usually in a variety of locations. Experience of
other types of Department of Employment work may
have been gained such as resettlement of the dis-
abled, occupational guidance, staff training, wages
inspectorate duties. Becoming a member of the ACAS
staff may be due to a number of reasons - an interest in industrial relations, the wish for a change,
the possibility of promotion. It has to be remembered that because ACAS remains, for administrative
purposes, part of the much larger Department of

The Organisation of the Advisory Function

Employment 'Group', as it is called, of activities, movement in and out of ACAS by able and ambitious personnel is part of the civil service way of life. The new recruit to ACAS may have joined the Service not as an adviser, but as an individual conciliator concerned with statutory individual employment rights and the work of industrial tribunals. This post is established at the IRO (HEO) grade but advisers, as mentioned, occupy both HEO and SEO grades. Experience as an individual conciliator therefore may afford eventual opportunities for a lateral move to HEO adviser but a later upward move to SEO-SIRO adviser. It must be stressed however, that promotion is far from assured. It is not uncommon to find seasoned HEO advisers who are older than their SEO colleagues.

While relative youth is not an automatic barrier to early promotion, it could be expected, as indeed is the case, that the ages of IROs would fall within a lower age bracket than that of SIRO advisers. An IRO is likely to be someone in the early thirties to mid forties age range, whereas a SIRO's age is likely to fall within the late thirties to mid-fifties span. Although the quality of the advice given is obviously of greater importance than the age of the advice giver, there appears to be broad agreement among advisers that below a certain age, thirty perhaps, an adviser could experience credibility difficulties. Grizzled clients bothered about knotty industrial relations problems would be reluctant to accept advice from someone of overly youthful appearance and associated limited experience. The youngest adviser we interviewed was aged 33. Civil service conventions also affect the age factor in that in relation to a hierarchy of grades, and the promotion processes that link them, certain age brackets are deemed appropriate even if not inflexibly applied. Age can be important in another way. Between regions marked variations can exist in the age profile of the advisers. For historical reasons, one region may have a high proportion of advisers in the fifty to sixty year old age group who will progress no further. Another region may be well blessed with young, energetic advisers who have an eye to notable achievement and promotion. Notable achievements can result from development work and it seems fair to claim, from the evidence we have, that on the whole younger advisers feel more comfortable than their older colleagues about carrying out development visits, which, by their nature, require the exercise of promotional skills to be effective.

Whatever the age of a newly appointed adviser he receives on-the-job and off-the-job training. The inexperienced IRO is likely to work for and with a seasoned SIRO. The 'for and with' can be critical in a close working relationship. Opinions vary as to whether there should be clear demarcation lines between an IRO's duties and those of a SIRO, related to rank and experience. In practice, from our own observations, the prevailing ethos would seem to be one of 'mucking in' rather than of standing to one side because 'that's not part of my job'. We came across no evidence that things were left undone as a consequence of differentiated responsibilities. Common sense appreciation of the differences in personal experience plays a large part in task allocation.

On-the-job training, perhaps learning would be the better term, is continuous for although there are similarities, no two industrial relations situations ever seem quite alike. Off-the-job training is designed, and for the most part carried out, by ACAS personnel. The residential training has tended to consist of short, concentrated courses, mostly at an appreciation level, at intervals during the early stages of an adviser's work experience. The courses are linked and together constitute a programme the aim of which:

> Is to provide (operational) staff with an adequate knowledge of industrial relations and employment policies and with the skills, experience and understanding necessary to identify, define and suggest possible remedies for current problems (involving either individuals or organisations) and for the causes of problems within organisations. 8)

Knowledge, for example, is provided by a course entitled Industrial Appreciation 1 covering the structure and organisation of industry, companies and trade unions. Industrial Appreciation 2 has a high industrial relations content. It also includes information and guidance about the ACAS advisory role and operational methods. While experienced ACAS personnel are probably as well equipped as anyone to discuss industrial relations in practical terms, and as well equipped as many to consider its theoretical aspects, ACAS, as an institution, acknowledges a need for help from other bodies on certain technical features of industrial relations. A course on management techniques is therefore organised on behalf of ACAS by the Engineering Employers' West of England Association. The subjects covered include cost control, stock control, work study - especially as applied in manufacturing industry. It is accepted that expertise cannot be established in the time available, but a useful measure of familiarity can. In a sense, of course, PASIROs also serve as consultants to ACAS during their employment with the service, and are used to assist with training courses. In addition to the topics already mentioned, ACAS in-house courses are also concerned with diagnostic techniques consisting of guidance on techniques, accompanied by case study work and exercises including the preparation and evaluation of reports. To the same general end of developing analytical ability, courses concerned with the development of social skills have been introduced.

Interspersed with the formal courses are periods of industrial attachment. These entail generosity on the part of companies, trade unions and other institutions which are prepared to play host to an adviser allowing him to study, in some detail, for example, the operation of a manufacturing company, the day-to-day work of a full-time trade union official, the features of a particular management technique, of a job evaluation scheme.

Most of the advisers we interviewed considered that training could be improved. Some of the criticisms were identical to those directed at teaching and training generally, having to do with length, content and level of courses and the competence of the instructors - internal and external. ACAS have been aware for some time of the need to improve training arrangements. The matter has been studied by a working party and certain changes have been made including the enhancement of the status of the training function in various operational ways.

A problem area remains the industrial attachment. Advisers' evaluations of this training activity ranged from 'an invaluable experience' to 'a complete waste of time'. There is no self-evident way in which the success of each attachment can be ensured. There are many evident ways in which things can go wrong. Despite careful preparation by host company and ACAS personnel at one level, there may be inadequate understanding and preparation at other levels within the company. The relatively inexperienced adviser himself may be too

polite or insufficiently assertive to point out to
host company personnel that he is not getting to
grips with the detailed workings of the complicated
piecework payment system in the way he had understood would be the case. Despite the disappoint-
ments voiced by individual advisers, the collective
view remained that the industrial attachment part
of the training should be retained.

We now know, if in very condensed form, something about the background from which advisers come,
and their early training. 9) To complete what remains a broad brush portrait it seems fitting to
add those touches of colour which lend greater
humanity to the portrait. Like everyone else advisers have personal qualities but there may be
particular personal qualities which are thought,
by them, to be especially important in the make-up
of an effective adviser. Furthermore, are there
special qualities that qualify a civil servant in
particular to be an effective industrial relations
adviser?

The personal qualities thought by the advisers
themselves to be important for the effective adviser appear to fall into four broad, overlapping
categories. These can be labelled, admittedly
somewhat simplistically, as - communication skills;
personality; self-reliance, and impartiality. A
good adviser needs a great deal of patience, to be
able to listen attentively, exercise tact and be
articulate in speech and writing. He needs to be
personable, persuasive and self-confident, without
being 'pushy'. He must be adaptable, resilient
and self-reliant as the job, as indicated, is often
a lonely one. He should be able to analyse situations in a clear headed manner, understanding the
different points of view present in many industrial
relations situations, and display impartiality.

The term impartiality occurred frequently in
answers to the question about the qualifications of
a civil servant, with little or no direct industrial or commercial experience, to be an industrial
relations adviser. The deeply ingrained civil
service practice of presenting relatively dis-
passionate assessments of a variety of optional
courses of action, is retained by ACAS advisers.
The social skills associated with the giving of
disinterested advice have been well developed, in
many instances by advisers' past experience in
employment exchange work, where great diplomacy was
often required to deal with the many, varied and
difficult human and technical problems that arose

(and still do) at the benefit counter. Advisers
believe that clients see them as civil servants
and therefore impartial in the civil service tradition of not representing a sectional interest
such as a firm of consultants, a trade union, an
employers' organisation. (Furthermore, to the
client the adviser presents no threat from the
State. He is not a civil servant who is inspecting,
enforcing, licensing, collecting money). Impartiality, in the sense of not representing a sectional interest would seem, prima facie, to be an especially important feature of ACAS advisory work.
Some of the evidence presented in Chapters Four,
Five and Six is pertinent to the impartiality
theme. Before that and other evidence can be considered, it is necessary to present a brief account
of the general approach to the research undertaken
and the methodology employed. This constitutes the
introduction to the next chapter.

NOTES AND REFERENCES

1. ACAS First Annual Report 1975, p.6.
2. ACAS Annual Report 1979, p.9.
3. For administrative purposes ACAS forms
part of the wider Department of Employment Group
of the civil service. Many ACAS personnel have
Department of Employment experience and some return
to the DE after a period with ACAS. 'The status of
the staff as civil servants has been confirmed by
the Government's decision to make the Service a
Crown body'. ACAS First Annual Report 1975, p.7.
4. ACAS First Annual Report 1975, p.7.
5. From listening in to telephone enquiries
and answers in a number of regions we were favourable impressed, for the most part, with the technical competence and diplomatic skills displayed
by the junior staff concerned. For further comment
see Chapter Seven.
6. ACAS Annual Reports 1977, p.6, 1978, p.7.
7. ACAS Annual Report 1978, p.8.
8. ACAS Training logbook.
9. Specialist courses, and attachments, for
experienced staff tend to be arranged on an ad hoc
basis.

Chapter Four

THE ADVISORY VISIT - CLIENTS' PERCEPTION

The central purpose of this chapter is to present an
analysis of the value placed by a sample of ACAS
clients on the advisory visit. Before setting out
that analysis it is clearly important to outline
the main characteristics of the sample, eg the number of organisations involved and their size. Other
factors pertinent to evaluation such as the origins
of the visit and the subject matter of the advice
given are also indicated. A detailed account of
the actual methodology employed to arrive at a sample of clients for visits, and for in-depth work,
is provided in Appendix A. For immediate purposes
it can be said that the sample of visits is drawn
from every ACAS region but not for the same period
of time. An earlier pilot survey of the advisory
visit, the results of which have been published, 1)
convinced us of the value of seeking the co-operation of ACAS clients in each of the nine regions
but in a way that afforded an insight into the nature of the advisory activity over a reasonably long
time span. Instead therefore of approaching clients
where visits had been made in the same given month
in each region, a timetable was devised which covered a sample of advisory visits undertaken between
August 1982 and May 1983 inclusive. In other words,
all clients where visits had been made in Region A
during August 1982 were invited 2) to co-operate in
the research. The same approach was made in Region
B for visits made in that region during September
1982. This incremental process was repeated until
Region I completed the cycle with visits made in
that region during May 1983. One exception to this
pattern was made. It was thought that the incursion
of Christmas and New Year holidays would reduce the
volume of visits for December 1982 and January 1983
and the visits for those two months combined there-

fore constituted the client sample to be approached for Region E.

There were two main reasons for approaching a month's sample of clients. Although variations between regions occur, during one month something of the order of an average of 100 visits are made in a region. 3) Assuming something of the order of 30 per cent response rate in terms of completed questionnaires (based on the pilot investigation), a total of 250-300 evaluations (from nine regions) of the advisory visit seemed a not insignificant sample. The second reason had to do with cost - the cost of producing and distributing more quest- ionnaires than would be returned, and the overall constraints of the research budget.

Some basic points about the questionnaire, its design, distribution and use, need to be mentioned. Some of the questions were designed to elicit factual information in ways that would be consist- ent with published ACAS statistics. Size of organ- isation, by number of employees, was an example of this kind. Similarly the 'subjects' of 'advisory work analysed by subject' (cf. ACAS Annual Reports) were also used. There was a devel- opmental structure to the questionnaire, questions being grouped under the following broad but linked themes - background information about the organisa- tion; origins of ACAS involvement; people involved in meetings that took place; subjects of advice; mode of advice presentation; advice implementation; evaluation of advisory assistance. Questionnaires were only distributed to clients who had given their written consent to co-operate in the research. That consent was sent directly to ACAS which had issued the invitation to co-operate to all clients who had been visited in the stated months and regions. This procedure was necessitated by the confidentiality bond existing between ACAS and each of its client organisations. Once the names and addresses of co-operating clients had been passed to the researchers, questionnaires were distributed. Completed questionnaires were returned directly to the researchers and an undertaking was given that no other party would be shown a completed question- naire. No completed questionnaire has been seen by any member of ACAS and no request to see one has been made. It can therefore be justly claimed that the findings of this chapter are based on facts and opinions freely given and in the knowledge that confidentiality will be respected. Such factors would seem not unimportant when the client's

58

evaluation of advisory work is itself evaluated.

Before presenting the main characteristics of
the responding sample of ACAS advisory visit
clients, it is as well to introduce the reminder
that during 1982 advisory visits accounted for
nearly half (47 per cent) of ACAS advisory activities. 4) Although that percentage may decline, as
intimated in Chapter Two, there is no reason to
suppose that the advisory visit will cease to be a
major consumer of the advisory resource.

Size of the responding sample

Across the nine regions and ten months concerned
ACAS issued 770 invitations to clients to co-operate
in the research. 5) More than half (411) of the
clients said they would help and nearly two thirds
of that number, 258, actually did by returning
completed questionnaires which could be processed
on a computer. In relation to the total potential
respondents, 258 constitutes an encouraging 33.5
per cent response rate. A number of clients who
had agreed to co-operate but did not return completed questionnaires still volunteered information,
by letters, phone calls or partly completed questionnaires. If these 31 additional returns are
added in, the response rate rises to 37.5 per cent.
On a completed questionnaire basis, the response
rate between regions naturally varied but most
figures clustered within the 28 per cent to the
34 per cent levels.

Main characteristics of the responding sample

Of the 258 visits represented by the total completed
questionnaire sample, 163 were requested and 95 were
non-requested visits. The proportion of requested
visits, 63 per cent in our sample, corresponds
almost exactly to the total 1982 experience of
ACAS as 'in 1982 they [the advisers] made some
10,800 visits, the majority (62 per cent) being in
response to a request for assistance and the remainder planned with regard to the potential needs
of the area and the effective development of the
Service'. 6) Such a close match 63 per cent: 62
per cent can only be a fortunate coincidence given
that a voluntary response from clients for part of
1982/83 is being set against the total advisory
visit experience for 1982. Even so, the comparison
does strongly suggest that on the dimension of
proportions of requested and non-requested visits,

The Advisory Visit - Clients' Perception

we have a representative sample.

The sample is reasonably representative on
another dimension. The 1982 ACAS Annual Report
shows that of all visits paid in the year, 1.9 per
cent were paid to trade unions. 7) (The corresponding figure for 1981 was 1.4 per cent). Of our 258
visits, 6 were paid to trade unions constituting
2.3 per cent of the total sample. The small number
of visits paid to trade unions may appear surprising but it does seem unlikely that trade unions in
their capacity as employers will seek advice from
ACAS. What cannot be readily demonstrated, at
least in figures, is the extent of trade union
involvement in advisory visits, many visits to companies entailing discussions with trade union representatives. In most cases however, it is the
role of the organisation as an employer that brings
about the advisory visit.

The distribution of the 159 employer requested
visits across industry groups is broadly consistent
with that shown in Table 2.5, p.25. Distributive
trades and Miscellaneous services accounted for 20
visits each, ie nearly 25 per cent of the total as
against 23 per cent for all visits made in 1982.
Our sample contained no requested visits from
Mining and quarrying or Vehicles and the modest
showing of these industry groups in the ACAS published tables has already been indicated in Chapter
Two. Distributive trades and Miscellaneous services also feature prominently in the total of 95
non-requested (mostly development) visits. A few
development visits were made to Mining and quarrying and to Vehicles. The only industry group not
to feature in our sample of development visits was
Agriculture, forestry and fishing.

As shown in Chapter Two and at Table 2.7 in
particular, ACAS relates the number of visits to
size of organisation - measured by number of employees. Using this measure, Table 4.1 compares the
results of our sample with the last five years of
total national experience (cf Table 2.7, p.29)

Table 4.1 indicates that on the dimension of
size of organisation our sample is broadly representative of the last five years of total national
advisory visit experience. Our sample appears to
be slightly over-represented in the size groups
1-49 and 200-299 and somewhat under-represented in
the 50-99 and 1500 and over size groups, but not on
a scale to constitute serious distortions to the
generally congruent pattern.

The nature of our questionnaire responses

60

Table 4.1: Advisory Visits by size of organisation, 1979-1983 percentage distribution

Size of organisation (number of employees)	Advisory Visits					Sample 1982/3
	1979	1980	1981	1982	1983	
1 to 49	22.2	20.7	23.2	23.9	24.0	26.0
50 to 99	13.2	16.1	13.6	13.6	13.6	11.0
100 to 199	14.4	16.5	15.0	15.6	14.8	15.4
200 to 299	9.8	10.2	10.5	10.0	10.4	13.0
300 to 499	12.8	11.8	11.9	11.6	10.7	12.2
500 to 1499	14.9	12.9	12.4	13.2	13.2	13.8
1500 and over	10.2	9.0	10.5	8.7	9.4	6.3
Trade unions	1.8	1.9	1.4	1.9	2.3	2.4
Employers' associations	0.7	0.9	1.5	1.5	1.6	-
Others	-	-	-	-	-	-
Total No. of Visits	12,602	15,222	12,484	10,841	10,892	254*

* 4 respondents did not give the size of the organisation

enables a refinement of Table 4.1 to be made. This shows, at Table 4.2, separate distributions for request and non-requested visits by size of organisation.

Table 4.2: Request and non-requested visits by size of organisation - percentage distribution

Research sample of visits

Size of organisation (number of employees)	Request	Non-requested
1 to 49	36.1	10.8
50 to 99	10.3	12.9
100 to 199	15.5	16.1
200 to 299	8.4	21.5
300 to 499	12.2	12.9
500 to 1499	11.0	19.4
1500 and over	6.5	6.4
Total No. of Visits	155	93

Table 4.2 shows that in our sample most requests came from the smallest firms whereas the distribution pattern for non-requested visits would seem to reflect the effects of the recent ACAS policy emphasis on making contact with a higher proportion of larger firms.

Whether advisory help is requested and given or results from a development visit, the figures in Tables 4.1 and 4.2 can in themselves tell us nothing about the numbers of people in relation to whom advice was given. In a small organisation the advice could apply to the entire workforce whereas in a large organisation the advice might concern only a small group of employees. The converse could apply - and so could many other permutations. With such possibilities in mind respondents were asked to estimate the number of employees to whom the advice related. Two hundred and thirteen responses were received. The number of employees to whom the advice related proved to be far in excess of 213 totalling 82,692. The 82,692 can be related to the respondents' total workforce of 122,747, constituting a proportion of just over two thirds, (67.37 per cent). In absolute and proportionate terms therefore, the advisory visit would seem, prima facie, to affect significant numbers of people. In regard to the visits to trade unions, the union membership in the relevant firms totalled

62

some 2,300 and the numbers to whom the advice related totalled 206. As will be seen later, the numbers and proportions of trade union members concerned change dramatically, in an upward direction, when in-depth work is considered.

As might be expected perhaps, when the distribution of the size of the group to whom the advice related was examined, the greatest frequency occurred in the 1-49 group. Fifty eight per cent of 'advised groups' came within this size band in the case of request visits and 30 per cent in the case of non-requested visits. Even allowing for the fact that the highest proportion of request visits came from the 1-49 size establishment (see Table 4.2) it does not follow that most good, in terms of advisory achievement, is necessarily done in the smallest sized firms. The issue remains open as the figures so far given cannot demonstrate the value of the advice. As we pointed out earlier;

> Revision of the particulars of employment for all 30 employees in one firm is an 'improvement' in the situation. But assistance with the easement of inefficient working arrangements involving 20 workers but adversely affecting 1200 others might be thought a greater improvement. 8)

To complete the account of the main characteristics of the responding sample, a few more features are indicated. The populations of responses to the relevant questions vary but remain substantial in each instance.

The very broad occupational groups employed at the establishments visited consisted of a majority of blue collar workers, in both requested and development visits but with white collar workers featuring more prominently in request visits. Predictably perhaps, the same sort of proportionate divisions are discernible in relation to the advised groups. In the case of request visits just over half (53 per cent of 161) were paid to establishments which were part of a wider company group organisation. In the case of the 95 non-requested visits the percentage rose to 77 per cent - indicating again perhaps the attention paid to larger companies through development visits. In relation to 146 requested visits, 36 per cent of the organisations concerned were members of employers' associations. The corresponding figure for development visits (86 respondents) was 64 per cent.

To a large extent it remains speculative whether
the 36 per cent of 'federated' firms who requested
help saw ACAS advice as additional to or in sub-
stitution for advice possibly obtainable from their
employers' associations, or head office where they
were part of a group. We do have some evidence
from comments made, that in an appreciable number
of instances companies saw ACAS as the first and
most appropriate source of help. Development
visits, being ACAS initiated, may raise different
questions in a potential client's mind concerning
the appropriate role of ACAS in relation to that of
other advisory institutions. Further comment on
this point will be made later.

In 56 per cent (of 141) request visit situations trade unions were recognised for collective
bargaining purposes at the locations concerned.
The proportion was larger, 69 per cent (of 88), for
development visits and this may be due to the higher
proportion of larger establishments in this sample.
In 60 per cent (of 133) request visits shop stewards, or their equivalent, played an active part in
local negotiations. The corresponding figure for
development visits was 74 per cent (of 86). In the
populations of both types of visit therefore, an
extensive degree of trade union organisation appeared to have taken place. While the presence of trade
union representation in a situation may or may not
alter the substantive advice given by an adviser,
it is almost certain to influence the manner of the
presentation of advice. This is yet another issue
for later comment particularly in regard to in-
depth work where there is a greater degree of trade
union involvement.

So much then for the main characteristics of
the samples of respondents. But how did the
adviser come to carry out each of the individual
visits concerned?

Origins of the advisory visit and people involved

While the basic nature of the development visit has
already been described, the character of the other
sub-division of non-requested visits needs to be
explained. 'Follow-up' visits, on a non-requested
basis, take place in order that the adviser may
discuss the outcome, if any, of an earlier visit.
The original recommendations may take time to implement, problems may grow or wither away. The
adviser may 'take the opportunity while in the
neighbourhood to pop in and see what the position

was now about...' the previously discussed topic/s.
Of the 20 follow-up visits in the sample 19 respondents said such visits had been worthwhile - with
one opinion to the contrary. The remaining 75 non-
requested visits were development visits of the
type already indicated. Sixty three respondents expressed an opinion about this unexpected ACAS
approach, 17 recording 'very interested', 35
'interested' and eleven 'unsure' as their reactions.
No-one recorded 'suspicious' or 'hostile' as a
reaction although these choices were offered.

Of the 163 request visits (the total population) 76.7 per cent (125) resulted from a company
request, the next highest category being joint
request at 9.8 per cent (16). Of 195 respondents
(drawn mostly from the request visit population)
almost half had had previous contact with the advisory service. Other important sources of awareness about ACAS work were - published information
and ACAS's own publications. The prominence of
previous advisory service contact in the answers is
at least suggestive of the phenomenon of satisfied
client seeking further help from the same source.

Where organisations had requested an advisory
visit they were asked to indicate the kind of circumstances that had brought about the request. A
choice of nine, broadly defined, situations was
offered from which respondents were free to choose
more than one if appropriate. Additions could also
be made by the clients. Many respondents made a
multi-choice decision. While these arrangements
increased the realism of the response, they created
complications in the presentation of results.
However, expressed in frequency of mention terms,
'a need to know more about employment legislation'
finished well ahead of second place 'an actual
industrial relations/employment problem'. There
followed in descending order of importance a
'pending problem' (of an industrial relations kind)
and an 'individual' as distinct from 'collective'
problem. A 'generally unsatisfactory state of
industrial relations' attracted fewest responses.

The choices made suggest that a request is
much more likely to emanate from an acknowledged
lack of specialist knowledge or from a problem
perceived as something tangible, specific and immediate - than from a generally unsatisfactory situation. There is also the possibility that people
are unable or unwilling to recognise or admit to a
state of 'poor' industrial relations. Less personal discomfort is likely to be experienced by a

client in admitting a lack of understanding of some
technical aspects of complex employment law than in
pointing out that industrial relations are bad in
an organisation for the management of which he is
partly responsible. If such speculations are valid,
an experienced adviser may see the specific problem
as a symptom of a deeper malaise and encourage the
client to consider the desirability of some in-
depth work being carried out. Choices from among
the nine situations referred to above were also
made by non-requested visit respondents. 'A need
to know more about employment legislation' again
headed the list, but by a narrow margin above
'another (unspecified) situation'.

The importance of employment legislation to
the role of ACAS in general, and to the advisory
and individual conciliation functions in particular,
is pointed up by the answers given to the question
concerning any previous contact clients had had with
ACAS. In the case of both requested and non-requested visits nearly 40 per cent of each respondent
group cited ACAS involvement in unfair dismissal
claims. Second in order of significance in both
groups was previous advisory help, again suggest ·
ive, in the case of request visits, of client satisfaction with earlier help.

Whatever the circumstances may be that bring
about a visit those present at the meeting can obviously have appreciable influence on what develops
out of a visit. If the visit is requested the
client will clearly decide who initially meets the
adviser. In arranging a development visit an
adviser may well wish to explain the nature of the
advisory role to someone at the most senior level
of management. The reality is likely to fall short
of the desire, especially in larger organisations
where middle management personnel specialists are
probably on hand to meet the adviser. Our development visit respondent sample confirmed this supposition. In 55 instances, (58 per cent of the total
non-requested visit population) personnel management were present as company representatives; the
percentages for line management and directors were
21 per cent and 16 per cent respectively. This con-
trasted with request visits when on a third of the
occasions a director was present. On most occasions, and this was true of both types of visit, the
number of managers present was small, usually one
to three. In 22 instances, mostly request visits,
trade union representatives, including full-time
officials on ten occasions, were involved. As might

66

be imagined, and as Chapter Five will show, the
extent of trade union involvement is much greater
in regard to in-depth work. With hindsight fewer
than 20 per cent of respondents (for each type of
visit) considered that it would have been right to
have involved more people in the visit. This compares to more than a third in the case of in-depth
work and probably reflects the greater complexities
of in-depth assignments compared to visits. But
whatever the status and numbers of those present at
a visit they are there to discuss particular industrial relations topics and advice is given concerning certain subjects.

Subjects of advisory visit

As Table 2.3 of Chapter Two (p.20) has shown, ACAS
Annual Reports identify 18 separate subjects in
relation to which advice has been given. As some
of these really amount to groupings of subjects, eg
'grievance, disciplinary, disputes and redundancy
procedures' we extended the list by separating the
procedures mentioned and by making similar refine-
ments elsewhere. Consequently the list was extended
to 34 subjects. Respondents were asked to specify
the subjects on which advice had been given, to
rank choices in order of importance where more than
one subject was concerned, and to add to the list
if necessary. In the event, not all of the 34
specific subjects were mentioned. No reference was
made to induction or training, job satisfaction or
'flexi-time'. Manpower planning featured once as
did negotiating procedures and safety committees.
Safety representatives were mentioned twice as was
job analysis. Reference to Table 2.3 (p.20) shows
that the single topics of job satisfaction and
manpower planning and the linked topics of safety
committees/safety representatives account for a
very modest amount of the total advisory activity.
     Turning to the subjects most frequently men-
tioned by the respondents Table 4.3 summarises
their responses by indicating all subjects that were
mentioned at least ten times (in request visits)
and the frequency with which those subjects were
first priority choice.
     Table 4.3 demonstrates very clearly, in rela-
tion to both types of visit, the significance of
collective procedural rules and of individual employment rules. (The 'rights of individual employees' and 'contracts of employment' are obviously
capable of being linked). The prominence of 'disc-

Table 4.3: Subjects of advice – order of frequency and importance

	Request visits		Non-requested visits	
	Total No. of occasions mentioned	Total No. of 1st importance mentions	Total No. of occasions mentioned	Total No. of 1st importance mentions
Disciplinary procedures	60	41	26	13
Redundancy procedures	47	37	11	6
Rights of individual employees	43	21	15	3
Grievance procedures	42	24	14	7
Disputes procedures	34	19	11	4
Payment matters/systems	22	14	10	5
Contracts of employment*	19	16	3	3
Absenteeism	14	3	13	5
Unsatisfactory industrial relations	12	8	3	1
Consultation	11	3	6	4
Local plant bargaining arrangements	10	3	3	–
Time keeping	10	2	4	1
	(158 respondents)		(90 respondents)	

* Subject introduced by respondents under   any other subject

iplinary procedures' may well reflect the concern
of the client and the adviser to align disciplinary
practices with the law as it relates to unfair
dismissal. It seems plausible that the economic
recession together with the latest and relatively
new legal rules relating to redundancy account for
redundancy procedures featuring in so marked a way.
    At first sight the emphasis on procedural sub-
jects in our sample may seem a little surprising
but reference to Table 2.3 (p.20) will show at
subject 2 in that table the importance, at least in
terms of frequency, of the procedural theme. It is
also worth bearing in mind that the data in Table
2.3 is compiled by ACAS itself from forms completed
by advisers who have themselves identified the
subjects of advice. In our sample the clients have
carried out the identification with an additional
indication of the relative importance of subjects.
Although the two populations of visits (Tables 2.3
and 4.3) are vastly different in size, the subject
evidence of our sample does suggest that it is
reasonably representative of the total subject
analysis experience for 1982 and 1983. The comparison also suggests that advisers and clients alike
perceive procedural matters in association with
individual employment rights to be prime subjects
of concern. A factor which conceivably contributes
to the prominence of these two subject areas may be
the client's perception of the civil service adviser
giving sound but essentially non-partisan information and advice on procedures, and employment rights
deriving from statute.
    But whatever the subjects of advice, their
relative importance in terms of frequency or order
of priority, the identification of subjects is an
early stage in the transaction of advice giving and
advice implementation - and in the evaluation of
that transaction. While the acceptance of advice
(to say nothing of its rejection) and its implementation in part or in whole, could be affected by
many factors, it seems reasonable to assume that
technical content apart, the manner in which the
advice is presented to a client could influence the
acceptance or the rejection of the advice.

Presentation of advice

It seemed fair to suppose that the manner in which
advice was given to a client could vary according
to the personality of the adviser and to the circumstances in which he found himself. In crude terms,

69

for the purpose of illustration, at one end of a
scale advice might be presented with an indifferent
take-it or leave-it attitude, and at the other end
with missionary zeal. It was also supposed that
clients would form views about the ways in which
advice was presented to them. Respondents were
therefore asked to indicate which of the following
approaches most closely approximated to the approach adopted by the adviser:

1. 'neutrally', eg these are the options and their
implications - but you, the client must decide what
is to be done.
2. 'positively' (Type 1) eg these are the options
and their implications but you, the client, might
think option A preferable to option B.
3. 'positively' (Type 2) eg these are the options
and their implications but you, the client, would
be strongly advised to adopt option A rather than
option B.
4. Some other way - please give brief indication.
Table 4.4 summarises the answers to these questions.

Table 4.4: Manner of advice presentation

	Request visits		Non-requested visit	
	No. of responses	%	No. of responses	%
Neutrally	62	40.5	38	57.6
Positive 1	45	29.4	15	22.7
Positive 2	30	19.6	4	6.1
Some other way	10	6.5	7	10.6
More than one way*	6	3.9	2	3.0
Total	153	100.0	66	100.0

*Category added as result of replies

The appreciably higher percentage of neutral
presentations in non-requested visits is notable.
The explanation may lie in the fact that most of
the non-requested visits were development visits.
As such visits are made at the adviser's request
it is likely that the adviser would 'set out his
stall' of potential advisory offerings in a careful
explanatory manner rather than that of a self-evident salesman. It is to be noticed that the largest

response in each group falls into the neutral category. Neutrally together with Positive 1 account for 70 per cent of the request visit responses and 80 per cent of the non-request visit responses. It would seem that only a minority of clients, albeit a significant near 20 per cent in the case of request visits, regarded the advice as assertively presented.

While the evidence does show that in the client's perception a variety of advisory styles is employed, perhaps the more important issue to determine is whether the chosen style is the right style. Respondents were asked whether 'the manner in which the advice was given was appropriate to the circumstances?' To this question 150 (98.7 per cent) request visit respondents said 'Yes' and only two 'No'. Sixty five (98.5 per cent) of non-requested visit respondents said 'Yes' and one 'No'. These results constitute very high success rates for the manner of advice presentation. But what of the matter? Was anything worthwhile achieved?

The extent to which an advisory visit brings about a change, and one regarded as beneficial by the client, is a much more difficult matter to evaluate even for those most closely involved, the clients themselves. To justify that claim, some of the subtle complications associated with the assessment of visits may be pointed out. Some advisory visits are made to pass on information, to increase the knowledge stock of the client. No immediate or near future action may be required. Some changes based on an adviser's recommendations may need to be implemented in stages. For clients in such situations our questionnaire might arrive at times when assessment was possible or when speculative prediction was entailed - or when some mixture of both circumstances obtained. Some advisory visits are requested because of an anticipated problem. For whatever reasons the problem may not materialise. Even these few illustrations should demonstrate the complexities associated with establishing the extent to which advice was implemented.

Advice implementation

Clients were invited to indicate the extent to which advice had been implemented on a graduated scale of to full extent, to appreciable extent, to some extent, to limited extent, not at all. As could be expected, the response rate was appreciably higher in the case of requested visits than in the case of non-requested visits many of the latter being of a development nature. Of the full population (163) of request visit clients, 148 (91 per cent) replied to the implementation questions. A summary of their answers is given in Table 4.5.

Table 4.5: Extent to which advice implemented

	Request visits No.	%
Fully	83	56.1
To appreciable extent	44	29.7
To some extent	9	6.1
To limited extent	2	1.3
Not at all	9	6.1
Implemented - but extent not specified	1	0.7
No. of respondents	148	100

As an initial assessment of the impact of the requested advisory visit, it is significant that the single largest category of response is full implementation - accounting for more than half the total number of cases. If the fully and appreciable extent **are combined then in 86 per** cent of the instances the advice has clearly been, on the criterion of acceptability to the client in practical implementation form, successful and influential.

In the case of non-requested visits just under half (46 per cent) of the total sample responded. Nevertheless, from the ACAS viewpoint that is an encouraging response rate because it suggests that development visits may well have borne fruit. Even during a non-requested visit the adviser concerned may well have been able to give advice in any dis-cussion that has taken place. Of the 44 respon-dents, 30 (68 per cent) said they had implemented the advice in full or to an appreciable extent. The largest single category was again full extent - 18 of 44 (41 per cent).

If the two populations of request and non-requested visits are added together, 157 of 192 respondents said that the advice had been fully or appreciably implemented. That success rate of 82 per cent, on evidence from all nine regions, can be compared to the equivalent rate of 78 per cent for one region for an earlier period in the pilot study 9) when separate figures were not given for the two types of visit.

Given what was said earlier about the possible implementation of advice in stages, it seemed sensible to ask questions about the possible future implementation of advice where this had not already been fully implemented. One indicator of the importance of pursuing this line of enquiry is given by the fact that in relation to requested visits a number of not at all implementers of Table 4.5 said that they would be implementing advice in the future. Only two respondents said they had not and would not implement the advice received. When responses on past implementation and implementation intentions were combined then of 148 respondents 135 (91 per cent) came into the fully and appreciable extent category of implementation. (The comparable percentage for non-requested visits, from a much smaller proportion of replies, was 86 per cent).

If again the populations of both types of visit are combined the total evidence demonstrates that of a population of 192 organisations, 173 (90 per cent) responded to advisory visits by implementing in full or to an appreciable extent, or expressing the intention of so doing, the advice received. At a level of 90 per cent incidence and in terms of advisory input in relation to positive response output, this must be considered an impressive achievement.

A limited amount of evidence was also gathered about the reasons why advice was not or would not be fully implemented. In regard to the 33 request visit respondents the most frequently cited reason (12 times) for non-implementation was the fact that the advice was of a character not calling for specific implementation, eg information for future use. Clearly that is support for rather than criticism of the value of advice. Next in frequency of mention were advice thought to be politically unsound and changes in organisational circumstances. (By 'politically unsound' was meant advice that was technically sound but incapable of implementation because of the climate within the organisation concerned). Of the 26 non-requested visit respondents, 19, by far the highest frequency of mention, gave future use as the reason for non-implementation. The predominance of this reason in regard to development visits could be expected. In the context of a general discussion a specific problem might not be identified but information might be given by the adviser which could be put to future use by the organisation concerned. What

73

should be reassuring to advisers, and of interest
to other parties, is that on only two occasions
(one request visit and one non-requested) was the
advice given held to be technically unsound and
therefore not to be implemented.

The evidence so far accumulated does indicate
a high level of favourable response to the advisory
visit. Even so, answers are needed to questions
concerned with the value placed by the client on
the visit and his assessment of the worth of the
changes brought about by the visit.

Clients' evaluation of advice

Respondents were asked to evaluate the general
quality of the advice given including information
provided to clarify issues and improve understanding. Table 4.6 summarises the responses.

Table 4.6: Evaluation of quality of advice/
information

	Request visits		Non-requested visits	
	No.	%	No.	%
Evaluated as				
Very good	101	65.8	25	37.9
Good	49	31.8	34	51.5
No particular views	2	1.3	7	10.6
Poor	1	.6	-	-
Very poor	1	.6	-	-
No. of respondents	154	100	66	100

The figures demonstrate very clearly that in
relation to its quality ACAS advice is highly valued by client and potential client alike. Even
where advice, or information, has not been sought,
as in the case of non-requested visits, its worth
is still recognised. If the figures for both types
of visit are added together then of 220 respondents
209 held the advice to be good or very good - an
impressive 95 per cent. As the 95 per cent derives
from a sample of work carried out in all regions
and over a period of ten months it can hardly be
considered a flash in the pan or freak phenomenon.
That view is strengthened by the fact that the
corresponding figure to 95 per cent, from a smaller
sample, in the earlier pilot study of one region,
was 91 per cent.

A high incidence of extensive implementation

74

of advice (see p.72) and a high appreciation of the
general quality of that advice may or may not bring
about significant changes to the clients' industrial relations systems. Respondents were therefore
asked:

> Bearing in mind that ACAS has a statutory duty
> to try to improve industrial relations and
> employment policies by advisory means, did
> the recent advice given to you bring about a
> change in the situation that was discussed
> with the adviser?

To that question 72.5 per cent, ie 95 of 131
request visit respondents said 'Yes' and the remainder 'No'. In the case of non-requested visits
the 'Yes' response was 59.5 per cent (22 of 37
respondents). If the two respondent populations
are combined the 'Yes' response becomes 70 per cent.
Part of the explanation for 'No' answers may reside
in factors already mentioned - situations where
advice had still to be implemented and instances
where the advice given was more akin to information
for possible future use than for immediate action.
Even so, a 70 per cent incidence of change among
168 respondents is significant especially when the
nature of development visits is kept in mind.
    It was perhaps to be expected that as questions
became more subjective and more difficult in the
sense of separating out the impact of advice from
the effects of other factors, the response rate
would drop. However, 93 of the 95 request visit
respondents who said there had been a change as a
result of advice implementation, were prepared to
evaluate the nature of that change. Fifty seven
(61.3 per cent) stated that the nature of the change
was 'significantly for the better' and 33 (35.5 per
cent) stated that the change was 'marginally for
the better'. The remaining three respondents chose
'marginally for the worse', 'significantly for the
worse' and 'uncertain' respectively. The 19 non-
requested visit respondents divided between eight -
'significantly for the better' and eleven - 'marginally for the better'.
    Some tentative explanation needs to be offered
concerning the short-fall between 93 request visit
respondents who reported change and the 138 clients
shown in Table 4.5 (p.72) who said that advice had
been implemented in some stated measure. Part of
the explanation may lie, as stated in the previous
paragraph, in the increased judgemental factors

called into the assessment of what took place. Much
could depend on a client's perception of change.
The linkage, in our question, of change with improved industrial relations could present a client with
difficulties of interpretation. For example, it is
certainly a plausible proposition that advice implementation might leave a particular industrial relations situation in a virtual status quo position
because the implemented advice prevented the situation from deteriorating or reduced imminent difficulties. Perhaps in the course of discussing with a
company its absenteeism problem in a particular department, the adviser may discover that the company's
grievance and disciplinary procedures are far from
adequate. With the adviser's assistance the procedures are suitably improved, industrial relations
continue much as before but with better safeguards
against their possible deterioration. In such circumstances, and the type of case cited is known to
happen, it is not self-evident that industrial relations have changed even though the advice has been
implemented and the advice appreciated by its reci-
pient. That last point may help to explain why,
as shown in Table 4.6, the general quality of advice
is highly valued and apparently 'scores' better, on
the given measures, than implementation and change.
There is also the simple practical supposition to
take into account, that an advisory visit of two
to three hours is unlikely to bring about dramatic
changes in a high proportion of cases.
     Whatever the validity of such explanations,
there was additional evidence from the questionnaire
responses that further changes based on advice were
still to be implemented and that when the implementation process was complete, it was thought that in
nearly 30 additional instances the changes
would be significantly for the better.
     Another way of attempting to evaluate the ad-
vice was to ask, as we did, what the consequences
might have been of not following the advice given.
Inevitably the answers had to be speculative and
for this reason it seemed better to allow answers
to be 'unforced' in the sense of not offering a list
of alternative situations from which a selection
could be made. Request visit replies totalled 113
of which 75 per cent in descending order of frequency of mention could be identified as 'a problem',
'worse industrial relations', 'legal complications',
'a dispute', 'a tribunal case'. Nearly the same
percentage, 73 per cent, of similar problems held
true of the 33 non-requested visit replies. The

76

overall message from both populations of replies would seem to be that but for the advisory intervention the industrial relations situation would have worsened. While that may not be a startling result it is consistent with the wider ACAS objective of improving industrial relations.

As part of the process of seeking the client's evaluation of ACAS advisory work, it was decided to broaden the approach by moving from the examination of a specific visit within the client's direct experience to what might be considered to be wider ranging policy issues. Respondents were therefore first asked to rank in order of importance the factors which, in their view, contributed most to the use made of the ACAS advisory service. Table 4.7 presents their answers.

Table 4.7: Factors contributing most to the use made of the ACAS advisory service

Factor		Request visits	Non-requested visits	Total
An impartial service ie attempting to be fair to all interests concerned	No. of times mentioned as being of			
	1st importance	84	47	131
	2nd importance	42	20	62
A technically competent service	1st importance	59	31	90
	2nd importance	44	20	64
An independent service, ie independent of government and sectional interests	1st importance	37	23	60
	2nd importance	41	24	65
A free service	1st importance	22	15	37
	2nd importance	26	11	37

The figures essentially speak for themselves and confirm, from a larger sample, the central message of the pilot survey that what principally matters to company clients is what might be termed the impartial competence of the advisory service. (It is noteworthy that in relation to both types of visit the distribution of choices between the factors remains basically similar).

The fact that the free nature of the advisory service is the least influential of the four identi-

fied factors is interesting and fortunately can be
elaborated upon by virtue of the answers given to
related questions. The question : 'do you think the
law should be changed to allow ACAS to charge for
its advisory work?' was answered by 246 respondents (request and non-requested visits combined).
Of the 246 93.5 percent (230) said 'No'. While
this would appear to constitute massive support for
the status quo of non-payment, the fee charging
issue and the possible money value of advice merit
closer examination. A multi-faceted attempt was
in fact made to elicit clients' views on these
matters. On the price value clients might possibly
attach to advice two questions were framed. 'In
principle would your organisation be prepared to
pay for ACAS advisory work?' and 'if at the time in
question ACAS had been a fee charging service is it
likely that an ACAS adviser would have become involved in your organisation?'
    Tables 4.8 and 4.9 summarise the answers to
the questions.

Table 4.8: No. of clients prepared to pay - in
principle for advisory visit

	Request visits		Non-requested visits	
	No.	%	No.	%
Yes	11	6.9	3	3.2
Probably	73	45.9	33	35.1
No	26	16.4	12	12.8
Doubt it	34	21.4	40	42.6
Doubt it very much	15	9.4	6	6.4
Total	159	100	94	100

    In relation to request visits it might be said
that just over half the clients might support a fee
charging service in principle a higher proportion, as could be expected, than in the case of non-
requested visits. However, principle and practice
are often and sometimes notoriously different.
Table 4.9 is pertinent to that observation.
    With hindsight it might arguably have been
better to have offered respondents the five choices
shown in Table 4.8 but the intention with the second of the two questions mentioned above was to encourage the client to concentrate on the issue of
whether the advice he had received in his specific
situation was the kind of advice worth paying for.

The Advisory Visit - Clients' Perception

Table 4.9: No. of clients prepared to pay - when advice given

	Request visits		Non-requested visits	
	No.	%	No.	%
Yes	31	19.3	7	9.0
No	67	41.6	46	59.0
Maybe	63	39.1	25	32.0
Total	161	100	78	100

If the 'Yes' and 'Maybe' answers are combined then 58 per cent of request visit clients might be thought to evaluate the specific advice received as worthy of payment. If, on the other hand, the 'Maybes' are equally divided between the 'Yes' and 'No' answers the 'Yes' per centage would drop from 58 per cent to 39 per cent. The higher proportion of 'No' answers in the case of non-requested visits was predictable perhaps given the nature of development and follow-up visits as already described.

Appreciable caution has to be exercised in the interpretation of the figures in Table 4.8 because some of the 'No' answers for example might be related less to the estimated money worth of the advice than to considerations associated with that homely but still apt phrase 'he who pays the piper calls the tune'. Clients in fact were asked - 'if payment was required for advisory help, do you think this would adversely affect the independent/impartial nature of the advisory service?' Table 4.10 summarises the answers to that question.

Table 4.10: Payment and possible adverse effect on impartiality/independence

	Request visits		Non-requested visits	
	No.	%	No.	%
Yes	91	57.6	44	47.8
No	34	21.5	24	26.1
Maybe	33	20.9	24	26.1
Total	158	100	92	100

If the unequivocal answers of 'Yes' and 'No' are considered then Table 4.10 suggests that payment per se, ie irrespective of its source, would

adversely affect the impartiality and independence
(as defined in Table 4.7) of the service. If the
'Maybes' are divided equally between the 'Yes' and
'No' replies the possible adverse effects on impartiality opinions would increase to 68 per cent
of the 'vote' in the case of request visits and
61 per cent in the case of non-requested visits.
The fact that a smaller proportion of non-requested
than request visit clients are apprehensive about
the possible effects of payment on impartiality is
probably attributable to the differences between
the two situations of actually needing advisory
help (the request visit) and listening to an account
of the availability of advisory help (the development visit). The degree of client involvement in
the two situations is obviously quite different
with the request visit client having a much sharper
and more immediate awareness of the nature and value
of advisory assistance. In development visits there
is obviously less at stake for the organisation
concerned and therefore perhaps less concern is felt
about the possible effects, of payments on impartiality.
     As was pointed out earlier, the vast majority
of answers have come from company clients and their
answers on the payment/impartiality theme are likely to have been influenced by the thought that they
would most likely become the payers if fees were
charged. If that proved to be the case what might
be the reactions of trade union representatives
with whom they had dealings? Simply to pose the
question is to indicate that the 'free v fee paying'
issue can rapidly promote complex considerations.
For this reason it is proposed to explore it more
fully at a later stage when all the clients' responses, including those involved in in-depth work,
have been analysed and evidence from employers'
associations, trade unions and other interested
parties has been assembled. For the moment it is
sufficient to counsel caution in considering one
factor or one question in isolation from a variety
of others when looking at the payment issue.
     Reverting to general evaluation considerations
the last question of the evaluation section was
concerned to test, from a different perspective, a
broad measure of client satisfaction with the advisory visit. The question posed was - 'from the
experience of the recent ACAS advisory visit would
your organisation, in principle, be prepared to use
the ACAS advisory service again?' Of the 162 request visit replies 159, (98.1 percent) replied

'Yes' and three 'Maybe'. Of the 88 non-requested visit replies 75 (85.2 per cent) said 'Yes', eleven 'Maybe' and only two 'No'. Of the total population of visits this represents a 94 per cent 'repeat order' measure of satisfaction.

Looking back through the total evidence presented in this chapter we believe that it strongly confirms the central interim conclusion that we formed from the pilot survey of the advisory visit. We then submitted that 'when the evidence is looked at in the round, it constitutes an emphatic vote of confidence by the client in the value of the advisory visit.' 10) Whether such an evaluation will hold true of in-depth advisory work will be examined in the next chapter.

NOTES AND REFERENCES

1. Armstrong and Lucas, 'A preliminary appraisal of the advisory visit'.
2. A full account of the research methodology is given at Appendix A.
3. Estimate based on a total of 10,841 visits made during 1982, ACAS Annual Report 1982, p.71.
4. ACAS Annual Report 1982, p.45.
5. The pilot study returns and results are not included in the figures shown. The results from what constitutes a second sample from one region, as part of the overall study, are included. A suitable lapse of time occurred between the two samplings.
6. ACAS Annual Report 1982, p.44.
7. Ibid, p.71.
8. Armstrong and Lucas, 'A preliminary appraisal of the advisory visit'. p.21.
9. Ibid, p.25.
10. Ibid, p.27.

Chapter Five

IN-DEPTH WORK - CLIENTS' PERCEPTION

In its 1982 Annual Report ACAS briefly described the differences between 'Short-term work' (which
includes advisory visits) and 'In-depth assistance.'
It is appropriate to quote from the latter description as a reminder of the nature of in-depth work.

> More intensive ACAS involvement depends on
> determining with the parties the form of
> assistance most appropriate to their needs.
> For statistical purposes exercises taking
> more than a single visit are classified as
> projects (a series of linked visits), surveys
> (continuous ACAS involvement, usually over a
> week or more, to conduct a diagnostic analysis),
> or extended training exercises (assistance
> with industrial relations training designed
> especially for the organisation). 1)

As to the scale of in-depth work, projects,
surveys and extended training exercises (ETEs)
accounted for 35 per cent of advisory services in
1982 and 32 per cent in 1981 (See also Table 2.2
p.18). As mentioned previously, an advisory visit
might entail a day's work but the average number of
man-days required for a piece of in-depth work,
total approximately twelve. Examples of in-depth
work in summarised case-study form, are given in
the more recent ACAS Annual Reports. These are
typically concerned with - 'the payment system',
'the communications structure', 'all aspects of
collective bargaining', 'job evaluation', 'an integrated wages structure'. During 1982, 123 surveys,
359 projects and 33 ETEs were completed.
In the context of the research undertaken,
'completed' is an important word. It has to be
recognised that in-depth work at a particular loca-

tion may be spread over a period of weeks or even months. Advisory recommendations to a client might need to be implemented in stages and a further period of time might need to elapse before a proper assessment can be made of the effects of the work carried out. For these reasons, and following the experience gained from a pilot study of one region, it was decided that our enquiries should be directed at all in-depth work completed in a year. To avoid artificiality and the possible exclusion of a piece of work almost near completion a marginal expansion of a year was permitted in appropriate cases. The chosen year was not a calendar year. The start and finish of a year for each region was different being one month later for each region in turn. The pilot study apart, which covered the period May 1981 to April 1982, our enquiries for the remaining eight regions spanned starting times from July 1981 to March 1982.

Because of the greater complexity of in-depth work, compared to advisory visits, and because of the more frequent and deeper involvement of trade unions in such work, it was thought desirable to design five separate questionnaires. The ETE is a distinctive type of activity meriting separate treatment. The other four questionnaires had many common features and many of these were identical to those of the advisory visit questionnaire. But given that a trade union is a different type of organisation from a private company or public authority and that it often features in in-depth work, technically separate but substantially similar questionnaires for trade unions and employers seemed sensible. The remaining two questionnaires were the same as the two just mentioned - apart from additional questions. These were designed to seek the respondents' views on the value of joint working parties (JWPs) where these had been constituted. JWPs had been given much prominence in the ACAS 1981 Annual Report and later publications 2) and it was therefore thought useful to seek the opinions of those involved about this particular method of industrial relations problem solving. However, in order not to divert the narrative flow of this chapter into too many channels, the analysis of information and opinions gathered about JWPs, job evaluation and ETEs is, unless otherwise stated, given in the aggregated data.

The methods of seeking client consent to cooperation in the research, of questionnaire distribution and the maintenance of confidentiality, were the same as described at the beginning of the previous chapter.

Size of the responding sample

One of the complexities associated with the analysis of completed questionnaires on in-depth work becomes immediately apparent when it is recognised that many more interested parties than pieces of advisory work are involved in the enquiry. As with advisory visits, the total population of clients concerned including the unions involved - were invited to take part in the survey. The 742 interested parties (ie employer client and involved trade unions) were associated with 519 pieces of in-depth work. While this opens up the encouraging possibility of receiving and presenting a multi-perspective view of particular projects and surveys, it does make for difficulties of analysis and presentation. A discussion of the multi-perspective view of certain situations is, therefore, like the discussion on JWPs, reserved for future work. Although the status of the employer client and the status of the involved trade union are different, and this point will be amplified later, for convenience the generic term of clients will be used to cover all the organisations which completed questionnaires. On this basis, from the 742 clients concerned 436 agreements to co-operate were received. In the event, 290 completed questionnaires were received, 208 of which had been completed by employers and 82 by trade unions. In relation to the total client population of 742 the figure of 290 represents a notable re-response rate of 39 per cent. The 290 questionnaires covered 246 pieces of in-depth work and the 246 expressed as a proportion of the total 519 pieces of in-depth work completed during the period under review, constitutes a very significant 47.4 per cent. During 1981 and 1982 ACAS completed 468 and 515 pieces of in-depth work. Our questionnaire response sample of 246 would therefore seem to represent the equivalent of six months of total ACAS in-depth work and must be considered a significant sample.

The 290 completed questionnaires were all those that could be processed by computer. In addition, partly completed questionnaires were returned as were explanatory letters in lieu of questionnaires. If this supplementary evidence is included the response rate from the total client population rises from 39 per cent to 41 per cent and from what has been intimated already this constitutes a sizeable body of evidence.

Main characteristics of the responding sample

The distinctions between projects and surveys, and the refinement of the JWP, probably matter more to ACAS personnel than to anyone else. They are all types of in-depth work which as a general category is different in a number of ways from the advisory visit where, from the perspective of the research, a distinction does need to be drawn between a visit which results from a client's request and a visit which is initiated by the adviser. While we shall not therefore be making constant separations of surveys, projects, etc., it is perhaps useful at this stage to indicate the sample sizes of the different categories of work within the 290 questionnaire responses. They are as follows:

```
No. of responses
163 projects    (131 employer : 32 TU)
 84 surveys     (50 employer  : 1 employers'
                 association   : 33 TU)
 35 JWPs        (17 employer   : 1 employers'
                 association   : 17 TU)
  8 ETEs
290
```

In view of what was said above, the heavy trade union response in the JWP category is of especial interest. So also is the fact, not shown in the table, that in 37 instances the views of two or more parties are available in relation to the same piece of in-depth work.

In regard to ACAS statistics it is not a straightforward matter to estimate the extent to which our respondent sample constitutes a reasonably representative sample of ACAS work. Reference to Table 2.1 (p.16) shows that from its formation in 1974 until the end of 1982, ACAS had completed a total of 921 surveys, 1865 projects and over a shorter period 235 ETEs. This shows a ratio of roughly 1:2 surveys to projects with appreciable variation year on year. If the years 1981-83 inclusive are taken, ie those in which the research period falls, the ratios are 1:2.7, 1:2.9 and 1:3.2; JWPs being separately categorised in 1983. The distribution of our population of 246 pieces of in-depth work is as follows. (Most JWPs constitute projects).

        72 Surveys
       166 Projects
         8 ETEs

    The ratio of surveys to projects in the sample
is therefore 1:2.3 and on that criterion the sample
would seem to be somewhat under represented in
respect of projects. As our sample comprises the
broad equivalent of half a year's work then our 8
ETEs suggest, compared to Table 2.1 (p.16) that
this feature of in-depth work is somewhat under
represented.
    All 208 employer responses identified the in-
dustry in which the organisation was located. Just
over half the responses (105) came from the following five industry groups - Food, drink and tobacco
(26), Miscellaneous services (22), Distributive
trades (21), Chemicals and allied industries (19),
Electrical engineering (17). Expressed as percentages of our sample and respectively as 12.5 per
cent (Food), 10.6 per cent (Miscl. services), 10.1
per cent (Distrib. trades), 9.1 per cent (Chemicals)
and 8.2 per cent (Elect. engineering) then compared
to the distribution of industry group figures of
Table 2.6, (p.26) and the more relevant years of
1981-82 inclusive, our sample, on the criterion of
in-depth work by industry group can be considered
reasonably representative. The exception to that
generalisation is Chemicals and allied industries
which appears to be over represented. No questionnaire was received from the Vehicles industry but
as Table 2.6 shows and as previously stated, little
in-depth work has been carried out in that industry
group.
    It is perhaps appropriate to indicate at this
stage the number and types of trade unions that co-
operated in the research. The 82 questionnaires
returned came from 22 different trade unions. As
might be expected perhaps, the two largest general
unions featured most frequently - TGWU 38 times,
GMBATU eleven times. Other unions which responded
more than once were ASTMS eight, AUEW five, NUTGW
four, RCN two, EETPU two. Other respondents included NGA, NALGO, APEX, NUPE, COHSE, NUFLAT and
the AUT (Association of University Teachers).
    It is impossible to say whether this list of
unions and the varying frequencies of involvement
are in any way a representative sample of overall
trade union involvement in in-depth work as ACAS
does not publish statistics of this kind. Even so,
a sample size of 82 and a cross-section of 22

different and major unions would seem to constitute
a sample of fair significance. That significance
is heightened when it is realised and kept in mind,
as it needs to be, that those completing the questionnaires were, in the great majority of cases,
full-time officials and shop stewards who had been
closely associated with the in-depth work in question. It should also be explained at this stage,
elaborating an earlier intimation, that the trade
union responses cannot strictly be classified as
client responses in quite the same way as those of
employers. Almost invariably the direct client
will be an employer and the work will be undertaken
on his premises. The in-depth assignment will commonly affect trade union interests and may prove
abortive without union consent to its being undertaken or being progressed beyond a certain point.
Trade union representatives and trade union lay
members become involved in discussions with advisers. Those representatives develop opinions about
the in-depth work carried out and it is from that
perspective of immediate, first hand experience with
an actual piece of work that the trade union view
is sought and presented in this chapter. However,
unless the work is done directly for the union in
its capacity as an institution in its own right -
and we have no examples of that kind - the union is
in the position of being an involved and interested
party rather than a direct client. (A discussion
of ACAS advisory work, as perceived by the union in
its general institutional role, as distinct from
specific workforce representation, will form part
of the next chapter.)

The fact that we have fair sized samples of
employer (208) and trade union (82) responses makes
both for difficulties of presentation and the possibility of tedium if, on every item of concern,
both viewpoints are presented.

It has therefore been decided to be selective
and to concentrate primarily on matters where it
is obviously important to have the evaluations of
both parties eg concerning the quality of ACAS
advice. By contrast we see little to be gained by
showing the size, by membership numbers, of the
trade unions concerned whereas there is point in
tabulating, as was done for visits, the distribution
by size of organisation, of employer respondents.
Table 5.1 shows this together with the last five
years of total national experience - based on Table
2.7, p.29.

Table 5.1: In-depth work by size of organisation,
1979-1983 Percentage distribution

Size of organisation (No. of employees)	1979	1980	1981	1982	1983	Sample 1981/83 related
1 to 49	15.3	10.3	13.2	21.1	23.5	23.9
50 to 99	12.9	15.5	13.7	19.2	18.8	10.2
100 to 199	16.6	18.1	16.9	17.9	13.9	18.0
200 to 299	9.4	11.4	12.2	10.5	13.7	10.7
300 to 499	15.5	14.5	13.5	11.3	9.8	15.1
500 to 1,499	16.6	17.0	15.6	10.9	12.4	14.1
1,500 and over	12.7	12.6	13.7	9.1	7.7	7.8
Trade unions	-	0.2	-	-	0.1	
Employers' associations	0.2	0.2	0.6	-	0.1	
Others	0.7	0.2	0.6	-	-	
Total No. of pieces of in-depth work	457	476	468	515	717	205*

* Total No. of employer ie direct client responses

Compared to the last five years' total experience our sample, which is spread over parts of two
of those years 1981 and 1983 and includes the whole
of 1982, appears to be somewhat over-represented in
the 1-49 size group and under-represented in the
size groups 50-99 and 1,500 and over. Overall
however, on the size of firm criterion the sample
appears tolerably representative of the most recent
and relevant ACAS global experience.
    The respondent employers of Table 5.1 employed
140,208 employees and the advice given related to
93,987 of them - a proportion of 67.03 per cent -
an almost identical proportion to that for advisory
visits which was 67.37 per cent (See p.62) While
such a close correspondence must surely fall within
the realm of coincidence, the fact that visits and
in-depth work alike seem to be concerned, on the
clients' own assessments, with two thirds of the
workforce of the employing organisations strongly
suggests that the advisory input, in terms of its
localised coverage, is likely to be widely influential. Supporting evidence that this is so is provided by the trade union respondents. Of their total
18,958 members in the organisations concerned the
unions estimated that advice related to 15,445 or
81.46 per cent of them.
    Reverting to the employer respondents' charact-
eristics, as might be expected from Table 5.1 and
from the advisory visit results, in terms of the
size of the advised group, the greatest frequency
occurred in the 1-49 size band. In 71 per cent of

instances (200 respondents) the main occupational
group was blue collar. This group also featured
most frequently as the one affected by advice. In
nearly two thirds of the cases, the establishment
where advice was given formed part of a larger
group organisation. Some 45 per cent of the companies were members of an employers' association.
As with advisory visits, such a percentage prompts
speculation about the clients' perceptions of the
respective advisory roles of an employers' association and of ACAS. In 71 per cent of instances (191
respondents) trade unions were recognised for
collective bargaining purposes at the locations
concerned. In 76 per cent of cases (177 respondents) shop stewards, or their equivalent, played
an active part in local negotiations. The union
estimate, relating to a smaller population of responses, was 100 per cent. Viewed from either body
of evidence and allowing for some overlaps where
employers and unions comment independently on shared
situations, in-depth work, far more often than not,
would appear to take place in organisations accustomed to collective bargaining.

Origins of in-depth work and people involved

Table 5.2 summarises, from the perspectives of both
complete populations of respondents the formal
origins of the in-depth work.

Table 5.2: Origins of the in-depth work

	Company view (Frequency)	TU view (Frequency)
Company request	107	6
Trade union request	3	23
Joint, ie company & TU	51	36
ACAS approach*	17	1
ACAS follow-up+	13	5
More than one origin specified	13	10
Some other way	4	1
Total	208	82

* Sixteen companies replied to the supplementary
question concerning their reaction to the ACAS
approach. Seven stated they were 'very interested',
five 'interested' and four 'unsure - but prepared
to listen'. No one gave 'suspicious' or 'hostile'
as an answer although those choices were offered.

+ To discuss outcome of previous involvement

    As the two sets of responses relate to a smaller number (246) of pieces of in-depth work, they cannot be combined for this would entail some double-counting in relation to type of origin. Furthermore, as our previous article showed, 3) when two parties, involved in the same piece of work, identify the origins of the intervention they may do so quite differently, for explicitly legitimate reasons. It is better therefore to look at the two response populations of Table 5.2 separately. It is of interest to note that in the trade union response the joint approach assumes far more significance than in the company's response and constitutes the most frequent origin in the trade union view. This is perhaps to be expected because where a trade union is present in a location this must increase the probability of a joint approach. Conversely, the high proportion of unilateral company requests may be partly due to there being no trade union present in an appreciable number of cases. Our earlier work also suggests that even where employer and union are joint parties to in-depth work at a particular company, each side may separately claim in good faith that it initiated the advisory intervention. There are certainly more complexities involved in identifying the origins of in-depth work than neat categorisation would lead us to believe.
    But establishing the formal origins of in-depth work is probably less important to the improvement of industrial relations than seeking to establish how the parties came to recognise ACAS as a possible source of advisory help. The employers' responses (some 80 per cent of the total population) in descending order of frequency were 'previous contacts with advisory service' (just over half the replies), 'published information, from non ACAS sources, about ACAS advisory service', 'ACAS involvement in concilation'. Of the 75 trade union respondents 49 gave 'previous contact with ACAS advisory service' as the main answer followed at an appreciable distance by 'ACAS conciliation'. The two lots of results do seem to suggest that the old adage 'success breeds success' could well apply to advisory work.
    Knowledge and/or previous experience of the advisory service do not of themselves indicate the specific reasons for the parties' involvement in the in-depth work associated with our enquiry. Res-

90

pondents were therefore asked, 'which, if any, of the following situations influenced the decision to consider ACAS advisory assistance?' Nine situations were illustrated and respondents were free to add others and to choose more than one if this suited their circumstances. As in the case of advisory visits 'a need to know more about employment legislation' featured prominently in employers' answers but it came second, in frequency of mention terms, to 'an actual industrial relations/employment problem'. These two situations were markedly more frequent than a cluster of others close together these being 'unsatisfactory state of employment policies/practices', and 'industrial relations collective problem' (as distinct from individual), an 'actual industrial relations dispute'. A significant re-ordering emerged when the trade union responses were analysed. 'Employment legislation' did not feature in the first five most frequently mentioned situations. An 'actual industrial relations problem' featured most often followed by a 'generally unsatisfactory state of industrial relations' and then 'a general unsatisfactory state of employment policies/practices'. An 'actual dispute' and 'collective problem' were somewhat behind in fourth and fifth places respectively.

In the pilot study article on in-depth work we speculated about the reasons for the differences between the company and union choices. The additional evidence gathered prompts no radical departure from those speculations that the volume and complexity of employment and industrial relations legislation of recent years continues to bother employers in the sense of learning how best to cope with the law's requirements; trade unions as representatives of collective values and standards are more concerned about general states of poor industrial relations. The larger body of evidence does indicate some shift of emphasis, both parties making more frequent reference to actual problems. When asked whether the organisation or union had had dealings with ACAS on previous occasions both parties made most frequent mention of 'unfair dismissal cases'. As in the case of advisory visits, (see pp.65-68) employment legislation would seem to be a major, formative element of the nature and volume of ACAS work generally. In passing, it would seem worth mentioning that overall the trade unions appeared to have had more frequent contact with ACAS than had the employers.

As pointed out in Chapter Four, whatever the
initiating circumstances of the advisory intervention the status and perhaps numbers of those drawn
into the discussions could be critical to the successful outcome of advisory work. Common sense
would suggest that this factor is likely to be especially important in regard to in-depth work which
may spread, at intervals, over weeks or even months
and entail far-reaching changes. Of 208 employers,
184 responded to the relevant questions concerning
who was principally involved in the in-depth work.
In just over a third of the cases, one manager was
so involved and in a similar proportion of cases
two managers. The largest number, at any one time,
one response, was 40. Director was the status of
the group most frequently mentioned followed closely by personnel management and line management.
One hundred employers'replies were received concerning the workers' representatives principally involved in in-depth work - on 36 occasions there was one,
on 23 occasions two, and on 15 occasions three. The
largest single number present on any occasion was
98. Shop stewards and lay officials were the representatives most frequently involved but full-time
officials and operatives were also quite often
cited.
From the trade union population of 82, 62 responses were received to the identical questions.
In 25 cases (40 per cent) one manager was involved,
in 17 cases two and 14 cases three. In the union
experience line management emerged as being principally involved, followed by directors and personnel management almost on a par. As to the trade
union representatives principally involved, on a
third of (67) occasions one was present, on 27 per
cent of occasions two, and 15 per cent of occasions
three. Again shop stewards were well to the fore
with lay officials and full-time officials almost
co-equal in frequency of mention.
What the figures of the last two paragraphs
suggest is that on the whole relatively small
numbers of managers and workers' representatives
are closely involved in discussions with the advisers. It may be, as is not uncommon in collective bargaining, that key meetings whether separate
or joint, are attended by directors and full-time
union officials with line management, personnel
management and shop stewards providing the continuity of discussion/negotiation. In frequency of
reference terms, the role of the shop steward, as
might be expected, was prominent if not necessarily

dominant. But as pointed out before, all those concerned, whatever their numbers and status, meet to discuss the industrial relations topics which are thought to warrant the help of the adviser.

Subjects of in-depth work

The way in which the list of ACAS subjects was modified for the advisory visit analysis was explained at p.67. The same modifications were adopted for the analysis of in-depth work.

As with advisory visits certain of the 34 specified subjects attracted nil or minimal attention. These included, safety representatives, safety committees, equal pay, sex discrimination, race relations, manpower planning and shift working. This could mean that advice on such topics is unnecessary but experience suggests that such an explanation merits a sceptical reception.

Very commonly more than one subject was involved in a piece of in-depth work and where this was the case, respondents were asked to rank the subjects in order of importance. Bearing that latter point in mind, Table 5.3 has been constructed to show all those subjects where in either the employer or trade union responses a subject attracted ten or more mentions of first importance ranking.

The importance attached by both parties to procedural issues is self-evident. The thought again arises as to whether such procedural prominence is in some measure due to the parties' perceptions of ACAS as a third and independent party which can provide fair minded procedural assistance to employers and trade unions in separate and shared situations alike. Within the joint overall concern for procedural reform revealed by Table 5.3, some interesting differences of emphasis between the parties' evaluations are discernible. In relation to the size of respondent populations from which they are drawn 'negotiating procedures' features far more significantly for trade unions than for employers. The same holds true of 'local plant bargaining arrangements'. It has, of course, to be remembered that not all the employer respondents had collective bargaining arrangements whereas almost by definition this would be the case, or the objective, with the trade union respondents. The difference of emphasis may also owe something to the fact that a trade union, while not ignoring individuals, is very much concerned with collective activities. Conversely the employer, because

Table 5.3: Subjects of advice - order of frequency and importance

| | In-depth work | | | |
| | Employer response | | TU response | |
	Total No. of occasions mentioned	Total No. of occasions 1st importance	Total No. of occasions mentioned	Total No. of occasions 1st importance
Disciplinary procedures	93	42	24	15
Grievance procedures	71	30	21	13
Payment matters/systems	68	45	30	25
Communications	42	19	27	16
Redundancy procedures	41	18	8	7
Disputes procedures	41	22	18	9
Absenteeism	40	17	10	7
Job evaluation	39	26	22	12
Rights of individual employees	39	20	6	2
Consultation	28	12	18	7
Negotiating procedures	22	13	18	14
Contracts of employment*	15	14	-	-
Generally unsatisfactory industrial relations	13	5	21	11
Local plant bargaining	8	5	16	10
	(207 respondents)		(81 respondents)	

* Subject introduced by respondents under any other subject

he engages people as individuals, has matters such
as 'rights of individual employees' and 'contracts
of employment' very much in mind as the figures
show.

Other subjects in Table 5.3 can be reasonably
linked together such as 'payment matters/systems'
with 'job evaluation'. These substantive matters
are obviously important, from the figures, to both
parties. From the trade unions 'payment matters'
receives the largest number both of mentions and
of 1st importance rankings. If all the trade union
1st importance responses which reach double figures
are related to their respective totals of frequency
of mention, then at a ratio of 25:30 (or 83 per
cent incidence) 'payment matters' sits at the head
of that league table with negotiating procedures
14:18 (or 78 per cent incidence) in second place.
While another subject pairing can be made between
'communications' and 'consultation', 'absenteeism',
although it has procedural implications, seems to
stand on its own serving to remind us perhaps that
some personnel management problems endure in all
kinds of economic conditions. It is noteworthy,
and consistent with earlier comments, that the subject 'generally unsatisfactory industrial relations'
features far more prominently in the trade unions'
than the employers' responses. All in all, although the Tables are not directly comparable, the
sample of subject matter responses of Table 5.3
follow the major contours of prominence of Table
4.3 given the latter's emphasis on procedures and
payment systems.

It is time now to consider the manner in which
advice was given about the subjects in question.

Presentation of advice

The reasons for putting questions on this aspect of
advisory work were given on p.69 and had to do
with the adviser's mode of operation and the potential acceptability of the advice he offered. The
actual questions put to respondents also appear on
p.70. Table 5.4 presents the responses in
summarised form.

Even allowing for the subjectivity of the process, for example, one client might evaluate the
advisory style as Positive 1 and another in relation to the same style Positive 2, the volume and
distribution of responses demonstrate that a variety of styles is used. Sometimes more than one
style is adopted in a given situation as evidenced

Table 5.4: Manner of advice presentation - in-depth work

| | Employer Sample | | TU Sample | |
	No. of responses	%	No. of responses	%
Neutrally	67	33.8	41	52.6
Positive 1	62	31.3	16	20.5
Positive 2	48	24.2	17	21.8
Some other way	9	4.5	4	5.1
More than one way*	12	6.1		
Total	198	100	78	100

* Category added as result of replies

in the category that had to be devised as a result of a fair sprinkling of company replies. All this would seem to point to a flexibility of approach on the part of the adviser and the deployment by him of a fair measure of social skills. Some support for that not unreasonable conjecture can be derived from what is perhaps the most interesting feature of Table 5.4, the far greater incidence of 'neutrality' in the unions' than in the employers' responses. Considering why this should be so gives rise to various speculations.

The difference of response might be associated with a range of different industrial relations situations or with the fact that a trade union is a different type of institution from a company or the difference might be related to a mixture of both conditions. A trade union, by definition, is a bargaining institution, a company may or may not be engaged in collective bargaining - and unions were not present throughout the company sample. It may be that a union, as a bargaining agent, would expect counsel from an ACAS adviser to be presented in a non-pushful, non-partisan way, knowing that ACAS has a duty to assist both sides of industry. Such speculations could run on, but of more immediate interest perhaps is the answer to the question of whether the style of advice presentation, whatever its nature, was right, was 'appropriate to the circumstances?' Of the 197 employers who answered this question 191 (97 per cent) said 'Yes'. Of the 76 union responses 70 (92 per cent) indicated 'Yes'.

Of the six who said 'No', five would have preferred a more positive approach. While that dissent does not seriously detract from the argument just advanced about the incidence of the neutral response in the trade union replies, it does point up again the importance of a 'horses for courses' approach to advice presentation. The high percentages, 97 per cent and 92 per cent, of appropriate style occasions testify to the fact that in the vast majority of cases the advisers chose the right horses for the right courses. That in turn bears further witness to the social skills of advisers, a point mentioned above, and occasions the thought that years of experience in an employment exchange (cf Chapter Three) may have contributed materially to the development of those skills.

The presentation of advice may or may not be admirable but the more searching questions about the implementation of advice and its contribution to desirable change have yet to be answered.

Advice implementation

As with advisory visits respondents were asked to indicate the extent to which advice had been implemented. Choices could be made on a graduated scale. An analysis of the employers' choices, with the scale, is given in Table 5.5.

Table 5.5: Extent to which advice implemented, In-depth work

Employers' responses

	No.	%
Fully	89	46.4
To appreciable extent	78	40.6
To some extent	15	7.8
To limited extent	5	2.6
Not at all	5	2.6
No. of respondents	192	100

8 ETEs excluded. Response rate therefore = 192 of possible maximum 200 replies = 96 %

In the terms stated of advice implementation the figures indicate a high level of achievement on the part of advisers. In 87 per cent of instances advice was fully or appreciably implemented. No

doubt there will be those who will fret about the
2.6 per cent 'not at all' employers but the overall
effect of Table 5.5 should be one of broad satisfaction for all those involved in the in-depth
activities. That satisfaction should increase when
the results of analysing future intentions about
further implementation are shortly considered.
Some of the 'not at alls' of Table 5.5 are conver-
ted to some measure of future implementation.
(It will be recalled that the recommendations of
in-depth reports to clients are often implemented
in stages). Table 5.5 shows that 103 employer
clients had not implemented the advice - fully. Of
these 103, 95 went on to complete what might be
termed stage two of the implementation questions,
those concerning future intentions. Of the 95,
20 expressed the intention of fully implementing
the advice or doing so to an appreciable extent.
When the completed and future intentions categories
of fully and appreciable extent implementation are
combined, a total of 176 employer clients is reached or 92 per cent of the population of Table 5.5.
Only one respondent remained in the 'not at all'
category.

Of the 82 trade union respondents, 79 completed the relevant implementation questions. Table
5.6 summarises the answers.

Table 5.6: Extent to which advice implemented
In-depth work
Trade Union responses

	No.	%
Fully	31	39.2
To appreciable extent	20	25.3
To some extent	9	11.4
To limited extent	7	8.9
Not at all	11	13.9
Yes (not specified)*	1	1.3
No. of respondents	79	100

* Category introduced by respondent
Response rate 79 of possible 82 = 96%

When the 64.5 per cent of full and appreciable
extent categories is expanded to include future
intentions, the total rises to 68 per cent. As the
corresponding figure for employers was 92 per cent

some explanation of the gap between the two assessments must be attempted. The two samples are, of
course, not the same either in size or in status,
in the sense of the relationship with the advisers.
Except in a minority of cases the pieces of work
to which the assessments relate are not identical.
But arguably the most plausible reason for the
difference derives from the issue of status briefly
mentioned above and touched on at p.87. It is the
employers who are the direct clients of ACAS. The
advisory work is done for them and not uncommonly in
co-operation with the unions concerned on site. The
union is therefore an interested or involved party -
but rarely is it the direct client. Reference to
the ACAS Annual Reports shows that during 1978-82
inclusive (figures before 1978 are not available)
only two pieces of in-depth work were carried out
for the trade unions as direct clients. It would
indeed be very surprising if trade unions in their
capacity as employers sought advisory help from
ACAS. In their capacity as bargaining agents within companies they may well agree on a joint employ-
er/union request to ACAS for help. Evidence given
earlier testifies to that fact as do ACAS Annual
Reports. But it still seems likely that the union/s
on site are less well placed than are employers to
assess the exact extent of implementation. They
cannot take the same overview of the total given
situation that an employer can. From some of the
questionnaire evidence it was obvious that in some
shared experiences, the trade union representatives
were less involved in the actual in-depth work than
their management counterparts. If several unions
are party to the same piece of in-depth work each
may see overlapping parts of the implementation
process but not the whole process. However, it must
be admitted that the explanation offered in this
paragraph for the differing assessments of advice
implementation remains conjectural.

   In addition to providing a broad assessment of
implementation, actual and projected, some respondents also gave information about the extent of implementation actual and projected, of the specific
subjects of advice they had earlier identified.
However, the volume and nature of the information
is such as to render clear conclusions hazardous.
Where the evidence is fullest and firmest, it comes
as no surprise to learn that employers most frequently fully implemented, in descending order of frequency - disciplinary procedures, grievance procedures, disputes procedures, payment matters/systems.

As with advisory visits, some evidence was obtained about the reasons why advice was not or would not be implemented. Respondents were asked to rank in order of importance any of 16 specific reasons - and to add others of their own where appropriate. Seventy five employers provided information and most of the answers can be grouped under five general headings. In descending order of importance these are - advice of a character not calling for specific implementation, eg information for possible future use: management resistance on various grounds, eg cost : changes in the organisation or management: 'political' climate not right : trade union/work force resistance of some kind. These reasons accounted for 91 per cent of the total reasons given. The reason of 'advice thought to be technically unsound' accounted for only 3 per cent of the total. The 29 trade union responses gave priority to management resistance, closely followed by changes in the organisation or management. Next, but at some distance removed came trade union/workforce resistance. 'Technically unsound' accounted for 6 per cent of the total number of reasons and the higher percentage compared to management's figure may possibly reflect the more critical stance of the professional negotiator.

Apart from the re-ordering of the reasons concerned, there is a fair amount of similarity between the two sets of assessments. It is noteworthy that both employers and unions acknowledge resistance within their own ranks to recommended change. Although 'management resistance' heads the reasons given by unions, both parties avoid the simplistic scape goat route of blaming the other side entirely for whatever degree of non-implementation there has been. Whether the avoidance of simple causal explanations and the presentation of a variety of causes owes anything to the joint nature of in-depth experiences and their commonly shared problem solving approach, is an open question but certainly one worth pondering. The evidence is insufficient to warrant firm conclusions but does provide pointers to further possible lines of enquiry. En passant, ACAS advisers should certainly take heart from the clients' view that their advice is seldom considered to be other than technically sound. With that closing thought to this section a more detailed examination may be made of the evaluation by the employers' and unions concerned of the advice given.

Employer and trade union evaluation of advice

In broad and aggregated terms the general quality of ACAS advice was evaluated by its recipients as shown in Table 5.7.

Table 5.7: Evaluation of quality of advice
In-depth work

	Companies		TUs	
Evaluated as	No.	%	No.	%
Very good	127	61.4	45	56.2
Good	66	31.9	27	33.8
No particular views	6	2.9	3	3.8
Poor	4	1.9	3	3.8
Very Poor	-	-	1	1.2
More than one category*	4	1.9	1	1.2
No. of respondents	207	100	80	100

* Category introduced by respondents

The above results manifestly demonstrate an impressive level of company and trade union satisfaction with the general quality of ACAS advice. That view is powerfully reinforced by the fact that only three respondents, one company and two trade unions, did not answer the question concerned. It will be noted that if the categories of 'very good' and 'good' are combined, the employers' evaluation and that of the trade unions are closely comparable at 93.3 per cent and 90 per cent respectively. This suggests, among other things, a skilful reading, by advisers, of industrial relations situations and an ability to be even-handed in providing good quality advice. But the key question concerning the effects of sound advice extensively implemented has yet to be addressed.

The question set out on p. 75 was put to all respondents, except those concerned with ETEs. Of the 188 employers who replied, 166 (88.3 per cent) acknowledged that as a result of the advice received there had been a change in the problem situation discussed with the adviser. (Again it has to be remembered that in a fair number of instances implementation of the advice had still to be completed). Of the 161 employers who sought to evaluate

the nature of the change, 109 (67.7 per cent) described the change as 'significantly for the better'
and 47 (29.2 per cent) as 'marginally for the
better'. The remaining five answers were spread
across 'marginally for the worse' (two), 'significantly for the worse' (one) and 'varied' (two).
Sixty five respondents ventured assessments in relation to the following question:

> If the change process is not complete because
> some advisory recommendations have still to be
> implemented, then assuming they will be, is
> the nature of the change at the 'end' of the
> advice implementation likely to be...

There followed a series of evaluation choices.
Of the 65 employers, 43 (66.2 per cent) considered
the likely outcome to be 'significantly for the
better', 15 (23.0 per cent) 'marginally for the
better' and the remaining seven (10.8 per cent)
found it 'difficult to predict'.
    Overall, the evidence from this section of the
enquiry does indicate that in a significant proportion of cases, the well valued advice has been
translated into action which has resulted in appreciable improvement to the pre-advice situation.
This raises the concomitant issue of what might
have happened had the advice not been followed.
Respondents were not offered a choice of admittedly
speculative possibilities but were free to define
their own forecasts. An encouraging response rate
of 76 per cent (152 of a possible 200 employers)
was achieved for this question suggesting that the
advice given was sufficiently important for the
possible effects of its non-implementation to be
seriously considered. The replies were varied but
could be grouped, with the main evaluations constituting 'worse industrial relations' (34 per cent)
and 'industrial relations problems' (27 per cent).
    For possible reasons already briefly discussed,
it is probably more difficult for a trade union
than an employer to assess the full effects of
implemented advice. Nevertheless, a good proportion
of the trade unions replied to the same questions
of change effects as were asked of employers.
Seventy of the full population of 82 trade unions
replied to the basic question of whether change
had occurred as a result of the advisory work.
Sixty three of the 70 (90 per cent) replied 'Yes'.
With three unions not specifying the nature of the
change, this left 60 valid replies for the next

question. Of these 37 (61.7 per cent) stated that
the change was 'significantly for the better' and
20 (33.3 per cent) 'marginally for the better'.
(The remaining three answers were - 'marginally
for the worse' (two) and 'varied' (one).) The
figures of 61.7 per cent and 33.3 per cent corres-
pond reasonably well to the employers' responses
of 67.7 per cent and 29.2 per cent - see above.
The evidence from both populations of respondents
would therefore seem to suggest that in over 60
per cent of instances, employers and unions alike
regard the implementation of ACAS advice as having
brought about a significant change for the better
in the industrial relations situations concerned.

The question aimed at the possible future
effects of advice yet to be implemented was answered by 33 unions. Seventeen (51.5 per cent) ventured 'significantly for the better' as the likely
outcome and seven 'marginally better'. Another
seven found it 'difficult to predict' and two stated
'significantly for the worse'. That last category
is especially interesting because it appears to
represent a deviation from the generally prevailing
pattern of changes for the better identified by
both employers and trade unions. While it would be
possible to shed evidential light on the deviation,
we are not convinced that it would be useful to do
so, as there would then result a need, in order to
preserve balance, to examine in more detail instances of 'significantly for the better' - and that
could make for a very long explication. What can
briefly be said, by way of illustration, is that a
trade union representative may accept a revised
job evaluation scheme as appropriate for the specific industrial relations situation but regard some
of the inevitable consequences as a change for the
worse for those of his members who may lose money
under the reformed payment system.

Responding to the question on what might have
happened had the advice not been followed, 17
(28.3 per cent) of the 60 responding unions said
industrial relations would have become worse, 15
identified problems of varying kinds, 15 a dispute
and 8 a strike. (The remaining five answers were
imprecise). The categories of dispute and strike
and the numbers in each category are notable. Such
results give a different dimension to advice evaluation by indicating that in some circumstances the
advice is held to be of sufficient value to merit
industrial action being taken to try and bring
about its implementation. Conversely such evidence

is a pointer to the probability that advisory work, as well as collective conciliation, can, on some occasions, avert industrial action.

As with advisory visits respondents were invited to answer a range of questions bearing on the general ACAS advisory role as distinct from the location specific advisory intervention with which the respondents had been personally involved. The first of such questions (see also p.77) concerned the factors which in the view of employers and trade unions contributed most to the use made of the ACAS advisory service. Table 5.8 summarises the answers given.

In the article on the pilot study of in-depth work we commented that 'it would be wrong to read too much into the findings from one sample'. However, the addition of eight more samples amply confirms the original tentative conclusion that:

> Perhaps the most interesting feature of Table [5.8 in the present case] is the far less weight attached by the unions than by the companies to the technically competent service factor. It seems plausible that the trade unions, seeing themselves as professional experts in industrial relations matters, regard the industrial relations expertise of advisers as less important than the advisers' impartial approach and independent status. These latter factors are highly evaluated by the unions, as the table shows. By contrast, the employers, and particularly those who from their own comments were inexperienced in industrial relations, greatly value technical competence. Impartiality remains, for both parties, the most important factor... [The table] does suggest that for employers, sound advice presented impartially is more important than the formal - in this case, independent as defined - status of the source of help. For the unions, however, the independent status of ACAS seems to play a more significant part. 4)

Overall, the free nature of the service seems to be the least important of the four factors - but not to the extent where it could be deemed insignificant. As stated earlier, it was decided to probe a little more deeply into the payment issue. Of 203 employers (nearly the total sample) only 14 (6.9 per cent) thought the law should be changed to allow ACAS to charge for its advisory

Table 5.8: Factors contributing most to the use made of the ACAS advisory service

Factor	In-depth work No. of times mentioned as being of	Employers	TUs	Total
An impartial service ie attempting to be fair to all interests concerned	1st importance 2nd importance	121 44	44 14	165 58
A technically competent service	1st importance 2nd importance	58 75	11 32	69 107
An independent service, ie independent of government and sectional interests	1st importance 2nd importance	31 49	37 13	68 62
A free service	1st importance 2nd importance	31 34	14 7	45 41

work while the remaining 93.1 per cent expressed the contrary opinion. The corresponding figures for the unions (81 of the total sample of 82 replied) were 3.7 per cent - yes, the law should be changed and 96.3 per cent - no, it should not. Thus, on this evidence there was almost no support from either employers or trade unions for a change to the law that would enable or even perhaps require ACAS to charge for the advisory services it provides.

This is not to say, of course, that employers and unions could not, if pressed a little, attempt to place some sort of price value on free advice. As mentioned before two questions were designed to elicit thoughts on this point:

i) in principle would your organisation be prepared to pay for ACAS advisory work?

ii) if at the time in question ACAS had been a fee charging service is it likely that an ACAS adviser would have become involved in your organisation?

Tables 5.9 and 5.10 supply the summarised answers to those questions.

Table 5.9: Nos. of employers and unions prepared to pay - in principle for advisory work

In-depth work

| | Employers | | TUs | |
	No.	%	No.	%
Yes	30	14.8	2	2.5
Probably	93	45.8	9	11.4
No	22	10.8	24	30.4
Doubt it	48	23.6	27	34.2
Doubt it very much	10	4.9	17	21.5
Total	203	100	79	100

On the evidence of Table 5.9 the employers' opinion might be crystallised as a cautious 'maybe' and the trade union view as 'almost certainly not'- and those are reactions to a question of principle when it is not known what the actual money cost might be. Furthermore, many of the employer 'maybes'need to be qualified by the knowledge that

106

the overwhelming majority of employers had already signified their opposition to a change in the law to enable ACAS to charge (see p.106). The message seems to be that in the abstract, advice received might be of sufficient worth to merit payment but a change to the statute to enable this to happen could be fraught with hazardous imponderables. Before considering opinions on what is arguably the major imponderable in relation to payment, ie its possible effect on ACAS impartiality (see Table 5.11), a further point may be made from Table 5.9. If the employers' 'Yes' and 'Probably' answers are totalled they comprise nearly 61 per cent of all the employer responses. This may be compared with the nearly 53 per cent for request advisory visits, see Table 4.8 p.78. The higher percentage for in-depth work may conceivably be related to a greater benefit accruing to the client from the greater advisory in-put of in-depth work. It is tempting to think so.

Moving from principle to practice Table 5.10 provides the answers to questions ii on p.106.

Table 5.10: Nos.of employers and unions prepared to pay - when advice given

In-depth work

| | Employers | | TUs | |
	No.	%	No.	%
Yes	58	28.9	6	7.8
No	60	29.8	52	67.5
Maybe	83	41.3	19	24.7
Total	201	100	77	100

As stated in the previous chapter, it might have been better to have retained the five choices of Table 5.9 but the reduction to three choices should hopefully have concentrated the mind of the respondent in relation to the specific situation in which advice was actually given. If, in the case of employers the 'Yes' and 'Maybe' replies are combined, then 70 per cent of the clients might be thought to evaluate the specific advice received as money worthy. This compares to 58 per cent in the case of request visits - see p.79, a difference which adds weight to the point made above about the

possible higher evaluation, by the client, of in-
depth work compared to a requested advisory visit.
(The respective clear 'Yes' votes are 29 per cent
in-depth, 19 per cent request visit)

The emphatic 67.5 per cent of 'Nos' in the
trade union response may owe less to concern about
the size of theoretical sums of money for the advice
received, than to policy considerations such as the
trade union movement as a whole being unlikely to
subscribe to the notion of a fee charging service
replacing a free one. If fees had to be paid, the
argument would run, it would be up to the employers
to pay them and this could well change the whole
approach to industrial relations problems by the
advisers. As pointed out several times before, it
is the employer who is the client with the trade
union or unions concerned having a different status
as involved parties. That distinction would be
very much sharper if payment were made by the employer. Some evidence about the possible disturbance
to the accustomed advisory role and people's perceptions of that role if payment was required,
resulted from answers to the following question:

> If payment was required for advisory help
> do you think this would adversely affect the
> independent/impartial nature of the advisory
> service?

Table 5.11 sheds some light on this matter.

Table 5.11: Payment and possible adverse effect on
impartiality/independence

In-depth work

	Employers		TUs	
	No.	%	No.	%
Yes	109	53.4	54	70.1
No	47	23.0	8	10.4
Maybe	48	23.5	15	19.5
Total	204	100	77	100

From the proportions of unequivocal 'Yes' and
'No' answers it would seem that payment for advice
would, in the directly concerned parties' perceptions, damage the impartiality/independence (as

earlier defined) of advisory work. And it needs to
be remembered that impartiality was seen by employer clients and unions alike as the factor which
contributed most to the use made of the advisory
service. If the 'Yes' responses of employers and
unions are added together then 163 of 281 respondents, 58 per cent, envisage harmful effects from a
payment system. It was predictable perhaps that
the union percentage of 'Yes' answers would be
higher than that of employers. Even so, the percentage of 'Nos' and 'Maybes' in the trade union
response is interesting and suggests a reaction
subtler than that of simply equating payment with
bias. It might also imply that some form of joint
fee paying arrangement was envisaged. As good
abstract grounds could be advanced for adding the
'Maybe' answers to either the 'Yes' or 'No' totals,
it is probably better, as an experiment, to divide
the 'Maybes' equally between the 'Yes' and 'No'
replies. If that is done, then the 53.4 per cent
of employers saying 'Yes' becomes 65 per cent, the
corresponding figure for unions being 80 per cent
and the overall 'Yes' reaction 69 per cent.

However, what cannot be over emphasised is the
importance of the many written comments that accompanied the 'Yes' and 'No' and 'Maybe' answers.
While the tables in this chapter, and the previous
one are necessary for providing significant pointers to the parties' thinking on the payment issue,
they do need to be placed, alongside other evidence,
in the context of a more extensive discussion.
This will be done in Chapter Eight.

To complete the evaluation section of the
questionnaire, the respondents were asked - 'from
the experience of the recent ACAS advisory assistance would your organisation, in principle, be prepared to use the ACAS advisory service again?' The
full population (208) of employers answered this
question, 200 (96.1 per cent) saying 'Yes', six
(2.9 per cent) 'Maybe' and two 'No' (1.0 per cent).
From the ACAS viewpoint that must be a highly encouraging reaction. Virtually the same encouragement can be derived from the trade union response.
Only two of the 82 total population of respondents
did not reply but of the 80 who did, 76 (95 per
cent) said 'Yes', three (3.8 per cent) said 'Maybe'
and one (1.2 per cent) 'No'.

Looking back through the chapter we would submit that the total evidence constitutes an expression of appreciable satisfaction by both the employers and unions concerned with the value of ACAS in-

depth work. For the most part, employers and
unions alike seem to be well pleased both with the
quality of the advice received and with the practical effects of its partial or complete implementation. The contribution these advisory activities
have made to the improvement of industrial relations more generally, is not the concern of this
chapter but clearly, in the opinion of sizeable
samples of consumers of the advisory output, some
good has been done. However, interests additional
to those of the direct consumer are involved in or
affected by ACAS advisory work and the next chapter
presents opinions about the ACAS advisory role
gathered from interested third parties, namely from
employers' associations, trade union head offices,
management consultants and professional bodies
active in industrial relations training. In this
way we shall be building up a highly relevant multi-
perspective evaluation of advisory work both for
its own intrinsic worth and for the contribution it
can make to the discussion on key advisory issues
such as that concerning payment for the advice.

NOTES AND REFERENCES

1. ACAS Annual Report 1982, p.46.
2. D. Evans, 'Joint working parties: the ACAS
experience', Employment Gazette, December 1982,
HMSO, pp.540-44. 'Integrated job evaluation at
Continental Can', Industrial Relations Review and
Report, 291, 8 March 1983, pp.9-15. J. Measures
and S. Norton, Joint Working Parties : A Case Study
of the ACAS Approach to Improving Industrial
Relations, Employee Relations, vol.5, no.3 (1983),
pp.10-12.
3. Armstrong and Lucas, 'A preliminary
appraisal of in-depth work', pp.28-29.
4. Ibid., p.33.

Chapter Six

ACAS ADVISORY ROLE - THIRD PARTIES' PERCEPTION

While the central objective of the research was to
gather evidence about advisory work from a significant sample of ACAS clients, it was recognised that
if a fuller assessment of the ACAS advisory role was
to be achieved, the views of other interested parties would need to be sought. Three such interested
parties were self-evidently - employers' associations, trade unions and management consultants.
    Although employers' associations vary greatly
in size and in the degree of influence they exercise on collective bargaining, they commonly provide services of an advisory nature to their member
companies. It therefore seemed sensible to ask such
associations, among other questions, whether they
considered the advisory role of ACAS to be complementary to or in competition with their own advisory role. The same question was obviously highly
pertinent to the work of management consultants who
require commercially determined levels of payment
from clients for advice that is given. A major
function of trade unions, as industrial relations
specialists, is to inform and advise their memberships about the host of matters that affect employment. How do such specialists regard the advisory
work of ACAS? Some answers will follow shortly.
    Including ACAS, it can be seen that four major
types of institution are in the business of dis-
pensing industrial relations advice. Two might be
thought to be partisan, employers' associations and
trade unions giving advice to their respective
constituencies from distinctive employer and employee viewpoints. They are also restricted in scope
because whether small or large organisations, their
respective client constituencies remain essentially
limited by the bounds of particular membership eli-
gibility requirements. The help of management

consultants is available to those who are prepared
to pay the required fees and the consultants'
client constituency is therefore essentially determined by commercial considerations on the part of
all concerned. In contrast, ACAS advice is available to the total 'universe' of potential industrial relations clients including those in the constituencies just identified. Because it does not
represent sectional interests in the way that employers' associations and trade unions do ACAS might
be regarded as non-partisan. And because ACAS is
required to give advice 'without charge' the
advice might be regarded differently from paid
advice. Observations pertinent to these and related
assumptions appear later in the chapter.
    To the four major kinds of advisory body out-
lined above, a fifth may be added. This is the
smaller but still significant group of professional/
education/training institutions which have a special
interest in industrial relations and employment
matters such as the Industrial Society, the Institute of Personnel Management, Employment Relations.
Some consultancy work may be undertaken by some of
these bodies but as a category they would seem to
be distinct from management consultants. Even so,
they could be expected to hold views about the
complementary or competitive role of ACAS advisory
work in relation to their own advisory activities.
    Obviously the CBI and the TUC as national
spokesmen and major industrial relations advisers
in their own right, will also hold opinions about
the ACAS advisory role but it was decided not to
seek such opinions directly and separately for the
reason given below. As the central co-ordinating
bodies of employers' and trade union interests, the
CBI and the TUC can be taken to support the advisory role of ACAS, because it is after consultation
with these two bodies that the Secretary of State
for Employment appoints the three employer members
and the three worker members to the ACAS Council.
The views of the CBI and the TUC about specific
aspects of advisory work are therefore expressed at
Council meetings and recorded in Council minutes.
Inevitably this tends to happen in a generalised,
overview way. It was thought that even if approached to do so, the CBI and TUC would feel unable to
elaborate on their formal Council positions.
    We thus arrive at a position where, CBI and
TUC apart, four quite different types of advisory
institution created by their own members or entre-
preneurial exertions, could be assumed to hold

various opinions about the advisory function of a
state created, statutory based, agency. However,
rather than build castles of conjecture on founda-
tions of assumption, we decided to seek answers to
specific questions from samples of the different
types of advisory group concerned. To that end,
three short but similar questionnaires were designed
for postal distribution. The differences between
the questionnaires only reflected the essential differences between the basic characteristics of employers' associations, trade unions and consultants/
trainers. The questions were designed to establish
the essential dimensions of the organisation concerned, the type of advisory role it carried out, the
nature and frequency of the organisation's contacts
with ACAS, opinions held about the ACAS advisory
role including the payment issue. What now follows
is an analysis of completed questionnaires returned
by:

    34 employers' associations
    29 trade unions
    10 management consultants
     7 professional/training bodies

Employers' Associations

In compiling a list of employers' associations to
whom questionnaires were to be sent, use was made
of the Department of Employment's Directory of
Employers' Associations, Trade Unions, Joint Organisations & etc. 1) On the assumption, supported by
the client survey experience, that something of the
order of 30 per cent response rate might be achieved, a distribution list of 103 employers' associations was compiled. Care was taken to choose a
number of associations from each major industrial
group and in a way that had regard to a distribution of associations by size and geographical location. But it would be impossible to say whether
our sample of returned questionnaires constitutes a
representative sample of the generality of British
employers' associations. What we do claim to have
is a significant sample and one that constitutes
a good cross section of industries and sizes of
bargaining units - ie the total numbers of employees in member companies coming within the industrial relations coverage of the associations concerned. This claim can be supported in a number of
ways. But before doing that, it must be made plain
that as the information was given to us in confidence, we have thought it right to aggregate figures

in such a way that a particular set of figures cannot be related to a named organisation.

The employers' associations (by industry group) which completed questionnaires were as follows:

Agriculture, Forestry, Fishing
Grimsby Fishing Vessel Owners' Association

Mining and Quarrying
Employers' side of West Midlands and Mid Wales Area Joint Industrial Council

Food, Drink and Tobacco
Food Manufacturers' Industrial Group

Chemical and Allied Industries
Chemical Industries Association

Engineering
Central Lancashire Engineering Employers' Association
Engineering Employers' West of England Association

Metal Goods
Sheffield Lighter Trades Industrial Section
Wire and Wire Rope Employers' Association
British Lock Manufacturers' Association

Textiles
The British Textile Employers' Association
The Confederation of British Wool Textiles Ltd
The Knitting Industries Federation Ltd
Hawick Knitwear Manufacturers' Association
Narrow Fabrics Federation

Clothing and Footwear
British Footwear Manufacturers' Federation

Bricks, Pottery, Glass, Cement, etc.
Association of Glass Container Manufacturers

Paper, Printing and Publishing
The British Paper and Board Industry Federation
Wallcovering Manufacturers Association
Newspaper Publishers Association

Construction
National Federation of Building Trades Employers
Scottish Building Employers' Federation
The Federation of Civil Engineering Contractors
Electrical Contractors' Association

114

<u>Transport and Communications</u>
General Council of British Shipping
British Association of Removers

<u>Distributive Trades</u>
Co-operative Employers Association
Employers Side of the Joint Council for the Whole-
sale Grocery and Provision Trade
Federation of London Wholesale Newspaper Distribu-
tors

<u>Insurance, Banking, Finance and Business Services</u>
Federation of London Clearing Bank Employers
The Federation of Scottish Bank Employers

<u>Miscellaneous Services</u>
Cinematograph Exhibitors' Association of Great
Britain and Ireland
National Union of Licensed Victuallers
Association of British Launderers and Cleaners Ltd
Motor Agents' Association

In relation to the 103 associations to whom
questionnaires were sent, the returns from the
above 34 constitute a 33 per cent response rate.
In addition letters, of an explanatory nature, were
received from another twelve associations.
Concentrating on the information contained in
the 34 completed questionnaires, two of the associations identified themselves as the employers'
sides of Joint Industrial Councils, three as trade
associations, eleven as employers' associations
and 18 combined employers'/trade associations.
Because the three trade associations had had some
industrial relations involvement and/or had made
comments on the ACAS advisory role, it was decided
to retain their questionnaires in the analysis.
In any event, these associations had been listed in
the Directory of Employers' Associations from which
our distribution list had been compiled.
In considering the size dimensions of our
sample, it has to be borne in mind that some associations did not give figures for number of establishments covered by the association, or number of
employees coming within the industrial relations
coverage of the association. In other instances,
estimates were given - between X and Y, with X the
lower figure. Where this was the case we have taken
the lower figure for inclusion in the aggregated returns. In short, the figures which follow are conservative in character. Between them the 34

associations:

> included 535 local organisations,represented
> 50,392 companies in 78,240 establishments
> which employed 2,144,300 workers coming within
> the industrial relations coverage of the
> associations concerned.

While the number of employees in particular is
the sum of approximations, the approximations were
made by those best placed to be as accurate as possible, the employers' associations themselves.
Overall, the sample is a sizeable one spread across
a variety of industries and catchment sizes of
industrial relations coverage. The smallest of the
latter comprised 600 employees and the largest
500,000. The distribution, by size of industrial
relations coverage, among the 30 employers' associations which gave figures on this matter, is given
in Table 6.1.

Table 6.1: Employers' associations
Size of industrial relations coverage by number
of employees

No. of associations	No. of employees
9	Less than 10,000
12	10,001 to 50,000
4	50,001 to 100,000
5	More than 100,000
Total 30	

In the questionnaire associations were asked
whether they provided industrial relations advice
and if they did, to identify from a given list,
the topics which they held to be the most important.
The list of topics provided was the same as that
which appeared in questionnaires sent to ACAS
clients consisting of the subjects appearing in
ACAS Annual Report statistics. As might be expected, considerable variations occurred between the
different association responses. The advisory coverage ranged from 'the Association provides
advice and direct assistance on all these topics.
Wages/salaries and conditions of employment are the
two regular areas of work' to 'we have no industrial relations activity' from a small association
identifying itself as a trade association.
    The weight attached to particular topics also

varied but an association's role in national negotiations in the industry, or industry sector concerned commonly featured prominently. In this group of
respondents, reference to procedures was understandably frequent. From the answers given it was
clear that not all associations, unlike the one
illustrated in the first of the two quotations
above, gave advice on all the listed topics. Two
inter-related and possibly overlapping explanations
can be offered for this occurrence. It could be
that advice on certain topics was unnecessary because problems requiring advice did not arise from
those particular topics. It could also be that
some associations considered that they had insufficient resources and/or expertise to advise member
companies about certain industrial relations matters. Associations were asked a question on that
latter point viz:

> If the Association finds itself unable to pro-
> vide particular industrial relations services
> for a member company does the Association re-
> commend to that company that it seek advice
> from -

a list of named alternative sources of help including ACAS and consultants. Supplementary questions
sought to elucidate whether some sources of help
were more strongly recommended than others by the
associations or whether the order of preference was
contingent on circumstances.

While all the associations except one in the
sample answered such questions, no particular pattern of response could be said to be dominant. Some
associations seemed to be entirely self-dependent:

> not applicable - always copes.
> has not yet ever been needed to refer members
> elsewhere.
> the situation does not arise.
> do not consider ACAS could offer anything we
> could not or that members could not do with
> their own staff.
> if we did need to seek external help ACAS
> would be the only one of those listed to be
> used.

A number of associations recommended both the
CBI and ACAS to their members as sources of help
but no other institution. Orders of preference between the two institutions varied. Nine associations

referred to consultants, sometimes as the only
source of recommended help, sometimes in combination
with the CBI and ACAS and other institutions. It is
perhaps worth mentioning at this point that of the
34 associations, three charged their own member companies for particular advisory services, ie payment
additional to the membership fee. The payment requirement appeared to be confined to the provision of
courses and seminars and the representation of
member companies at industrial tribunal hearings.
Two of these three associations came within the
self-reliant group and the third recommended only
consultants to its membership. Two of the smallest
associations referred to solicitors specialising in
industrial relations as other recommended sources
of help.

The general picture that emerges from this aspect of the enquiry is one of an extensive variety
of practice and one that is perhaps more influenced
by pragmatic than ideological considerations in
that the source of help recommended to member companies by associations will commonly be influenced
more by an assessment of an individual company's
particular need than by an overall view of a particular institution's advisory role.

Although ACAS was seen by a fair proportion of
associations to be one of a number of alternative
sources of additional advisory help, contact between
the associations and ACAS was apparently not frequent and was usually connected with the conciliation and arbitration work of ACAS. Only two of the
associations assessed the contact as 'frequent'
and six as 'fairly frequent'. Twenty two maintained
that contact was infrequent and four that there
was none at all. Reference was made to conciliation twenty five times (14 collective : 11 individual) and to arbitration on ten occasions. Advisory work was mentioned on four occasions and reference was also made, twice, to ACAS involvement in
JIC work. Where the contact was held to be frequent or fairly frequent this was almost exclusively
concerned with individual conciliation associated
with individual employment rights. Not surprisingly
perhaps, this conjunction of greatest frequency of
mention and individual conciliation came from associations whose members employed, in total, large
numbers of workers.

Turning to policy directed issues, employers'
associations were asked three questions identical to
those that had been put to company clients and to
trade union representatives involved in advisory

118

exercises. The first question read:

> ACAS Annual Reports indicate that a substantial
> amount of advisory work is carried out by ACAS.
> Which of the following factors contribute most,
> in your view, to the use made of the ACAS ad-
> visory service?
> Please rank in order of importance No. 1 =
> most important.

The factors - and the answers are given in Table
6.2.

Table 6.2: Factors contributing most to the use
made of the ACAS advisory service

Employers' Associations

Factor	No. of times mentioned as being of	
An <u>impartial</u> service ie attempting to be fair to all interests concerned	1st importance	12
	2nd importance	7
An <u>independent</u> service, ie <u>independent</u> of government and sectional interests	1st importance	7
	2nd importance	11
A <u>free</u> service	1st importance	8
	2nd importance	3
A <u>technically competent</u> service	1st importance	3
	2nd importance	8

   The central message of Table 6.2 seems clear -
that employers' associations, in our sample, evaluate
the impartiality and independence of ACAS as the most
important factors contributing to the use made of the
ACAS advisory service. The 19 respondents who placed
either impartial or independence first constitute 18
associations as one association rated each factor as
equal first. Looking at the eighteen associations
they represent a spread of industries and services
and their industrial relations employment coverage
ranges from 600 employees to 350,000. In fact, in
this group of respondents each of the size ranges of
Table 6.1 is well represented except the largest,

ie that with more than 100,000 employees. Only one
of the five largest associations puts either impartial or independent in first place. It is interesting however, that the remaining four largest associations all make their first choice as free service. It seems plausible that from their position
of being large and essentially self-reliant organisations, they regard a free advisory service as
being particularly valuable to smaller organisations. It is interesting that a further three associations in the first choice/free service category
should all come from one industry which has suffer-
ed massive contraction in the last decade but which
still contains small firms struggling for survival.
Advice, free of charge, could obviously be regarded
as of prime importance in such circumstances.
        The lesser importance attached to technical
competence may reflect the understandable hesitancy
of an employers' association, in its advisory role,
to evaluate the advisory competence of an agency
whose potential client market may overlap that of
the association's membership who may also look to
ACAS for the provision of conciliation and arbitration services. As a comment on the question given on
p.119, one small employers' association stated -
'your (the researchers) mixing of factors for preference is perhaps unfortunate. For example, it is
taken for granted (and found by experience) that
ACAS is competent'. (This association rated, impartial first and independent second and free
third). Relevant to the overlapping of interests
issue mentioned above, and the understandable sensitivity no doubt felt by ACAS and other interested
parties on this matter, one employers' association
official commented - 'In my experience I have always
found ACAS staff meticulous in not undermining
services provided by federations under agreed procedures with trade unions'.

        A widespread and possibly the dominant reaction
to the question that led to the formation of Table
6.2 can be represented by the following observation
from an employers' association with an industrial
relations coverage of 30,000 employees:

        Largely, member companies'experience of the
        advisory services of ACAS is limited, their
        services being mostly associated with concilia-
        tion/arbitration. Of those having used ACAS
        advisory services the most advantageous factor
        given was this overriding impartiality, and

The concomitant acceptability of their status
by all parties.

The question of acceptability - to all parties
- is clearly of central importance to an agency
which has a statutory duty to provide advice to
anyone involved in industrial relations.
Whether changes to the law could affect the acceptability of ACAS was commented upon in answers to
the next two questions on the questionnaire.
To the question : 'do you think the law should
be changed to allow ACAS to charge for its
advisory work ?' 28 associations gave direct replies.
Four associations answered yes and 24 no.
Among the four who answered yes were two of the
three associations which made some charge for
particular services to member companies such as
representation at industrial tribunal hearings
(see above). The associations supporting a
change in the law represented companies employing
upwards of 215,000 workpeople (one of these four
associations gave no industrial relations catchment
area figures). Some comments to support the 'Yes'
decision were advanced 'would overcome "unfair"
competition with consultants and associations'
(association, 100,000 plus employee coverage),
'charging should be discretionary. Only major
projects', (association with 5,000 employee
coverage). 'Begs the question of who pays?'
That begged question will, of course, be discussed.
Opinions were also expressed by some among
the 28 associations who had replied no to
changing the law so that ACAS could charge for
its advice. (Figures in brackets denote the
size of overall industrial relations coverage
measured by number of employees concerned).

I don't see the benefit in ACAS charging
for its advice, as it seems to be
adequately funded. (not given)

(No) unless this is necessary to maintain
the service. The fact that it is free makes
it more attractive to both sides of the
industry. (50,000)

Cannot see the point. They then become
just another consultancy, possibly not
able to attract staff of the same
calibre as the major consultancy firms.
(200,000 plus)

I have rarely used ACAS for advisory work but a charge may deter others. (600)

In our view individuals and companies would make less frequent use of ACAS if fees were involved. (20,000)

Many smaller companies would not even seek advice and guidance if they had to pay. The service provided helps promote a better industrial relations climate and this is worth more than the exchequer cost of running ACAS. (35,000)

One respondent made a distinction between types of advice:
If this advice is to individuals then 'No'. If it is for complex work for companies then 'Yes' in areas such as large scale studies on absenteeism etc. (65,000)

The second payment question on the questionnaire read (as it had on client questionnaires) as follows - if payment was required for advisory help, do you think this would adversely affect the independent/impartial nature of the advisory service? To this question 30 associations replied, the divisions of opinion being twelve associations deciding no, nine yes, and nine maybe. (The respective industrial relations coverage populations were upwards of 474,000, 286,300 and 490,500). These bald statistical 'voting returns' merit amplification but unfortunately, relatively few comments were made. The following observations are from associations which considered that impartiality would not be adversely affected by a payment system.

I think it would probably affect the demand for the service with people looking elsewhere for advice. (No. of employees not given)

Probably not, but this might call the impartiality into question. (50,000) (This could justify a transfer to the maybe constituency)

Other roles of ACAS would be a stronger influence. (20,000 plus)

Turning to the comments made by associations which thought a payment system for advice would damage its impartial status, there is only one but it is detailed and considered:

> Fundamentally our objection to any charge being
> made for ACAS advisory work - or, indeed, any
> of its services - is that there would be a
> perceived loss of impartiality and independence
> leading to a sapping of its major attraction -
> ie acceptability. Companies would assess the
> services available on a commercial footing,
> and would perhaps not even consider them (par-
> ticularly in the case of small companies). A
> view was expressed that charging a fee would
> enable larger companies to get advice quicker
> and thus avoid any unnecessary delay. This
> would mean ACAS coming into direct competition
> with commercial business consultancies. How-
> ever, this was a minority view. (30,000)

The maybe reactions were accompanied by the
following cryptic observations,

> Customer/client risks involved. (160,000)
> Would reduce demand for ACAS services.
> (30,000)

and one fuller response:

> The question is speculative and the answer
> would depend to some extent on the scale of
> charges. We think that on balance it is
> right that fees are not charged. It would
> probably not affect the service or client's
> attitude to it if modest or nominal charges
> were levied as part of the government's policy
> of cost containment. However, commercial rates
> would probably prove to be a deterrent to some
> clients. (23,000)

Such thoughtful comments provide a useful tran-
sition to a consideration of the answers given to
the question as to whether associations saw the
ACAS advisory function as being complementary to
or in competition with the advisory work undertaken
by other institutions, including employers' associations. Of the 31 associations which replied, 23
saw the ACAS advisory role as complementary, one as
competitive and seven as possessing a mixture of
the two qualities.
The association that had evaluated ACAS advice
as competitive did not amplify this view. The associations perceiving ACAS to perform both comple-

mentary and competitive roles commented as follows:

> Depends on the adequacy of an industry's pro-
> cedure agreements. (No. not given)

> There are times when ACAS involvement inter-
> feres with the smooth operation of the
> (industry's) national grievance/disputes mach-
> inery. (120,000)

> Again, no experience. It must complement the
> work done by some if only in terms of scale and
> coverage whilst being in competition with
> others in the consulting field. (200,000 plus)

> Complementary to my own association, but might
> compete with organisations with greater re-
> sources. (5,000)

Those of the complementary role persuasion who
commented did so as follows:

> ACAS is very useful for confirming points of
> doubt in employment law, obviously without
> bias. (No. not given)

> We do not see it as ACAS's function to be in
> competition with employers' associations -
> this would not be conducive to promoting good
> industrial relations. (23,000)

> Surprised to see possible idea of competition.
> ACAS is regarded as the 'expert' body. It is
> assumed that (for example) employers' associa-
> tions in many cases do not have the same exper-
> tise. (No. not given)

> ACAS advisory services are seen as being comp-
> lementary to advice available from other org-
> anisations, including employers' associations.
> This is consistent with their stance of im-
> partiality, and the view is held that their
> services would be missed (again, particularly
> by smaller companies). (30,000)

> In view of the quality of ACAS services we do
> not regard it as being in competition with the
> (association). The neutral position of ACAS
> staff frequently means that they do not feel
> able to give the positive guidance that the
> employer requires. (30,000)

124

Where companies employ consultants on a direct
basis the service given by ACAS provides a
check on the accuracy of the consultants' work
thus acting as a regulator on an impartial
basis. (35,000)

To round off this analysis of the employers'
association's perception and evaluation of the ACAS
advisory role, the concluding comments from questionnaires are given. These have been grouped around
particular themes or aspects of the advisory role.

Value to small organisations - and the
unorganised
Must be valuable to the small employer/trader
especially and also employees not in trade
unions. (160,000)

I would think it must be very useful to small
companies not having specialist advisers and
not being prepared to pay consultants' fees
at to-day's levels. I am sure they perform
an excellent, necessary function. However,
large employers will usually have their own
resources. (200,000 plus)

Free advice
The availability of such a free service is an
important aid to employers and employees,
given today's complex employment scene.
(120,000)

The Association would hold the view that ACAS
functions quite effectively in the industrial
relations climate that prevails and would not
wish any structural changes of the type queried
in this questionnaire to be adopted. (97,000)

Impartiality
The fact that ACAS is an independent body and
is free from bias ensures that it has the respect of both employers and trade unions.
(No. not given)

ACAS has built up a reputation for independence
and impartiality which is respected by both
sides of the industry. (50,000)

Unbiased and prompt. (4,000)

General appraisal
We have had no adverse comments on the role
of ACAS. (500,000)

First class. (6,000)

We have always been favourably impressed with
the soundness of advice given by ACAS officials. We consider it helpful to have an impartial and authoritative body at national
level which makes general pronouncements on
good industrial relations practice eg through
the medium of the Chairman's Annual Report and
the Council's evidence to the Megaw Enquiry
into the determination of Civil Service pay.
(23,000)

Trade Unions

Questionnaires designed on very similar lines to
the one sent to employers' associations were distributed to 105 trade unions affiliated to the TUC.
Twenty nine unions returned questionnaires constituting a 28 per cent response rate. Listed alpha-
betically the respondent unions were -

Amalgamated Association of Beamers, Twisters and
Drawers
Amalgamated Society of Wiredrawers and Kindred
Workers
Amalgamated Textiles Workers Union
Amalgamated Union of Engineering Workers - Roll
Turning Section
Association of Broadcasting and Allied Staffs
Association of Professional, Executive Clerical
and Computer Staff
Bakers, Food and Allied Workers Union
Banking, Insurance and Finance Union
British Actors' Equity Association
British Airline Pilots Association
Civil Service Union
Educational Institute of Scotland
Electrical, Electronic, Telecommunication and
Plumbing Union
Inland Revenue Staff Federation
Institution of Professional Civil Servants
Iron and Steel Trades Confederation
National Association of Schoolmasters and the Union
of Women Teachers
National Society of Metal Mechanics
National Association of Theatrical, Television and

Kine Employees
National and Local Government Officers Association
National Union of the Footwear, Leather and Allied
Trades
National Union of Mineworkers
National Union of Scalemakers
National Union of Tailors and Garment Workers
Northern Carpet Trades Union
Scottish Union of Powerloom Overlookers
Screw, Nut Bolt and Rivet Trade Union
Society of Telecom Executives
United Road Transport Union

Between them, and based on their own figures,
the 29 unions represented a total membership of
nearly two and a quarter million (2,242,101). The
smallest union had a membership of 101 and the largest 600,000 plus. For the purposes of protecting
the identity of individual unions, while presenting
comments made by them, it has been decided to adopt
a slightly different convention from that employed
for employers' associations. The union population
of responses has been divided into three groups by
membership size - small, medium and large. Unions
with fewer than 5,000 members have been designated
- small, unions with 5,000 or more but less than
100,000 members are categorised as medium and those
with 100,000 members or more as - large. This
classification method establishes seven unions as
small, 16 as medium-sized and six as large. Such a
distribution together with the total membership
figure suggests that the sample is a sizeable one
reflecting a reasonable cross-section of the trade
union movement by size of organisation.
White collar unions, particularly in the public sector, are well represented in the sample,
but blue-collar unions are less evident. In fairness, it must be said that letters were received
from two large general labour unions, and from
others, explaining why questionnaires could not be
completed. Reasons advanced included 'inappropriate in present circumstances, our principal involvement with ACAS has been in the area of industrial disputes and much of the information sought by
the questionnaire is not within the experience of
our relationship with ACAS', and, similarly 'we
have not used the advisory facility our involvement
with ACAS being in the fields of concilation and
arbitration'.
As could be expected, unions gave advice on a
wide range of industrial relations topics, high

priority choices frequently being payment matters,
negotiating procedures and individual employment
rights. When it was thought necessary to seek advisory help from outside sources, in the great majority of cases and with almost equal frequency
reference was made to the TUC or Scottish TUC and
ACAS as the sources of help. Where orders of preference were expressed, the TUC/Scottish TUC finished only slightly ahead of ACAS. Other sources
of help mentioned were consultants (six times)
and the GFTU (General Federation of Trade Unions
four times), legal advisers, academic institutions,
Labour Research Dept, the Industrial Society, the
Health and Safety Executive. As with employers'
associations the choices made are often contingent
on circumstances 'we get advice from the TUC and
ACAS on different types of problem' (medium).
'One would approach the TUC for information etc.
ACAS for help in resolving a problem' (large).

As in the case of employers' associations, the
majority of respondents claimed that contact with
ACAS was infrequent. 'Frequent' contact was mentioned only twice, both times in connection with
collective conciliation, while 'fairly frequent'
occurred eight times, three instances featuring the
advisory function. Overall, conciliation, of both
types, was the most frequently mentioned topic.
Advice was mentioned by half a dozen unions but
from comments made (see below) some of the advice
given might be more accurately described as information.

Replies to the questions on policy issues
showed, as could be expected, rather different emphases from those of employers' associations. The
trade union equivalent to Table 6.2 (p.119) is
shown in Table 6.3.

Although the emphases on impartiality and independence are slightly greater in the trade union
than in the employers' association response, it is
interesting that the overall patterns of response
from the two groups of respondents is basically
similar. For both groups impartiality and independence are the factors which contribute most to the
use made of the ACAS advisory service. All sizes
of union were represented in the groups that evaluated impartiality and independence as being of first
or second importance. One union from each size
group, small, medium and large made up the three respondents who placed greatest emphasis on the free
nature of the service.

All twenty nine unions answered 'no' to the

Table 6.3: Factors contributing most to the use
made of the ACAS advisory service

Trade Unions

Factor	No. of times mentioned as being of	
An impartial service, ie attempting to be fair to all interests concerned	1st importance 2nd importance	13 12
An independent service, ie independent of government and sectional interests	1st importance 2nd importance	15 5
A free service	1st importance 2nd importance	3 3
a technically competent service	1st importance 2nd importance	3 5

question on whether the law should be changed to
allow ACAS to charge for advisory work.
A number of amplifying comments were made:

> Advice by ACAS is, and should remain, a
> legitimate charge on public funds. (medium)

> The service benefits both sides of industry
> (public and private) and it is rightly a
> function of the state to provide the funds.
> (medium)

> Who authorises payment and from what funds?
> (medium)

> ...where charges may be made (and they would
> not be nominal?) We suspect such charges
> could discourage both organisations and indi-
> viduals from using ACAS services. (medium)

> To our union, the major advantage of ACAS and
> its advisory role is that we are always aware
> that it is there even if we seldom need to use
> it. The fact that it is free is important to
> us because in simplistic terms we are poor and
> our employers are rich. (medium)

> If there was a charge we probably would use
> other sources of advice, especially as we are
> often unsure in advance whether or not they
> can assist us.   (large)

> I think that if there was a charge the employ-
> ers would possibly be more reluctant to use
> them. (small)

> Despite 'free service' only ranking No 4 (in
> our assessment of factors) we do regard this
> service without cost as being desirable. The
> fact that ACAS is independent, impartial and
> free makes it more attractive and money is
> saved by the avoidance of disputes through
> their intervention. (medium)

> This (a change in the law) would change the
> ACAS/TU relationship for the worse. (medium)

> It is not felt that charging for services
> would enhance ACAS's reputation for indepen-
> dence/impartiality. Charges would be detri-
> mental to less well-off unions and employers.
> The fact that the service is free allows for
> ready access without fear of incurring 'costs'
> and once there for more relaxed discussions
> without fear of higher costs imposing time
> constraints. (large)

The question concerning the possible adverse
effect of a payment requirement on the independent/
impartial nature of the advisory service was also
answered by all 29 unions. Two unions thought that
paying for advice would not have an adverse effect,
18 thought it would and nine replied 'maybe'. This
is a different pattern of response, as could be expected assuming a greater union sensitivity on the
subject, from that of employers' associations - see
p. 122 . The two unions, one small, one medium
that replied no did not add any comments.
Comments were made by some of the nine 'maybes'.

> It (payment) would not affect the quality of
> the service - it would lead to a fall-off in
> demand. (medium)

> It would also affect the frequency with which
> some unions turn to ACAS for assistance.
> (large)

It would depend to some extent on the proportions of its income that ACAS derived from
employers and unions. (medium)

Would ACAS officers be influenced by who pays?
(medium)

In industrial relations there is good and bad
advice. The bad advice is more unacceptable
if it is paid for. ACAS would become wary and
even less decisive. (medium)

Maybe where a charge is made, conceivably/un-
wittingly ACAS staff could advise applicants
what they wish to hear. (medium)

Some of the above comments seem to reflect the
difficulty of assessing whether proven impartiality
could completely withstand the insidious influence
of a payment factor and its source.
Unions which thought impartiality would be
impaired by a payment system commented:

To have to pay may dissuade some parties from
using the service as well as adversely affecting the impartiality, or at least the 'felt
fair' atmosphere. (medium)

I feel they would feel obliged to give some
advice rather than honestly point out their
own uncertainty in some areas if a charge was
involved. Such advice could cause more problems than it is worth. (large)

Only one side might be able to afford to buy
advice. The employers would be in a stronger
position to refer matters to ACAS. TUs could
be constrained by the cost. (large)

Whoever pays the piper etc. It would have a
vested interest to subscribers if advice were
charged for. (medium)

If a charge were made the old adage regarding
the 'piper' could apply. (small)

In passing it may be noted that the 'old adage'
- he who pays the piper calls the tune - was frequently used by ACAS clients to describe their
assessment of the impartiality/payment issue. To
allay possible apprehension on the point, it is not

the intention to reproduce all those particular
quotations in Chapter Eight when the total evidence
on the payment issue is summarised and examined.
    All 29 unions saw the ACAS advisory function
as complementary to advisory work undertaken by
other institutions, including unions themselves.
Comments on this point and on the advisory role of
ACAS generally are given below:

> I often use them with regard to areas of some
> uncertainty as part of a double check with
> other organisations. On the whole I have
> found them very competent and helpful. We use
> them more as a source of information than ad-
> vice as such. (large)

> ACAS useful in cases involving breaches of
> statutory legislation ie an independent body
> able to clarify the situation for the emp-
> loyers and unions. (small)

> When ACAS has given advice this has been help-
> ful to trade union officials in trying to con-
> vince their members to follow a course of ac-
> tion with which ACAS advice coincides.
> (medium)

> Within the confines of our experience with
> ACAS and our use of their services, we do
> find the guidance and advice given most help-
> ful and on a number of occasions this has
> been the main contribution to resolving in-
> dustrial disputes. (medium)

> ACAS codes tend to be useful aids in address-
> ing the topics covered by them. Generally
> helpful in providing jointly agreed 'appeal
> courts' on various issues. Always found ACAS
> officials very helpful. (large)

> The Union sees the role of ACAS purely in
> terms of its function of arbitration and
> conciliation. (large)

> The (union) welcomed the seminar mounted in -
> by ACAS to discuss the work undertaken by the
> service in conciliation, arbitration and in
> tribunals. (medium)

> Because of the impartiality it suffers com-
> ments as 'toothless'. Advice is sound.

Seldom breaks new ground and usually enables
employers to see from an independent viewpoint.
(medium)

...they (advisory service) are not used to
their full potential. (small)

ACAS should be given a greater role in the
field of industrial relations and more power
if necessary. (medium)

They do a very good job. (medium)

The last quotation was deliberately placed in
that position in order to pose the issue of the extent to which such an evaluation might be shared by
institutions which could be thought to be in keen
rivalry with the advisory function of ACAS, namely
management consultants.

Management Consultants

The questionnaire distribution list for management
consultants was compiled from the Directory of Management Consultants in the UK 1983-84. 2) This
Directory lists consultants by size, ie by the
number of consultancy staff employed. On the reasonable assumption that the larger consultants were
the ones most likely to regard ACAS as a competitor
institution, the questionnaire was sent to all
those organisations which employed 20 or more consultancy staff. Although it was known that a number of those companies specialised in fields other
than industrial relations, we could not be sure that
they had no involvement with industrial relations or
personnel management. Questionnaires were therefore
sent to the total population of 31 large (as defined) consultancy firms including eight which employed more than 100 consultancy staff each.
Ten companies returned completed questionnaires. A further eight replied to the effect that
they were not involved in industrial relations or
had 'insufficient contact with ACAS to comment'.
If these eight companies are deducted from the
original 31 approached, the questionnaire response
rate, ten of 23, (assuming all non-respondents to
have an industrial relations interest, which is
doubtful) becomes an encouraging 43 per cent. To
preserve confidentiality and to avoid the possible
linkage of particular comments to particular organisations, it has been decided not to name the con-

sultants concerned. Some indication of their size
and main characteristics can however be given.

Between them the ten companies employed 873
consultancy staff - ranging between six and 200.
Five of the respondents employed more than 100 consultants each. For three of the five companies in
this group industrial relations/personnel management constituted the major part of their consultancy work. For the remaining seven respondent companies it was minor. Some refinement of the above
figures is necessary. Of the total 873 staff
roughly 172 could be called upon to undertake industrial relations/personnel management consultancy
work. Across the companies these specialists
ranged in number from two to 65. (In one instance
the figure would increase markedly if industrial
relations training was included) In nine out of
ten instances by far the greater part of the consultancy work was carried out in the private sector
as distinct from the public sector.

The frequency of contact (by respondents) with
ACAS personnel including advisers and conciliators
was variously described as none (six times),
very rarely (once), no formal contact, as yet (once)
and contact on an ad hoc basis only, usually
for clarification of legislation or procedure, and
two to three times a year - on training matters.
In a few instances, consultancy assignments had
arisen from ACAS having suggested the name of the
company concerned, along with the names of other
companies, to a company or trade union with which
ACAS had been involved. The comments made were
'normally about once in two years to resolve disputes on standard times between union and employer'
'resolution of parity disputes by independent job
evaluation exercises' but infrequently.

Although the number of respondents involved
is small, in the interests of consistency, the
practice of presenting, in tabulated form, the pattern of responses to the free/impartiality factors question, has been maintained. Table 6.4
depicts the consultants' assessment.

The prominence of free service even within
a small sample, is perhaps to be expected given
that the responses are from companies which earn a
living from advisory work. Of the four companies
evaluating free as of first importance, three are
the largest and most specialised industrial relations consultants referred to above. From the
logic of a commercial viewpoint, the free nature of
ACAS advice must seem a major reason why ACAS at-

Table 6.4: Factors contributing most to the use
made of the ACAS advisory service

Management Consultants

Factor	No. of times mentioned as being of	
An impartial service, ie attempting to be fair to all interests concerned	1st importance 2nd importance	2 6
An independent service, ie independent of government and sectional interests	1st importance 2nd importance	2 3
A free service	1st importance 2nd importance	- 1
A technically competent service	1st importance 2nd importance	- 1

tracts the large amount of advisory work that it
does. By the same logic of the paid professional,
it is not the technical competence of the amateur,
in the sense of unpaid advice supplier, that attra-
cts business. Overall however, the frequency of
reference both to impartiality and to independence
remains notable.

Of the ten companies only three (including one
of 'the big three') thought the law should be changed to allow ACAS to charge for advisory work.
Opinions were divided as to whether payment would
adversely affect the impartial nature of the advisory service. The divisions were Yes (two), No
(five), Maybe (three). A number of pertinent
comments were made:

Where a paymaster is involved it becomes increasingly difficult, though not impossible,
to maintain an independent position.

No (to changing law) because ACAS would then
be perceived to be working for the side which
was paying. The service would lose its
important image.

No (re law change) for queries, enquiries and
industrial tribunal conciliation. And surely
payment must destroy impartiality. It would
hardly be practical to charge individuals for
advice. The employer, as paymaster, would inevitably expect to be advised on how to get
out of the problem which could be contrary to
'natural justice'.

As consultants, whether ACAS or independent
companies, we are ethically bound to give an
independent view. However, to satisfy the
needs of both parties the funding should be
split equally between trade unions and
industry.

The considerable amount of legislation tends to
attract some companies to ACAS because of
ACAS's detailed knowledge of the legislation.
Some companies are only interested because it
is free.

If ACAS charged for its work some companies
would try and handle the problem without outside assistance. When an independent outsider
is required it is advisable to be able to
offer a free service.

We rate ACAS staff too highly to be influenced
by fees.

A charge would improve professional standards
which in turn would lead to an improvement in
the selected standard of ACAS staff.

(Payment) could well deter some use of the service. It might also prove difficult to collect
the payment if a satisfactory solution was not
provided.

If this were the case (paid advice) then the
advisory services offered by ACAS would have
few distinctive features.

No (to changing law) they would merely compete
more with the private sector.

Where clear answers were given to the question
concerning the complementary or competitive nature
of the ACAS advisory function, five consultants
saw the ACAS role as being complementary to their

own and two (two of the big three) as ACAS being
competitive:

> Generally speaking we would see ACAS as a
> competitor. However, there are occasions
> when clearly ACAS act in an arbitrary role.

> Assistance with job evaluation and pay struc-
> ture development is in direct competition.

> Basically we see it as complementary but have
> occasionally felt that ACAS has impinged on
> the consultant's role. We see a distinct
> difference in our respective roles but some-
> times it has become blurred.

Something of the ambivalence experienced and
felt about the complementary/competitive nature of
the ACAS advisory role is reflected in two general
comments:

> (ACAS) Not always as technically competent as
> one would like.

Presumably, if the technical competence was
improved, ACAS advisers would constitute greater
competition - and

> We do believe there should be a closer relation-
> ship between ACAS and management consultants.
> Our experience suggests that when a dispute
> reaches ACAS there is usually a fundamental
> problem and the 'instant' solution tends only
> to 'paper over the cracks'. We have sometimes
> felt that ACAS should be more positive about
> the more fundamental problem and when appropri-
> ate recommend consultants.

On occasions ACAS may provide a client with a
list of consultants from which to choose. Clients
may also be referred to other sources of help, some
of which feature in the next section.

Other industrial relations advisers

The type of institution to which 14 questionnaires
were addressed is indicated in the titles of the
seven organisations which replied, these being:

Employment Relations Ltd
Industrial Participation Association

Institution of Industrial Managers
Institute of Manpower Studies
Institute of Personnel Management
Institute of Supervisory Management
Production Engineering Research Association

Although each of the above organisations (as their titles imply) has its own distinctive interests, the provision of industrial relations training, the supply of information about research into the use of the manpower resource, commonly constitute important elements of their activities.

Generically, and for convenience, this group of respondents will be referred to as training institutions. Between them the seven organisations had 72 personnel who could be called upon to act in some form of industrial relations advisory capacity. In only one instance however, was industrial relations consultancy per se regarded as a major part of the organisation's work. This organisation had regular meetings with ACAS staff about training matters. In other instances, contact with ACAS personnel was infrequent and varied in nature from ACAS staff attending conferences organised by another training institution to an institution advising its individual manager members with personal personnel problems to apply to ACAS for information and help. In two cases, and on one or two occasions, ACAS had suggested to enquiring companies that the institutions in question be approached for specialist help which ACAS could not supply.

Again in the interests of consistency, the equivalent of Tables 6.2, 6.3 and 6.4 for the other three interest groups of this chapter, is given as Table 6.5 (There were only six respondents and as elsewhere, some respondents ranked more than one choice as being of equal importance).

Impartiality again emerges as the most prominent factor, fairly closely followed by the free nature of the service. No respondent thought the law should be changed to allow ACAS to charge for advice but opinions differed as to whether a payment requirement would adversely affect the impartiality/independence of ACAS advice. Two respondents said yes, four no, and one maybe. In regard to the payment issue a number of comments were made:

> Generally managers are not members of any
> trade union, where full advice is readily
> available and representation available.
> Professional organisations can advise but not

represent individuals. A knowledgeable third party, easily accessed and without charge is clearly desirable and certainly for initial advice.

Table 6.5: Factors contributing most to the use made of the ACAS advisory service.

Training Institutions

Factor	No. of times mentioned as being of	
An impartial service ie attempting to be fair to all interests concerned	1st importance 2nd importance	3 3
An independent service, ie independent of government and sectional interests	1st importance 2nd importance	- 3
A free service	1st importance 2nd importance	3 1
A technically competent service	1st importance 2nd importance	2 -

Their impartiality should not be affected; however number of cases would diminish and individuals, at a time of stress, would have added burdens as to whether to consult solicitors, consultants or other sources.

Would require that charging be full recovery and not subsidised. In practice I suspect that ACAS advisers must retain a large element of free advisory work if they are to have influence where it matters. Unfortunately, a mixed charge/free service would be confusing and conflicting in its objectives.

Current Government thinking would seem to imply that all functions be self-supporting. However, as a personal opinion I feel that charges would reduce the credibility of the organisation.

Of the seven training institutions, five saw the ACAS advisory function as complementary to their own activities and one as competitive. The seventh

institution regarded the function as both competitive and complementary.

Comments of a general nature were made by
several respondents:

> There has not been (from members) any reports
> of dissatisfaction with ACAS.

> It is unfortunate that ACAS is usually seen as
> being involved primarily in conflict situati-
> ons, attempting to reconcile conflicting
> interests. This limits its possible role as
> a promoter of common interests.

> Excellent as a last resort.

Conclusion

Having presented and briefly discussed the views of
the ACAS advisory role held by significant samples
of employers' associations, trade unions, management
consultants and training institutions, it is appropriate to attempt some general assessment of those
views. The assessment will be very brief because
much of the evidence of this chapter, especially the
quotations, has been of a res ipsa loquitor nature
calling for little or no elaboration from the
researchers.

Without going into evidential chapter and verse
detail, praise for the ACAS advisory function would
seem to outweigh, by an appreciable amount, adverse
criticism of that function. In fact, the consensus
evaluation by the samples of the four interested
party groups concerned, appears to be one of a broad
measure of satisfaction with the status quo position
of the ACAS advisory service. While such a result
may be gratifying to ACAS, especially when taken in
conjunction with the results of the clients' survey,
it does not follow that the advisory function is
operating at optimum effectiveness or that there are
no advisory issues and problems meriting more detailed discussion. The next two chapters are concerned with a number of such matters.

NOTES AND REFERENCES

1. Department of Employment Directory of
Employers' Associations, Trade unions, Joint
Organisations & etc., HMSO, 1983.
2. Directory of Management Consultants in the
UK 1983-84, compiled by Management Consultancy
Information Service, Ilford.

Chapter Seven

ISSUES OF SPECIALISM

In Chapter Three it was pointed out that the varied
duties of providing advisory, individual and collective conciliation and arbitration services within
each region, called for the development of a flexible and adaptable manpower resource, not least because of the constantly changing levels of demand
for each type of service. A brief explanation of
the broad choices available to a regional director
to organise his staff on a generalist or specialist basis was also given. While the choices that
are made are not crucial, they remain important
even when allowance is made for the influence exerted by the geographical nature of a particular region. Their importance is related to what are
thought to be the advantages and disadvantages of
each approach to the advisory and conciliation functions as such and the contribution that each approach is held to make to the effective deployment of
the region's manpower. The efficient use of advisers is certainly of concern to ACAS management, to
Department of Employment survey teams, and should,
it is hoped, be of some interest to taxpayer fund-
ers of ACAS. It is therefore thought useful to
elaborate, without going into fine detail, the generalist v specialist debate touched on in Chapter
Three and to associate that debate with other aspects of the management of the advisory service
especially where these relate to the issue of specialism.

Specialist organisation?

The advantages that are claimed, by an advocate of
specialism, for deploying staff as specialist conciliators (collective) or specialist advisers include the attainment of a higher level of skill and

141

expertise in the given specialism. Specialists become experts and because of this they are able to achieve better success rates and to project a more telling and influential ACAS image. The specialist adviser can carry out his assignment without distraction. Such concentrated activity becomes increasingly important as the proportion of in-depth work, and particularly of JWPs, increases.

By contrast, the generalist SIRO may fall between two stools, achieving limited expertise in both collective concilation and advisory work. A generalist adviser may receive only a limited number of conciliation cases, his advisory potential will thereby be diminished and his conciliation experience and skills hardly enhanced. By specialising, conciliators can respond immediately to urgent requests to help resolve disputes. Similarly, a specialist adviser can respond quickly to requests for advisory assistance. A generalist whose main work may be advisory can experience difficulties in breaking away from a partly completed advisory task in order to deal with a pressing request for conciliation. He may therefore hesitate to become extensively involved in in-depth work. His hybrid duties may nudge him in the direction of contingency planning in the sense of setting aside periods of time for conciliation work which may or may not then materialise. That in turn could reduce the volume of advisory work undertaken. It is thought that specialist conciliators can establish good relationships with trade union full-time officials. If, in contrast, such officials meet a number of generalist conciliators dispersed across several geographical 'patches', the lack of continuity of contact with one well-known ACAS officer may arguably diminish the official's readiness to use the conciliation service.

The same regional director advocate of specialisation who made the above points did however acknowledge that advantages could be claimed for the generalist approach. These were seen to be as follows. Collective conciliation work loads inevitably fluctuate and spare capacity can be occupied with advisory work. Otherwise a lean period for a specialist conciliation section could lead to an under-utilisation of resources. Conciliators carrying out advisory work could be better placed than specialists to keep up to date and in closer touch with the wide range of industrial relations activities occurring in a locality. Generalist conciliators would be more likely than their spec-

142

ialist counterparts to spot opportunities for potential in-depth work in dispute situations which they were attempting to resolve. A single generalist SIRO could provide multi-functional services to particular firms, to particular localities and thus present a comprehensive and perhaps more comprehensible form of help to companies and unions. Time and money might be saved by using the same officer for a variety of purposes. (It is also worth pointing out that conciliation skills are needed in advisory work, especially in the JWP and industrial relations audit type of activity).

To add to the range of relevant factors, it is necessary to recall that the most specialist of the specialist advisers is almost certainly the period appointment adviser (PASIRO) recruited, as he commonly is, for his experience and knowledge of work study, payment systems, incentive schemes. It is considered important that his expertise should have been developed in non-civil service employment and preferably in private industry. After all, most ACAS clients are to be found in the private sector and the possession of direct, appreciable experience of commercial competition, of industrial practices, by a PASIRO is therefore considered desirable and in some cases essential. The long exposure of a technical expert PASIRO to management oriented approaches to problems may have occasionally caused difficulties for himself, and others, when, in an ACAS role, he is expected to be even-handed to all parties concerned in or affected by a piece of in-depth work. Similar difficulties may also have arisen in the case of a PASIRO recruited from a trade union background. The movement from a sectional interest stance to one closer to some conception of neutrality proves harder for some individuals than for others.

All the civil service advisers we interviewed believed that it was right to recruit experts from industry with immediate and relevant experience. Anecdotal evidence volunteered by some advisers indicated that some PASIRO appointments had been unfortunate - while others had been extremely successful both in terms of what had been achieved for clients and for adviser colleagues with whom PASIROs had worked. Some advisers expressed the view that PASIROs should be brought into closer and more frequent contact with a greater number of colleagues in order that part of the PASIRO's expertise could be more widely shared. The view was also advanced that some PASIROs guarded their expertise quite carefully and were reluctant to share their skills, techniques and knowledge with civil servant advisers.

Whatever his individual ability and whatever perception he holds of his role, the PASIRO presumably remains conscious of his transient status within the advisory labour resource, and increasingly aware of his approaching need to find other employment. Differing views are held about whether a PASIRO's personal capital of marketable experience and skills increases or decreases as a result of his stay with ACAS. On one view the PASIRO joins ACAS with immediate and relevant experience of industry. By definition the value of that experience, to ACAS, must diminish the longer his appointment as a PASIRO. On another view, his overall experience is seen to increase given that in an adviser's role he is likely to encounter industrial relations problems and use his expertise in a variety of industries and types of organisation that would not have been possible in his previous position. What is clear from our interviews is that some PASIROs would welcome a continuing career as established ACAS advisers, and that a good proportion of the civil service advisers would welcome the retention of the best PASIROs, while acknowledging the unions' understandable concern to protect the conditions of established civil servants and their promotion opportunities by limiting the intake of outsiders.

Reverting to the generalist v specialist debate, in which the role of the PASIRO constitutes a significant element, the advocate of specialism alluded to above claimed, as a further advantageous consequence of the specialist approach, that it made for an ease of management and elegance of organisation, control, recording and accountability. Doubtless this was meant to be a contentious point and in so far as regional directors permit themselves to bridle, the generalists among them may have done so at the implied inelegance of generalist arrangements. But, a serious point remains - that of the effective management of the advisory resource allied to other ACAS resources in shifting demand conditions in a region, in which varying sized employment concentrations may be widely dispersed. While there may be little to choose, in intellectual terms, between the respective merits of the generalist and specialist approaches, at the end of the day the dispersion referred to, together with cost-benefit considerations, may determine

144

that one experienced all-rounder rather than two
specialists is sent to the locality concerned when
separate advisory and conciliation problems require
attention.

As outlined in Chapter Three, the day-to-day
management responsibility for the deployment of
both specialist and generalist resources is very
much in the hands of the PIRO concerned, even allowing for the strong element of self-management in
advisory and conciliation work. It is established
within ACAS that the PIRO's job is essentially one
that calls for the exercise of managerial skills.
In some instances it is apparent that such skills
have been developed by, for example, the PIRO having at some time been a manager of a sizeable employment exchange or in charge of a department
within some other part of the DE Group. Latterly
however, the development pattern has changed with
suitable personnel being promoted from within the
service to PIRO positions. This has meant that an
appreciable number of newly appointed PIROs have
had no recent management experience. ACAS acknowledges that this lack of experience necessitates
the provision of particular training inputs which
in turn requires a pre-training analysis of what
the PIRO job entails. Senior and junior personnel
are very well aware that it is far from being
enough to claim that : 'effective fieldwork,
advisory and conciliation, is all that really matters - anyone can manage'. Effective striving for
the optimum use of that fieldwork resource does require managerial ability. It may be of interest
therefore to set down part of a Principal's role as
described by the Civil Service Department a few
years ago and the ACAS identification of key tasks
in the Principal IRO's advisory role.

First the CSD:

The Principal's task is varied and demanding
and not confined to one type of work. The
qualities expected are a penetrating and clear
mind, the capacity for critical analysis and
judgement, good powers of expression on paper
and orally, and the ability to make ready and
easy contact with other people.

Some key PIRO tasks in the management of advisory work were described by an ACAS working party
as follows:

Ensuring understanding and compliance with

advisory work policy.
Planning ahead and managing and organising
resources to achieve objectives.
Teaching and counselling staff to develop
"Professionalism" and quality of service.
Maintaining regular training schedules, pre-
paring staff for training and following up
afterwards, identifying any gaps in training
and arranging additional training via internal
seminars, formal courses, attachments etc.
Promoting discussion of appropriate operation-
al methods and dissemination of experience
within the region/with other regions.
Encouraging flexibility of approach.
Authorising in-depth work (time cost and
methods).
Supervising case work, report writing etc.
Monitoring and evaluating progress towards
objectives.
Organising conferences/seminars.

It was also envisaged, by the working party,
that the PIRO would have an important, direct operational involvement in advisory work by setting
up in-depth exercises, presenting survey reports
and chairing other meetings with the parties concerned, and speaking at conferences as part of a
marketing of the advisory service strategy.
In addition to the notable emphasis on the
training and development of staff for whom the PIRO
is responsible, two other features are of particular interest in the duties listed above. These are
the references to "professionalism" and advisory
work policy. The latter topic will be discussed
in the next chapter but a few thoughts on professionalism can be expressed now. Professionalism,
as a word, was placed in quotation marks in the
document concerned - and was left undefined. However, as it is associated in the list of duties
with quality of service, it seems reasonable to
suppose that the implied intention was that advisers should seek and be encouraged to attain widely
recognisable high standards of competence in dealing with industrial relations and personnel management matters; in short to become practical experts
in the industrial relations field. While that is
a sensible enough objective, particularly when the
value for public money notion is kept in mind, it
may be wondered whether the objective could be more
readily achieved if the institutional status of
ACAS itself was altered. This requires some expla-

nation.

As previously mentioned ACAS remains, for administrative purposes, part of the DE Group within the wider structure of the civil service. Although '...the Service shall not be subject to directions of any kind from any Minister of the Crown as to the manner in which it is to exercise any of its functions under any enactment.' 1) the Service does not enjoy the independence of being able to determine unilaterally, within some publicly funded budget, its own staffing levels or graded labour force composition. In regard to such matters the Service remains subject to Department of Employment monitoring. It remains the practice, as promotion opportunities occur, for some ACAS personnel to move to jobs outside ACAS but within the DE Group. Movements in the reverse direction also take place. 'Shop floor' ACAS advisers, and other field staff can be heard to grumble that there have been too many instances of career 'high fliers' from the DE being transferred into senior posts at ACAS head office. It is alleged that too few among such personnel have had any significant industrial relations experience and having introduced a few experiments, to make their career mark, they soon disappear to pastures that have become greener than those of ACAS.

Whatever the merits of such claims, and we are reporting rather than assessing some shop floor perceptions, ACAS is undoubtedly affected by the traditional civil service practice of staff mobility. While this certainly extends the range of experience of a significant number of individuals and facilitates career progression, the question can fairly be posed, in the ACAS case, as to whether it really helps the formation of a corps of experts on industrial relations and of the professionalism referred to above. The same question prompts the associated thought of whether the ACAS staffing links with the DE Group should be weakened, even severed, so that ACAS could enjoy more independence in relation to its staffing requirements. The implications of any such change merit far more detailed and lengthy discussion than can be undertaken here, but a few of the possible implications can be mentioned.

Without doubt a strong case could be made for staffing a specialist industrial relations institution entirely with industrial relations experts, with people who wished to work exclusively and continuously in the industrial relations field.

Among the advisers we interviewed there were a
number who would fall into such a category.
Others would see value in advisers, and others,
acquiring a variety of experience in other parts
of the DE Group before becoming advisers, stressing
again the importance of developing social skills,
something that was perhaps harder to do, and more
necessary, than gaining knowledge about the structures, institutions, procedures and techniques of
industrial relations. From this viewpoint, once a
basic understanding of the content of industrial
relations has been acquired, it was not self-evident that an adviser with experience of a variety
of jobs in the DE was, or should be, any less
effective, less conscientious, less professional
than an adviser who originally joined ACAS because
of his own personal interest in the activity of
industrial relations.
    Another implication that would attract close
scrutiny would be whether ACAS, being a relatively
small institution, could or even should devise an
employment structure that offered career opportunities for staff comparable to those that currently
exist, linked as ACAS is in the manner described,
to the DE Group. The issue of the status of the
staff of a specialist, more sharply separated, institution would arise as would questions bearing
on staff terms and conditions of employment. Such
considerations can easily lead to others - for example, whether the role of the Secretary of State
for Employment in relation to ACAS should also be
re-examined. It is this minister who appoints the
members of the directing ACAS Council, who approves
or withholds approval of draft Codes of Practice
that ACAS prepares, who requires ACAS to conduct
inquiries into the operation of wages councils.
These and related issues are relevant to any discussion on the extent to which the advisory function and the institution of ACAS should become more
specialist. It is at least arguable, if also dis-
putable, that the advisory function could become
both more specialist and more professional if it
was completely separated from ACAS and required to
operate, as do consultants, in a commercially viable
way. We shall return to this issue later.

Specialist advice : the published and spoken word

Whatever view is held of the specialist nature of
the advisory service and its organisation, there will
undoubtedly be a widespread expectation that ACAS

is especially well placed to publish specialist
advice. 'What does ACAS have to say about...?'
would be a common enough way of expressing that
expectation. As will be widely known, ACAS has the
statutory authority to issue Codes of Practice
(Section 6, EPA). To date three such codes have
been issued these being,

1. Disciplinary practice and procedures in
employment
2. Disclosure of information to trade unions
for collective bargaining purposes
3. Time off for trade union duties and
activities

The wording of Section 6(1) of the EPA is of
interest. 'The Service may issue Codes of Practice
containing such practical guidance as the Service
thinks fit for the purpose of promoting the improvement of industrial relations.' The overall statutory authority of ACAS in relation to the issuing of
codes is therefore enabling and discretionary.
However, Section 6(2) employs the word 'shall' in
relation to the ACAS duty to issue codes in regard
to two specific topics. ACAS has a mandatory duty
to issue codes regarding **disclosure of information**
to trade unions, and, time off facilities for trade
union representatives. The difference between the
discretionary and mandatory duties was, of course,
related to the Act's wider objective of extending
the influence of trade unions and collective bargaining. The legal status of all three codes, and
of any others that may be made, is defined in
Section 6(11). While not legally binding in themselves, they are admissible in evidence in any proceedings before an industrial tribunal or the
Central Arbitration Committee, 'and if any provision
of such a Code appears to the tribunal or Committee
to be relevant to any question arising in the proceedings it shall be taken into account in determin-
ing that question.'
The two codes that ACAS was required to issue -
disclosure of information, and time-off, were
published in 1977 and came into effect in August
1977 and April 1978 respectively. Code Number 1 -
Disciplinary practice and procedures, the code
chosen by ACAS itself for issue, came into effect
in June 1977. Since that time, seven years have
gone by, at the time of writing, without ACAS having
published, even in draft form, another code. Does
this mean that there are no other matters on which

codified advice needs to be given with a view to
improving industrial relations? Or does it mean
that although suitable industrial relations subjects
can be identified, it proves impossible even to
start the process of codifying advice because of the
absence of a sufficient measure of consensus among
those who influence and determine such matters, including the ACAS Council and any parties such as
trade unions and employers' associations who chose
to make representations about any draft code prepared? Or does it mean that the codes so far produced are thought to have very little influence in
the direction of improving industrial relations?
Comprehensive answers to such questions would entail
further and detailed research but from our conversations with advisers we can provide a few pointers
to what fuller answers might contain.

The majority of advisers interviewed considered
it to be appropriate for ACAS to issue codes but
only a modest number among them readily suggested
additional specific topics for codified advice.
These consisted of collective bargaining, communications, participation, redundancy. Several advisers believed that the original and general Industrial Relations Code of Practice should be up-dated.
This Code was issued in 1972 by the Department of
Employment under the Industrial Relations Act 1971.
The code 'survived' the repeal of that highly controversial act but parts of it have been superseded
by the ACAS codes. The advisers who referred to
this 1972 code took the view that practitioners valued the code, one adviser seeing parallels between
it and the advice given in Shakespeare's Hamlet by
Polonius to his son Laertes before the latter's
departure from parental care. That famous collection of precepts includes the lines:

> Give every man thine ear, but few thy voice
> Take each man's censure, but reserve thy
> judgement.

Well, maybe so, but it remains an interesting proposition that the nearest a government has come in
recent times to defining good industrial relations
is the formulation represented by the 1972 code of
practice.

Returning to what might constitute the themes
for any new codes, a common view held by advisers
was that even if a subject could be agreed upon by
the ACAS council and that was unlikely, it was even
more unlikely that the council would be able to
150

agree about the contents of any new code. The reasons for such a possible state of affairs probably have much more to do with the general political climate surrounding industrial relations in recent years, than with the intrinsic worth of genuine differences of opinion among council members about various technical or other aspects of industrial relations.

As to the impact of the existing codes, it was notable that in a number of instances, advisers could remember the themes of only two of the three codes the forgotten Cinderella among them most frequently being the disclosure of information code. It is known that a certain amount of work was done within ACAS during 1981 with a view to a possible revision of that code in order to improve its operational effectiveness. This attempted revision of disclosure of information for <u>collective bargaining</u> purposes would appear to have been placed within a broader context of greater disclosure of information by companies to employees. However, the original code has remained unchanged.

Varying reactions were expressed by advisers interviewed to the time-off code. In the experience of some advisers it had featured significantly but in the experience of others, hardly at all. The view was unanimous that the most useful code by far and the one with the greatest impact was the disciplinary code. Its wide influence was thought to be due to its close association with unfair dismissal proceedings before industrial tribunals. It was the advisers' view that if any ACAS document was to be found in active use in a personnel manager's office it would almost certainly be the disciplinary code.

It is worth recording that most of the advisers interviewed believed that ACAS was not the appropriate body to issue codes of practice on matters such as picketing and the closed shop. It was considered that attempting to codify guidance on such controversial issues would conflict with the perceived and actual independent status of ACAS. It is also, of course, extremely unlikely that members of the ACAS council could agree either to the idea of such codes let alone their contents. Despite the reservations mentioned about advice on thorny issues like the closed shop, many advisers felt that if ACAS was to be regarded as a prime source of guidance on good industrial relations practice, it should be much more ready than had so far been the case, to give authoritative voice to its opinions

about a whole range of industrial relations matters.
The publication of discussion papers was seen by
some advisers as a way of introducing influential
guidance which could not be achieved by codes because of the tri-partite nature of a council which
remained acutely conscious of a highly politicised
industrial relations atmosphere. The first discussion paper - Developments in Harmonisation - appeared in March 1982. The introduction to this paper
indicates the educational as distinct from prescrip-
tive nature of the planned series of papers. A
second discussion paper entitled - Collective bargaining in Britain : its extent and level - has also
become available.

As an institution ACAS presented its own views
on codes of practice to a House of Commons Select
Committee on Employment in October 1981. It saw
codes as being intended to influence industrial
relations practice in two ways - first as persuasive documents (after due consultation with interested parties and the approval of Parliament) - and,
secondly, as guides to considerations which should
be taken into account in relevant employment
legislation proceedings. In regard to codes as
persuasive documents it was the ACAS view that
while codes should lead opinion and urge adoption
of best practice they could not be tco far
ahead of general practice. This posed drafting
difficulties especially on controversial topics.
If codes were to be read and used they needed
to be brief and to the point but not so general as
to be meaningless. The issue of too many statutory
codes might be counter-productive bearing in mind
that other state institutions, notably the DE, produced codes deriving from employment legislation.
The burden on employers, particularly the smaller
ones, had to be kept in mind.

At the time (1981) the above evidence was submitted, ACAS claimed that there was no systematic
evidence then available about the impact of codes
in the employment field. Since 1981 a number of
independent studies have been completed which are
concerned with disclosure of information and employee reporting and to some extent with the role of the
disclosure code within the general debate about disclosure of information. One article is especially
concerned with the role of codes in labour relations
and in particular with the disclosure code. 2) This
article concludes that from four SSRC studies on the
operation of the code at the workplace, the code had
no significant direct effect although it may have

had an enlightening effect indirectly. For ACAS
there would seem to arise the question of whether
good practice can be identified. The real problem
seemingly is the absence of consensus about the
disclosure issue itself.

In addition to producing codes of what will
hopefully be broadly acknowledged as good practice,
ACAS tries in a variety of other published forms to
give sound advice, clear information and explanations to those willing to read. A full list of such
publications (apart from the inquiry reports) is
given at Appendix B. What cannot be known is the
full list of people influenced by such publications
or the nature and extent of any influence. We can
offer, from the research, only a few observations
based on interviews with advisers.

Two general points emerged from these interviews. First, it was right for ACAS to publish
advice. ACAS had a duty to make its mark with the
written word for its clients' and its own sake. In
fact, many advisers were in favour of more imaginative efforts being made to publicise the range of
ACAS activities and scale of work undertaken.
Secondly, it was claimed by advisers that many of
the explanatory leaflets, eg 'This is ACAS' and the
advisory booklets, eg 'No 3 Personnel records'
served the important purpose of visiting cards,
especially in relation to development visits.
Those visited apparently frequently expressed surprise at and interest in the variety of work undertaken by ACAS. It was not unusual for a potential
client's perception of ACAS to change from that of
being, as the media so often summarises its functions - 'the government's conciliation service', to
one more closely resembling its independent provision of a range of services. The retention, by the
potential client, of some of the free ACAS literature may be helpful, it is thought, in bringing
back to mind the conversation with 'that chap from
ACAS' when, at a later stage, a manager facing
industrial relations problems may be looking for
help.

In regard to specific ACAS publications advisers tended to single out Advisory Booklet No 1
Job Evaluation for special commendation. Although
only an introduction to the subject it was held to
be an especially useful one. By contrast, the
Industrial Relations Handbook, even though relatively cheap at £5, was thought to be of almost no interest to clients but of some use to advisers when
seeking, for instance, information about collective

bargaining arrangements in particular sectors of
employment. Advisers believed that ACAS should
bring out such a reference work. The publication
was probably useful to students of industrial relations but through no fault of the authors, significant parts of it were obsolescent, even obsolete,
from the day the book appeared, the recent changes
to industrial relations and employment law having
been so numerous and so rapid. The great majority
of advisers supported, with varying degrees of
warmth, the widely distributed and extensively publicised leaflet - Improving Industrial Relations -
A Joint Responsibility. This was thought to set
out sensibly enough a check-list of points to ob-
serve if industrial relations were to be handled
in a civilised and humane way during an economic
recession. While sceptical of the actual beneficial
impact of such a publication, advisers nevertheless
acknowledged that ACAS, of all institutions, had a
responsibility to propagate the ideas and philosophy
expressed in the leaflet. At the personal level, it
just became rather difficult to do so, when advisers
all too often found themselves in situations where
companies were fighting desperately for survival,
and the managers concerned were pre-occupied with
problems of costs, customers and markets.

Although the above evidence is modest in volume and limited in scope, it was accumulated systematically from a series of structured interviews
with advisers. It therefore provides some clues
to the advisers' evaluation of part of their collective published advice and information. What we
cannot provide is the clients' evaluation of ACAS
publications. This is because we considered that
there are limits to the number of questions that
can reasonably be put to questionnaire respondents.
Questions on publications, and for that matter on a
range of other issues, were therefore omitted from
the questionnaires. For the same reason, we did
not ask clients questions about any experiences
they might have had with ACAS enquiry points, even
though such points are vital distribution centres
of information and advice. What now follows are
our own observations, not those of clients.

The enquiry point

Although the number of enquiries handled within the
regional and head offices by telephone, letter or
meeting callers at the offices, has declined over
the years, some 279,000 such enquiries were dealt

with at ACAS enquiry points during 1983. 3) This
activity accounted, in the same year, for twelve per
cent of the total time spent by advisers on advisory
work. The enquiry point thus remains an important
consumer of advisory time and of resources more
generally, as nationally, the full-time equivalent
of some ten executive officers and twenty five
clerical officers are engaged on enquiry point work.
It is the cost-effectiveness of this staffing arrangement that causes concern among more senior
levels of ACAS staff not least among the regional
directors themselves. For many enquirers their
first point of contact with ACAS will be the enquiry
point itself. Given what may develop out of a telephone enquiry - an advisory visit, even a piece of
in-depth work - it is clearly important that the
manner and the matter of the response to the enquir-
er's telephone call is an appropriately professional
one.
     Each regional office has an enquiry point the
size of which will vary according to the needs of
the region itself. As the London and South East
regions share the same premises, they also share an
enquiry point, controlled by the London region.
This is by far the largest enquiry point consisting,
in 1983, of eleven people nine of whom spent their
whole working time answering enquiries. An estimated 68,500 enquiries were handled by this point in
1982. Although this point was staffed largely with
clerical staff, each IRO in turn in the two regions
spent a week on the point to deal with the more complex enquiries. These commonly had to do with unfair dismissal. Similar organisational practices
with smaller numbers of staff, and with an executive officer in charge of the enquiry point, are
adopted by the other regions. Some of the clerical
officers manning the enquiry point will also be engaged in clerical duties. For the executive officer
concerned, supervising the enquiry point may constitute just one part of his work. Regions endeav-
our to have an IRO available on a regular basis for
more difficult enquiries but it sometimes becomes a
question of finding out if any adviser happens to
be in the office at the time in question.
     From these few simple descriptions it is easy
to imagine that an agitated caller, by telephone or
in person, may not always, at the first time of
enquiring, receive the optimum advice or information
to meet his employment problem enquiries. Stripped
of their contextual material, and often confused
presentation, those enquiries could typically

155

include:

> Am I redundant? What is my entitlement to pay
> and notice? The boss is trying to impose a
> cut in wages and change my conditions and I
> don't like it. What can I do? Is there a
> minimum wage for a clerical worker? I'm laid
> off. What is my entitlement to guarantee pay?
> Do I get holiday pay when I leave?

Enquiries, including those frequently made by
small employers, related to individual rights in
employment are legion. Some of the answers to the
queries raised may be found in the series of employment legislation booklets published by the DE.
Large stocks of these are held by ACAS offices and
where appropriate copies are sent to enquirers.
Quite frequently enquirers will have to be directed
to other public bodies for appropriate information
and guidance, eg to the factory inspectorate, the
wages inspectorate, the inland revenue, the Department of Employment, the EDC, the Citizens Advice
Bureau, a trade union. Although most enquiries
would seem to be made by individuals, employers
sometimes seek in effect, a knowledgeable second
opinion about a particular course of action they
are proposing to take. Similarly, they may seek to
bounce off their ideas, their interpretation, their
reading of a situation, against the viewpoints of
the industrial relations specialist institution -
ACAS; in reality, at least to begin with, a clerical officer of perhaps modest industrial relations
knowledge and less experience. To add to the
range of enquirers, and complexities, some solicitors, with their clients present, will ring ACAS
for advice and information.
Although clerical officers who feel they are
being drawn into too deep water are required to
seek help from more experienced or senior colleagues, their position seems such that a wrong answer
could easily damage an image of ACAS professionalism. Taking into account on and off the job training, it is estimated that it takes a full twelve
months before a clerical officer becomes fully
effective on the enquiry point. It may be questioned whether such work should really be classified as
clerical work for it contains little that resembles
routine clerical practice. It is true that records
are kept of enquiries but this does not happen in
any uniform way and when the demand for telephone
answers is high, it is known that by no means all

enquiries can be logged and classified.
As intimated above, ACAS itself is a little
uneasy about the staffing of enquiry points.
Civil service socialisation processes may well develop the social skills necessary for an effective
enquiry point clerical officer, but a few bad
technical mistakes, where influential institutional
enquirers are involved, could soon do harm to the
professional standing of enquiry work. ACAS management are alive to this danger and enquiry point
arrangements, with attendant training implications,
recently came under internal review.

Specialist analysis : the expired legacy of the CIR?

On 22 April 1975 the following advertisement appeared in The Times:

ACAS Industrial Relations Officers
In addition to providing an advisory service
and facilities for conciliation and arbitration ACAS undertakes detailed inquiries into
industrial relations problems from company to
national level. There are opportunities for
employment in this work based at the ACAS
Head Office ...Officers will be required to
lead or participate in small inquiry teams
studying and analysing complex problems in
the general field of collective bargaining
and putting forward recommendations for their
solution.

Although supported by Section 1(2) and Section
4 of the Employment Protection Act 1975, the major
statutory authority for the above advertisement is
Section 5 of the Act - Inquiry. Subsection (1) of
Section 5 reads:

The Service may, if it thinks fit, inquire into
any question relating to industrial relations
generally or to industrial relations in any
particular industry or in any particular undertaking or part of an undertaking. (underlining
added)

Sub-section (2) continues:

The finding of any inquiry under this section,
together with any advice given by the Service
in connection with those findings, may be published. (underlining added)

Because of its generalised wording Section 5,
within the overall duty of improving industrial
relations, enables various types of inquiry to be
undertaken. One type continues the long established practice of appointing a committee of inquiry,
or panel of investigation to use a more recent
phrase, to analyse a serious industrial dispute,
actual or pending, and to make recommendations for
the basis of a settlement or improvement in the
situation. Other inquiries might be seen as in the
mould of a number of the CIR investigations into
states of bad industrial relations in particular
companies. To complete the inquiry picture, ACAS
is required, under the Wages Councils Act 1979, to
conduct, for the Secretary of State for Employment,
inquiries as to whether or not a particular wages
council should be abolished or perhaps altered in
terms of its operational scope. Reports from this
type of inquiry constitute advice in the sense that
in the light of what ACAS discovers and comments
upon, the Minister is better placed than he would
otherwise have been, to make a more considered
judgement about the future of a particular wages
council.
Taking all forms of inquiry together, the 1983
ACAS Annual Report lists 21 published reports of
inquiries. 4) Of these nine are concerned with
wages council matters. The remaining twelve are
industrial dispute or industrial relations problem
centred Some are concerned with the problems of
individual companies, eg Scottish and Newcastle
Breweries (Report No 9) and some with industry wide
matters eg ACAS evidence to the Royal Commission on
the National Health Service (Report No 12). The
last inquiry of this type, ie into industrial relations 'in any particular industry or in any particular undertaking' was into Industrial Relations in
the Coaching Industry - Report No 16. This report
was published in 1979 following the appointment of
the committee concerned in September 1976.
Given what has just been related, it may be
wondered why, for the latter half of its life-span
to date, ACAS has undertaken no searching inquiries
of the type conducted by the CIR and foreshadowed in
the advertisement cited at the beginning of this
chapter. It could be that the type of problem to be
tackled via the route of Section 5 of the EPA has
diminished. But even casual acquaintance with or
awareness of turbulent or troublesome aspects of
industrial relations of the past few years, makes
such an explanation sound implausible. It could be

158

that ACAS itself, for whatever reasons, decided to make very sparing use of Section 5. It could be that Section 5 type problems can be tackled in ways other than by inquiries. The latter two possibilities sound more plausible and will be considered more closely.

It will be recalled that the Donovan Commission recommendations for the improvement of disorderly industrial relations placed heavy emphasis on the need for procedural reform so that the 'two systems' of workplace and industry wide bargaining could be brought into a more effective and harmonious relationship. The process of self-help reform should be assisted by the formation of an independent institution which could investigate general and specific industrial relations problems. The Labour Government of the day acted upon this proposal and in March 1969 the Commission on Industrial Relations (CIR) was established. Initially the CIR's case load of inquiries was determined by government. Later the National Industrial Relations Court was also empowered to refer cases to the CIR. It is worth bearing in mind that although it could lobby for particular problems to be referred to it for examination, the CIR was never free to choose the composition and nature of its work load. This contrasts strongly with the position of ACAS under Section 5 of the EPA which virtually gives the service carte blanche authority to inquire into any aspect of industrial relations - 'if it thinks fit' (underlining added).

There can be no doubt that during the CIR's relatively brief existence (1969-74) its work attracted much interest and not a little controversy. The CIR staff certainly included able people with a strong commitment to the reform of industrial relations along Donovan recommended lines. However, the extent to which the CIR actually improved industrial relations in specific instances, or more generally, is much more difficult to determine. The most notable attempt made at such an assessment has been that of John Purcell, a former member of the CIR who was closely involved in a number of the key procedural inquiries conducted by the CIR (Purcell's work features below).

CIR procedural inquiries appear to have been much influenced by the methods adopted earlier by the National Board for Prices and Incomes which also looked at a number of industrial relations problem areas during its life time of attempted price and income influence (1965- 70). A typical

CIR study of bad, ie conflict torn industrial relations in a specific location or locations would
entail a close scrutiny of discrete factors such
as payment methods and earnings levels, procedures, disputes, management organisation, trade union
organisation, production methods and the views of
the interested parties. The analysis would bring
out the inter-relationships between such factors,
indicate how conflicts arose and how well or how
badly disputes procedures coped with the conflicts.
From such an examination it became possible to
propose reforms and hopefully obtain agreement to
them from discussions with the parties involved.
On the face of it, this seems a rational enough way
of proceeding but its overall effectiveness has
been seriously questioned by Purcell.
    Purcell returned to the companies where the
CIR's first nine procedural inquiries had been
carried out, in order to establish what the CIR's
interventions had achieved. Purcell formed the
clear impression that although the managers and
union representatives concerned generally agreed
that the CIR's diagnoses of their problems had been
substantially correct, in possibly only two of the
nine companies concerned had the CIR played a
primary role in bringing about reform. In the other
situations it was essentially economic survival
crises that had fostered improved mutual accommodation between the antagonistic parties. In relation
to the promotion of reform via government created
agencies Purcell observes:

    It may be considered that there is little
    point in trying to encourage reform through
    lengthy and expensive inquiries if the agency
    has only a secondary role to play. If,
    however, it can be shown that the limited
    impact of the CIR can be explained in large
    measure by the methodology it employed, and
    that an alternative approach to reform exists,
    then the case for third party intervention
    can be restated. 5)

    Part of the CIR's methodology could be seen as
its practice, flowing from a policy decision, to
publish highly detailed accounts of its case-study
work in companies with bad industrial relations
records. This practice was considered to serve
wider educational interests and possibly owed
something to the zeal of the reformers associated
with inquiry work. Section 5 of the EPA allows a

160

different approach to be taken by ACAS:

> The finding of any inquiry under this section,
> together with any advice given by the Service
> in connection with those findings, may be
> published by the Service if -
> a) it appears to the Service that publication
> is desirable for the improvement of industrial
> relations, either generally or in relation to
> the specific question inquired into; and,
> b) after sending a draft of the findings to,
> and taking into account the views of, all the
> parties appearing to the Service to be concern-
> ed, the Service thinks fit.

Of the published ACAS inquiry reports referred
to earlier, only two - Scottish and Newcastle
Breweries (No 9) and St. Stephen's Parliamentary
Press (No 14), might be thought to fall into the
company type inquiry of the published CIR kind.
Report No 14 appeared in 1978. The 1981 ACAS Annual
Report tells us 6) that six other company inquiries
had been carried out but their associated reports
have not been published.

From the above account, it is tempting to believe that after an initial impact on the modus oper-
andi of ACAS inquiries, the influence of the CIR
inquiry approach waned and then disappeared. It is
necessary to recall that on its abolition the CIR's
inquiry functions passed to ACAS as did a number of
the CIR's inquiry staff. Some among them were not
career civil servants but had been recruited on
short term contracts against job specification criteria similar to those in the cited ACAS advertisement - studying and analysing complex problems in
the general field of collective bargaining and putting forward recommendations for their solution.
This recommendation process which, in the CIR experience, often envisaged and emphasised structural
changes in the industrial relations systems concerned, was part of the methodology which Purcell
questioned. He suggested that a better approach
could be that whereby a third party 'process agent',
eg ACAS, concentrated on identifying the factors
which inhibited the parties from finding their own
solutions. The third party would assume the role
of a 'strategic mediator'. By helping the parties:

> In carefully staged joint meetings or through
> joint working parties, agency staff (would)
> help stimulate attitude changes by creating

the opportunity for trust to grow. The role
is to help the combatants reach an understanding of the problems and, through this, help
alter attitudes as a prelude to the negotiation
of longer term changes in structures, roles
and remedies. It is up to the parties to find
their own solutions. 7)

This, of course, is a very different methodology from that of conducting a searching analysis,
making numerous, wide-ranging and probably valid
recommendations - then disappearing from the scene
while denouncing industrial relations sin from a
published and sometimes widely publicised report.
The 1981 ACAS Annual Report made reference
to Purcell's ideas and indicated that in regard to
its inquiry work, ACAS in its turn had become
'interested in the possibility of different
approaches as a result of its experience with CIR-
type company inquiries, as well as with collective
conciliation and in-depth advisory work generally.'
8) What this interest meant in specific terms was
a much greater emphasis being placed on the formation, where appropriate, of joint working parties.
'The aim is to foster as far as possible a rational
team approach to the solving of problems which
yields results compatible with the objectives of
both parties.' 9)   Reference to subsequent annual
reports reveals continuing ACAS commitment to the
perceived value of the JWP which in the 1983 report
features for the first time as a separate category
in the statistical tables.
What may be seen as a company inquiry methodology that evolves from the CIR mode to the ACAS
mode, 10) does contain other formative elements
from those indicated. As mentioned before, the CIR
staff included keen reformers who were not averse
to seeking difficult assignments and telling the
world of their discoveries and ideas. In moving to
ACAS they joined colleagues who, from a DE background, probably had a more pragmatic and cautious
civil service approach to the improvement of industrial relations and its attendant publicity. It
would seem that the latter culture has prevailed.
Certainly the great majority of advisers we interviewed, while considering that it was right for ACAS
to have a statutory authority to inquire into problems, did not believe that reform attempts grounded
in missionary zeal were particularly effective.
Individual companies, and unions, publicly criticis-
ed by third parties for their industrial relations
162

shortcomings had felt resentful and this had sometimes hampered further work. However, in fairness
to the CIR it has to be recalled that the Commission
received its investigatory assignments from either
the Secretary of State for Employment or the NIRC,
an arrangement which probably encouraged managements
and unions in the publicly designated 'black spots'
to be unhelpful to those actually conducting the
inquiries. (It may be remembered also that as the
result of the NIRC's involvement with the CIR, the
TUC ceased to co-operate with the Commission). In
contrast, ACAS devises its own portfolio of inquiry
work, and would be unlikely to press for an inquiry
unless there appeared to be a reasonable pre-dispo-
sition on the part of all those concerned, to co-
operate in the inquiry. In any event, similar ends
to those envisaged for inquiries are presumably
being achieved, at least to some extent, by different means, by JWPs and other forms of joint involvement with a third party presence.

Organisational factors have also contributed to
the limited use, made by ACAS, of the inquiry power.
Because of its potentially far reaching consequences, inquiry work is conducted from ACAS head
office. But this inevitably entails some overlap
with regional advisory work. Various questions
arise - whose should be the responsibility to identify potential inquiry situations, head office or
the regions? How large a head-office inquiry team
should be constituted and to what extent might that
team duplicate the advisory resource in the region
in which the problem company is located? Would a
head office inquiry really be so very different from
a major diagnostic survey carried out by regional
advisers? Most companies falling into a problem
category would probably prefer a confidential diagnostic survey carried out by a possibly familiar
regional staff to an inquiry conducted by an unfam-
iliar ACAS head office team, which might support
more strongly the idea of a published report. For
such reasons, coupled with the commitment to the
methodology of JWPs, the concern to conduct company
inquiries has diminished and the role of head office
in this type of activity has changed to one of co-
ordination and support for regional activities where
a major piece of work involving the same company in
different regions is carried out.

While the inquiry style changes described
appear to be sound enough in themselves, the question of whether adequate use is made of Section 5 of
the EPA still seems a somewhat open one. It will be

remembered that the service has the discretionary
authority (see p.157) to inquire into any question
relating to,

    a)   industrial relations generally
    b)   industrial relations in any particular
industry
    c)   industrial relations in any particular
undertaking
    d)   industrial relations in part of an
undertaking

Even allowing for the apparent effectiveness
of JWPs and other forms of in-depth work, Britain
would seem to have a sufficient number and variety
of industrial relations problems to warrant greater
use being made of the Section 5 inquiry power.
Putting the issue somewhat differently and more
broadly, is ACAS sufficiently assertive with its
advisory activities? Should there not be a clear,
authoritative ACAS view about ...and...and...?
Such questions raise policy issues and it is to
some of these that we turn in the next chapter.

NOTES AND REFERENCES

1.   Employment Protection Act 1975, Schedule 1,
Section 11(1).
2.   P. Willman, H. Gospel, 'The role of codes
in labour relations : the case of disclosure',
Industrial Relations Journal, vol.14, no.4 (Winter
1983), pp.76-82. See also Roger Hussey and Arthur
Marsh, Disclosure of information and employee
reporting,(Gower 1983). B. Towers, M. Wright,
'Pay reference arbitration and the disclosure of
information', Industrial Relations Journal, no. 3
(Autumn 1983), pp.82-96. and no.4 (Winter 1983),
pp.83-91.
3.   ACAS Annual Report 1983, p.41.
4.   Ibid. pp.83-4.
5.   J. Purcell, 'The lessons of the Commission
on Industrial Relations' attempts to reform workplace industrial relations', Industrial Relations
Journal, vol.10, no.2 (Summer 1979), p.18.
6.   ACAS Annual Report 1981, p.55.
7.   Purcell, 'The lessons of the Commission on
Industrial Relations', p.19.
8.   ACAS Annual Report 1981, p.55.
9.   Ibid. p.56.
10.   The ACAS diagnostic survey approach remains close to the CIR inquiry methodology.

Chapter Eight

ISSUES OF POLICY AND PAYMENT

> Staffing provision has also been made for the
> Service to undertake longer term investiga-
> tions...This was the role given to the
> Commission on Industrial Relations when it
> was first established in 1969. I very much
> hope that the Service will secure the co-oper-
> ation of management and unions in investiga-
> tions of this kind. It will be for the
> Council to decide on the publication of the
> results of such inquiries. 1)

The above expression of fact and hope was made
by Mr Michael Foot when, as Secretary of State for
Employment he wrote, on 8 August 1974, to the first
chairman of ACAS, Mr J E Mortimer, outlining the
nature of the duties of the new service.
The implied expectation that CIR type inquiries would continue, has not been realised for
reasons which were advanced in the previous chapter.
Those reasons, in their totality, could be inter-
preted as a change of policy in relation to the inquiry aspect of advisory work. But does ACAS have
a policy in the sense of a general plan of action
for the whole of its advisory function? If such a
policy exists, what is it and is the policy a good
one? If ACAS does not have a policy, does it need
one and if so, what should that policy be? Such
are the sort of questions that seem to merit an
airing.

The issue of policy

The adviser in the field may see limited need for an
advisory policy. He responds to requests to reform,
for example, procedures and payment systems. Giving
advice on such eminently practical problems would

not seem to entail, let alone require, policy considerations being taken into account to any significant extent. The situation would naturally be
very different if ACAS took a policy decision that
wherever possible, when payment systems were to be
overhauled, job evaluation should be introduced in
preference to any other method of payment. Such an
affirmative policy decision has not been taken and
the adviser remains free, within an arguably
laissez-faire policy, to assess the merits of particular payment systems in relation to the reforms
that appear to be necessary.

In broad terms it would seem that the same
'horses for courses' approach can be adopted by
the adviser, for all the subjects of advice listed
in the ACAS Annual Reports. It is true that for
some subjects there exist certain benchmark standards for assessment purposes. The influence of
the Code of Practice No 1 Disciplinary practice and
procedures, has already been commented upon and it
would seem extremely unlikely that an unjust or
deficient disciplinary procedure would be improved
without reference to that code. Other guidance on
the substantive content of advice which might be
thought to have a policy content resides in ACAS
publications generally. But although an adviser
is hardly likely to give advice which is seriously
at odds with the ACAS published word, the various
documents are so drafted that they should not res-
trict the adviser's freedom to shape the substantive advice he gives to meet the requirements of
each given situation.

If, therefore, the field adviser feels largely
free of policy pressure as far as the content of
the advice he gives is concerned, the same cannot
be said of the policy pressure which is exerted on
the process whereby he gives advice. From what
has been described earlier, it would seem that a
policy decision has been taken to promote JWPs,
wherever appropriate, as the head office preferred
method of conveying and implementing advice. The
evidence to-date on the soundness of that policy
decision is encouraging for those who formulated
the policy and made the decision. That can fairly
be said despite the reservations expressed on operational rather than policy grounds by some of the
advisers we interviewed. Those reservations were
usually associated with the setting of targets for
different types of advisory work and the related
danger of the numbers game being played as mentioned in Chapter Three.

166

Another important reason why the field adviser,
and others, may see limited need for an advisory
policy is central to the nature of the advisory
function. As mentioned before, advisory work is
essentially demand related and not determined
either in volume or in distribution of content by
ACAS selection criteria. Rarely will a request for
advice be refused. If a request was clearly at
variance with the statutory duties to improve industrial relations, the potential client's request
would be met with a polite refusal. Some requests
for advice may be turned down because the work involved is beyond the industrial relations remit of
ACAS or the technical competence or scale of the
advisory resource locally available. In such circumstances, would-be clients are often given information about possible alternative sources of advisory help. In short, it is true to say that ACAS
does not turn advisory business away except in a
limited range of situations. The service takes on
all kinds of advisory work without reference to
policy decisions which conceivably could determine
for example, that requests for assistance from
firms below, or above, a certain size should be
automatically referred to other organisations.
What has just been indicated, ie seeking to be
constructively responsive to all requests for
advice, could itself be interpreted as a policy
decision. However, it seems more likely that this
policy is less a deliberate and unique ACAS formulation than a continuance of pre-ACAS practices by
CAS and its predecessors. In any event, the EPA
requires ACAS to give advice - on request - if the
Service thinks fit and the limited circumstances in
which this discretionary authority tends to be exercised have been outlined.
In stating that the advisory service is essentially demand related, the use of 'essentially'
indicates that some factor other than client demand
is involved. That factor is, of course, demand
stimulus, as largely represented by the number,
nature and quality of development visits carried
out. By their very nature development visits require decisions to be made about the sample of
organisations to be visited. The decisions could be
left to each individual adviser. Samples might or
might not be constructed in haphazard ways. They
could also be planned and the planning could be
affected by policy decisions of the ACAS Council
that in a given year, and while allowing for regional variations, particular attention should be paid,

167

for stated reasons, to companies in a particular
industry, or to companies of a particular size. In
recent years, as Chapter Three indicated, this indicative planning has been associated with the issuing
of advisory guidelines authorised by the ACAS
Council. More will be said about the policy aspects
of guidelines shortly.

The EPA (Section 4 (1)) decrees that advice
shall be given on request, or <u>otherwise</u> (emphasis
added). The phrase 'or otherwise' is interesting
for it seems to intimate that ACAS has the authority to take initiatives and not simply wait passive-
ly for requests for advice to arrive before seeking
to improve industrial relations. One initiative
has, of course, been the development of the development visit itself. Another initiative, stemming
from a policy decision, but one not directly related
to the 'or otherwise' phrase, concerns the <u>depth</u>
of ACAS involvement in any piece of advisory work
and attention has already been drawn to the policy
decision, reaffirmed in recent years, to increase
the proportion of in-depth work carried out and to
increase the proportion of JWP style activities
within the category of in-depth assignments. But
have other policy initiatives been considered? 2)
Should other initiatives be placed on a discussion
agenda?

During 1980 a thought provoking paper, prepared
by an ACAS Council member, was discussed by members
of the Council. The paper's theme was the possibility of formulating, after six years' practical
experience of advising, conciliating and arbitrat-
ing, an ACAS strategy. The strategy would address
itself to two basic issues - the kind of industrial
relations system the Council wished to see develop
and the kind of operational needs that would follow
from some perceived desirable system. Policy
objectives could include the extension of collective bargaining in terms of extended coverage of
the labour force and of a bargaining agenda enriched
by new topics; the improvement of collective bargaining structures; the improvement of procedures
and the extension of good practice procedures to
industry sectors where the provision of such procedures was currently poor; the role of improved
industrial relations in increasing national productivity and competitiveness. It was pointed out that
all such objectives were closely bound up with the
service's advisory work and if pursued would have
a number of operational implications such as the
need to adopt a more analytical approach to some

subjects, improved methods of evaluation of work
carried out, more sophisticated training for
advisers. The difficulties of achieving tri-partite
Council commitment to specific as distinct from
general policy objectives were acknowledged. Even
so, it was thought that the time had come for a
stocktaking of ACAS objectives and their concomitant
operational implications to be undertaken.

The extent to which this paper influenced the
Council to consider some movement from an essentially reactive approach to advisory work to a style
with a larger pro-active content, is unclear, but
the discussion on the possibility of adopting a more
positive advisory approach certainly continued and
continues. What might be regarded as movement in
the direction of a more positive advisory policy
has been slow in pace and modest in scale if, as
seems reasonable, the advisory guidelines are taken
as the expression and measure of policy changes. A
faster rate and greater degree of change seems unlikely given the difficulties of achieving a consensus within Council about some of the thornier
issues of industrial relations. The tendency therefore has been to make slow but arguably sure progress towards a more assertive advisory policy.

The claim, made in 1980 during internal ACAS
discussions, that the introduction of guidelines had
given a much more positive thrust to advisory work
was perhaps overstated. But the fact that the
guidelines have been changed each subsequent year,
with a view to their improvement, suggests that they
remain important to the cautious evolutionary development of an advisory policy. To use the description of cautious, evolutionary development is to
state fact rather than to imply criticism. Given
the tri-partite composition of the Council and
the politicised industrial relations climate of
recent years, it would be greatly surprising if
bolder and more radical advisory policy changes had
occurred.

In so far as advisory policy is formulated and
used for operational and therefore practical purposes, as distinct from being akin to a statement of
industrial relations beliefs, the advisory guidelines can be taken to be that formulation. While
it would not be particularly productive, for present
purposes, to trace through and comment upon the
changes that have occurred to the guidelines since
their introduction, some comparisons can briefly
and usefully be made. The guidelines for 1982 were
given on p.44. Those for 1983 and 1984 now

follow, accompanied by short comments, from the researchers, where change of some interest or significance has taken place.

1983 7. To manage regional resources to improve the scope and quality of advice given and assess effectiveness by systematic follow up of completed work.

1984 1. To manage advisory resources effectively so as to maximise the contribution of the service to the improvement of industrial relations and to evaluate systematically the results achieved.

Comment. This is a conventional statement of good management practice. The omission of 'regional' in 1984 can conceivably be read as the managerial responsibility being service wide, ie including head office!

1983 1. To involve management and employee representatives jointly wherever practicable in ACAS work.

1984 2. To involve management and employee representatives jointly in ACAS work wherever appropriate.

Comment. The replacement of practicable by appropriate is interesting and seems to emphasise the 'horses for courses' approach. Employee representatives, has, of course, a wider connotation than trade union representatives and the phrase is one of a number of ACAS indicators that the boundaries of industrial relations are not set by the limits of direct trade union activity.

1983 2. To maximise the amount of in-depth work undertaken.

1984 3. To give priority to in-depth work, particularly where lasting improvements in industrial relations can be achieved.

Comment. This would seem to represent a considerable refinement of the 1983 formulation.

1983 3. To encourage systematic examination of policies, practices and procedures to effect an improvement in industrial relations.

170

1984   4. To encourage systematic examination
of policies, practices and procedures to effect
an improvement in industrial relations.

Comment. Can be seen as part of the continuing attempt to foster the industrial relations/personnel
management practices recommended in the ACAS leaflet, Improving Industrial Relations - a Joint
Responsibility.

1983   4. To offer help in identified organisations or industries where industrial relations
problems exist or are apprehended and where
the independence of ACAS has particular advantages.

1984   5. To ensure constructive links between
advisory and conciliation work which help to
identify organisations where industrial relations problems exist or are apprehended.

Comment. The 1984 wording appears to be much sharper in its specific application because of the
declared link with conciliation which is widely
recognised by employers and trade unions as being
of independent status. Implicit in the 1984 guidelines is the recognition that there could be more
effective liaison between collective conciliation
and advisory work and that conciliators could possibly generate more advisory work. It is a feature
of the conciliated settlement of some disputes that
appropriate advisory work be undertaken.
    The omission of 'industries' is notable. In
earlier guidelines specific industries had been
cited, sometimes because of their troubled industrial relations or economic importance. (Regions
now determine their own 'priority industries'. This
is an implied element of the 1984 guideline 6).

1983   5. To undertake an agreed programme of
contacts to ensure that an adviser is known to
most employers and full-time trade union
officers in his/her area.

1984   6. To undertake a planned programme of
contacts taking account of the IR needs of
each region and the need to ensure that an
adviser is known to most employers and full
time officers in an area.

Comment. Arguably another subtle change of emphasis

- from an agreed to a planned programme of contacts
for 1984. The introduction of ' taking account of
the IR needs of each region ' is also indicative of
more detailed planning.

> 1983 6. To deal with enquiries and supply
> advice by the most appropriate means and to
> use such contacts to widen knowledge of ACAS
> advisory services.

> 1984 7. To provide enquirers with relevant
> and up-to-date information on IR matters and,
> where appropriate, to use such contacts to
> promote the advisory services.

Comment. The 1984 guideline seems a more considered re-formulation of the 1983 version with greater
weight attached to marketing considerations. It
concentrates on the provision of information.

> 1984 8. To arrange the collection of informa-
> tion on specified subjects for analysis of
> developments and trends in IR as determined
> with Head Office.

Comment. This has no direct equivalent in the 1983
guidelines. It seems to indicate a concern for
improved intelligence gathering and analysis, and
possibly reflects the trend, previously mentioned,
to exercising more influence on field operations
from the centre. The concept of a national institution providing a coherent and consistent service
remains a powerful one.

> 1983 8. To develop a store of knowledge of
> good industrial relations practice and to
> ensure that this is made generally available
> both within the Service and outside.

> 1984 9. To develop a store of knowledge of
> good IR practices and to ensure that this is
> made generally available both within and
> outside the Service.

Comment. Apart from a stylistic change, the 1984
guideline is identical to that of 1983.
    Whether considered individually or as a collec-
tion, the guidelines seem unobjectionable and unex-
ceptional. They will surely fall well short of the
ringing declarations on advisory policy that might
be welcomed in some quarters. Nevertheless, the

172

guidelines do seem to represent the limits of what
has so far been feasible as an internal expression
of policy which can also be carried out in operational terms.

The issue of payment

We intimated earlier that although the issue of
payment for advisory help was not a central pre-
occupation of the research, it was an important
matter which warranted fairly detailed discussion.
The relevance of the discussion is heightened by
the present government's commitment to the process
of privatisation. Although the government has made
no mention of subjecting ACAS to that process, an
important case can be made for requiring ACAS to
charge for its advisory service. An important case
can also be made against that proposition. The
resultant debate can be carried out at two levels.
At one level the discussion is conducted from
the basis of people's opinions and value judgements
deriving from their general experience and view of
life. eg whether what is paid for is valued. The
conjectures and assumptions inevitably inherent in
such a process may be supplemented and supported
by impressions and anecdotal evidence. However,
the outcome of such a discussion may owe more to
ideology than to established facts. At a second
level, the discussion is hopefully informed and
influenced by a sizeable body of evidence which has
been systematically assembled. The various deduc-
tions that can be drawn from that evidence may or
may not cause varying degrees of discomfort to one
or more of the perspectives that have informed and
coloured the first level debate. Be that as it may,
we would repeat an earlier claim that as the result
of our research, the debate about the payment issue
should now be a better informed one. In business
terminology, market research has replaced, to a not
insignificant extent, guesswork. However, in what
now follows we plan to summarise the contents of
the debate at the two levels mentioned, in order
that readers may more readily decide for themselves
whether a free or a fee charging advisory service
would better meet the objective of improving industrial relations.
In some ways it is a little unfortunate that
the basic case for introducing a fee charging system
can be made with far fewer words than the case
against. But there is some comfort in believing
that no automatic correlation exists between the

volume of words employed and the power of the
argument with which the words are associated.
Having entered this important reminder, the case
for charging a fee can be regarded as having two
main strands of support - improved cost effectiveness and increased professionalism in the service
provided.

In times of economic stringency involving cuts
in public expenditure, which have also affected
ACAS, charging for advice might help to prevent
further cuts, preserve and even build up the advisory resource. The pursuit of self-sufficiency for
advisory work could improve ACAS's bargaining position with government, when negotiating the funding
of the service. If clients were required to pay
for advice, this would quicken their interest in
the advice given and probably enhance the chances
of the advice being implemented. People tend to
value what they pay for. If fees were charged, the
arrangement would probably be of a non-profit making
nature and this would place the service in a very
competitive position with management consultants.
Operating commercially, even if on a non-profit
making basis, would put pressure on the service to
attract custom. This in turn could result in pressure on advisory staff both to become more professional in their approach and to make greater efforts
to tap all the potential markets for advisory work.

The concern about the possibly damaging effects
of payment on impartiality could easily be overstated and any problems might well be overcome if
employers and trade unions shared the cost of advisory fees. As 'fire-fighting' conciliation was
a quite different activity from 'fire prevention'
advisory work, it should be quite feasible and not
cause any special difficulties to levy a charge on
the advisory work. It was conceivable that a separate advisory unit could be established to take
on fee charging work. The unit could have its own
staff and in these ways the impartiality problem
could be overcome.

The above arguments can be met with a variety
of counter arguments. Charging for advisory work
would not necessarily protect that work, or ACAS,
from economies in public expenditure. The grant-in-
aid, which funds ACAS, could well be cut by the
Treasury, by the amount of income derived from fee
charging work. Even if advisory work became self
supporting it was most probable that conciliation
work, if it was to remain credible and acceptable,
would still need to be paid for from public funds.

174

The government would thereby retain an interest in
ACAS resources generally. In recent years, it was
governments which had been responsible for introducing many changes to statutory employment rights
and obligations and this strengthened the claim
that the service should continue to be a free public
source of advice and information for individuals,
their representatives, and employers of every size
and description. An important part of the duties
of ACAS as a public service was to spread knowledge
about good employment practices. This process
could well be hampered, especially where such knowledge was most needed, if fees were charged.

To charge fees might bring about a situation
whereby only those companies with the resources to
do so, would pay. Companies in serious financial
straits, possibly because of poor manpower policies
and practices, and greatly in need of advisory help,
would be unable to afford it. Where joint work was
concerned the notion of the employer and trade
union sharing the cost would present difficulties.
Most local trade union representatives would be
unlikely to have the authority to authorise payments
at the probable level entailed by a self-supporting
advisory service. Seeking authorisation for payment
from higher levels of a union hierarchy would almost
certainly be self-defeating and certainly time con-
suming. Such difficulties would be appreciably
worse where problems were being tackled in a multi-
union plant. The question of paymaster on behalf of
involved employees who were not represented by a
union would also have to be addressed.

In considering the cost implications and impact
of fee charging on companies and unions, it has to
be remembered that ACAS receives an appreciable
amount of free help, eg through industrial attachments, and free information from firms and trade
unions. Such help from those quarters might not be
so readily available under a fee charging regime.
The effect of such a regime on management consultants would also have to be considered. If fees were
set on a self-sufficiency, ie non-profit making
basis, they might be such as to under-cut the commercially based fees of consultants leaving ACAS
open to the charge of constituting unfair competition.

Common sense and common experience suggests
that in a fee charging system payment would most
probably only be obtained from the company and not
from an involved union. This could result in advisers being regarded as becoming more management

oriented being dependent on management fees.
Clients would become customers and as such would
understandably expect solutions to be given to
specific problems. The change of status in the
relationship from free adviser/client to paid
adviser/customer presumably has contractual implications. This change could conceivably cause difficulties in the area of individual employment
rights involving ACAS in legal responsibilities for
advice which might be thought prejudicial to the
ACAS role of conciliation in, for example, unfair
dismissal cases. The changed relationship to paid
adviser/customer, with a consequent reduced status
for any union involvement, might move advisory work
away from a central pre-occupation with industrial
relations to a greater involvement, than at present,
with production and operating efficiency concerns.
This would add to the perception of paid advisers
being increasingly management oriented.

Such changes of perception would not leave the
process of conciliation unimpaired. Assuming that
conciliation, individual and collective, would
still be provided free, the distinction between
free conciliation and paid advice could prove confusing to anyone wishing to use both services especially if the adviser/conciliator was a generalist.
A manager beset with his own industrial relations
problems might find it puzzling, even irritating,
that he had to pay 'that chap from ACAS' for some
visits but not for others. For the reasons given,
trade unions would inevitably come to regard paid
advisory work as drifting in the direction of management bias. This in turn would affect the readiness of unions to use ACAS for individual or collective conciliation purposes. This would probably
still be the case even if advisory work and conciliation were carried out by separate organisational
units. Although feasible at a technical level, such
a separation would obviously make it difficult for
a collective conciliator to achieve, as a feature
of the parties' negotiated settlement of a dispute,
the inclusion of a joint commitment to co-operate
in a piece of in-depth work to be undertaken by
fee charging, management oriented advisers, the
conciliator's services having been provided free of
charge. In short, a revenue raising advisory service could undermine the confidence of unions in
ACAS conciliation.

The confidence of unions, and not only of
unions, in the work of ACAS is held, certainly by
ACAS itself - vide the Annual Reports, to reside in

its impartiality. Advice is not bought by management but is available freely to any and all parties
concerned. This facilitates joint work. However
good ACAS advice might be, it would be unlikely to
be effective unless accepted and implemented jointly.
Consultants sometimes experienced difficulties in
gaining that joint commitment. On a realistic reading of the situation, only employers would be prepared to pay for advice. This would create the impression of employers controlling the advisory function of ACAS thus seriously damaging the impartial
third party advisory role and leading to a loss of
confidence in the impartiality of ACAS conciliation
work.
    Needless to say, much of the defence of the
status quo of a free advisory service has been
provided from ACAS sources, from the directly interested party. It is valuable therefore that some,
if not all, of the arguments can be tested against
the opinions of others closely involved, those at
first hand being a sample of clients and those at a
further remove being a sample of employers' associations, trade unions, management consultants and
training institutions. The fact that not all of
the arguments for and against paid advice can be
tested by evidence, is because the payment issue,
although obviously important, was not the prime or
sole concern of the research. As earlier chapters
have shown however, our payment issue questions have
concentrated on key policy concerns. The evidence
about these concerns will be summarised below in
tabulated form.
    At the end of the day, the opinions of the
clients, for the most part the companies concerned,
would seem to be the most important as almost inevitably they would be the organisations called upon
to pay any fees required by a fee charging advisory
service. The reactions of union representatives at
workplace level are also very important and for
these reasons a selection of observations made by
both groups, on the payment issue, has been reserved
to this chapter. Again because the clients' position is pre-eminent when considering the payment
issue, it has been decided to re-order the presentation of the aggregated responses to the payment
questions, compared to earlier chapters. This means
that the focus of attention will be directed first
on client company and local trade union responses
before being broadened to include the views of the
interested parties of employers' associations, national trade unions, consultants and trainers. Table

8.1 which starts this process is therefore concerned with the total client response to the payment in
principle question.

Table 8.1: No. of clients prepared to pay - in
principle - for advisory work

	Visits Request and non-requested		In-depth work Employers		TUs		All respondents	
	No.	%	No.	%	No.	%	No.	%
Yes	14	5.5	30	14.8	2	2.5	46	8.6
Probably	106	41.9	93	45.8	9	11.4	208	38.9
No	38	15.0	22	10.8	24	30.4	84	15.7
Doubt it	74	29.2	48	23.6	27	34.2	149	27.8
Doubt it very much	21	8.3	10	4.9	17	21.5	48	9.0
Total	253	100	203	100	79	100	535	100

On the basis of the aggregated responses it
would seem that just under half, 47.5 per cent (Yes
and Probably answers combined) of respondents would,
in principle, be prepared to pay for advisory work,
leaving 52.5 per cent who would not. Of the 79
trade union respondents involved in in-depth work,
86 per cent recorded, in effect, a No vote to the
idea of payment, a result which does little to encourage the belief that in a fee charging situation,
the unions would share the cost, with the employers
concerned, of the fees charged. Such a response obviously has implications for the issue of advisory
impartiality being affected if only one paymaster
is involved. It is also worth pointing out that
where unequivocal expressions of support for or
opposition to the payment principle are expressed
by companies, the support votes total 44 compared
to 60 votes of opposition.

As could be expected, the aggregated results
of the responses about the 'money value' of the
advice at the time it was given present rather different results. These are due in part to only three
choices of response, instead of the five of Table
8.1, being offered to respondents. (The reasons
for this were given on p.78). Table 8.2 shows the
aggregated responses to the question designed to
elicit client judgements, if only in a very broad
way, as to whether the specific advice given was
of sufficient value to justify payment being made
for it.

Compared to Table 8.1 it is noticeable that the

Table 8.2: No. of clients prepared to pay - when
advice given

| | Visits Request and non-requested | | In-depth work | | | | All respondents | |
| | | | Employers | | TUs | | | |
	No.	%	No.	%	No.	%	No.	%
Yes	38	15.9	58	28.9	6	7.8	102	19.7
No	113	47.3	60	29.8	52	67.5	225	43.5
Maybe	88	36.8	83	41.3	19	24.7	190	36.8
Total	239	100	201	100	77	100	517	100

proportion of clear Yes responses, all respondents,
has more than doubled from 8.6 per cent to 19.7 per
cent. This may suggest that in 20 per cent of instances
where specific advice has been given that advice
was held to be of sufficient value to justify payment. And yet there is stronger contrary evidence
if the No votes - all respondents of Tables 8.1 and
8.2 are compared. While 15.7 per cent would vote
against payment in principle, 43.5 per cent would
vote against payment in practice. The extent to
which the respondents of Table 8.2 were at all
influenced by policy considerations obviously cannot be known. By policy considerations is meant
the conjecture that a number of respondents may
have reasoned to themselves - the advisory intervention in question may have been worth paying for,
but not by us, on grounds of principle, the State
having provided a free advisory service. To answer
'Yes' to the question could indicate support for
a fee paying system which we do not favour. Such
considerations may also have turned some 'Yes'
votes (Table 8.2) to 'Maybes'. It seems a reasonably
tenable presumption that similar thoughts would
have influenced the trade unions involved in in-
depth work. It is their vote which has materially
affected the total No vote and supporters of a fee
paying system may still be heartened by the distribution of responses from employers in regard to
in-depth work. Even so, it would be hazardous to
conclude that because a given number or percentage
of clients considered that particular pieces of
advice were payment worthy, they would necessarily
make use of a fee charging advisory service. It is
obvious, as earlier Tables have shown, that other
factors, besides that of a free service, come into
play when decisions are taken to seek advisory help.
Those factors and the weightings attached to them
by the total client respondent population and by the

interested parties is given at Table 8.3. We would
maintain that because of these added dimensions and
the fact that respondents are taking a general view
of ACAS advisory work, rather than assessing a specific advisory intervention, or principle, Table 8.3
constitutes the best of the various indicators which
are relevant to the payment issue.

Before drawing implications from Table 8.3, two
points about the presentation need to be made. Because of the multiple factors involved and the multiple choices allowed by the question, together with
the fact that a number of respondents ranked some
factors as of equal importance, it could be misleading to try to present the absolute figures in
percentage terms. In any event, the level and distribution of responses is sufficient to reveal significant and different patterns of assessment. Secondly, it was thought better not to aggregate the two
totals of client and interested party responses for
the following reasons. For the most part, the
former total consists of an accumulation of single
employer and single workplace trade union perspective responses - the management and shop steward
viewpoints essentially, whereas the latter grouping,
certainly so far as employers' associations and
national trade unions are concerned, represents
institutional and collective viewpoints. In broad
terms, the client group constitutes a participant
group whereas the other group essentially consists
of sectional interest observers.

The patterns of assessment associated with the
various factors are readily discernible. It is
obvious that for the client group as a whole, and
for the interested parties group, impartiality is
the factor which contributes most to the use made
of the advisory service. The stress on this factor is particularly pronounced in the client group,
with a 'score' of nearly 300 against 1st importance,
nearly double the equivalent score of the next
highest ranked factor of technical competence.
Interestingly, technical competence is held by the
interested parties group to be the least important
of the four factors offered for evaluation. The
quite different weights attached by the two groups
to the technically competent factor may be related
to the direct experience of advisory competence by
the client group and the largely indirect knowledge,
via their membership, of employers' associations and
national trade unions. There is the additional and
subtle element in the equation, that employers'
associations, management consultants and training

Table 8.3: Factors contributing most to the use made of the ACAS advisory service

Factor	No. of times mentioned as being of	Request and non-requested visits	In-depth work		Total Clients	Interested Parties				Total Interested Parties
			Emps	TUs		EAs	National TUs	Consultants	Trainers	
An impartial service, ie attempting to be fair to all interests concerned	1st importance	131	121	44	296	12	13	2	3	30
	2nd importance	62	44	14	120	7	12	6	3	28
An independent service ie independent of government and sectional interests	1st importance	60	31	37	128	7	15	2	-	24
	2nd importance	65	49	13	127	11	5	3	3	22
A free service	1st importance	37	31	14	82	8	3	4	3	18
	2nd importance	37	34	7	78	3	3	1	1	8
A technically competent service	1st importance	90	58	11	159	3	3	-	2	8
	2nd importance	64	75	32	171	8	5	1	-	14

institutions offer advisory services which might,
to a certain extent, be held to be in competition
with the ACAS advisory service. A certain caution,
of a self-interest nature, may therefore have influenced the judgement made about the technical worth
of the competition. As claimed previously, trade
unions are in business as industrial relations experts and for them the technical competence of ACAS
advice would appear far less important than the impartial and independent status of the advice givers.
    While by no means held to be insignificant, the
free nature of the service appears to be the least
important feature of the advisory function for the
client group. By the interested parties group it is
placed slightly higher in third position, employers'
associations and consultants understandably giving
particular weight to the appeal of free advice to
small companies. Quotations were given in Chapter
six which illustrated that viewpoint. For the interested parties group, the independent status of
the service is the second most important factor and
is third in the rankings of the client group where
it is well ahead of the fourth placed free service.
    To the client group the impartial provision of
sound advice appears to be what matters most and to
the interested parties group it is the combination
of impartiality and independence that primarily at-
tracts clients to ACAS for advice. These claims
can be put forward with some confidence not only
because of the distributions of replies among the
factors but because respondents had the opportunity
to identify other, additional factors of their own
free choice but none did so. To consider whether
more weight should be attached to the views of one
respondent than to those of another, on grounds, for
example, of size or status, would be to wander into
a morass of contentious imponderables. In broad
terms, the evidence sustains the claims made at
the beginning of this paragraph.
    Those claims derived from a particular
set of circumstances, existing circumstances
in point of fact. If those circumstances
changed in some material way, then the claims
themselves might require revision. A major
change of circumstance would be the replacement
of a free advisory service by a fee charging
one. It will be recalled that respondents were
asked two questions on this point. The first
read - do you think the law should be changed
to allow ACAS to charge for advisory work? Table
8.4 summarises the answers from all respondents.

182

Table 8.4: Opinions as to whether law should be
changed to allow ACAS to charge for advisory work.

	Yes No.	No No.
Client Group		
Visits - request and non requested	16	230
In-depth work Employers	14	189
TUs	3	78
Total	33	497
Interested Parties Group		
Employers' Associations	4	24
National Trade Unions	-	29
Management Consultants	3	7
Training Institutions	-	7
Total	7	67

The response rate from the client group was a
very high one, 530 replies of a possible 548, ie
97 per cent. Of the 530 respondents 94 per cent can
be said to be in favour of leaving the law unchanged
so that advice continues to be given without
charge. The corresponding percentage for the interested parties group is 90 per cent. It is perhaps
not surprising that a higher proportion of clients
than of the interested parties group should be in
favour of retaining free advice for it would be the
client and not the third party, except perhaps in
the unlikely case of trade unions, who would become
the fee paying customer if the law was changed.

The second payment question is the following
familiar one - if payment was required for advisory
help, do you think this would adversely affect the
independent/impartial nature of the advisory service? Table 8.5 summarises the answers to that
question from all respondents.

Again there was a 97 per cent response rate
from the client group, 531 respondents of a possible
548. Given that the extra choice of 'maybe' was
offered as a possible response, it was hardly likely
that the distribution pattern of answers would
closely parallel the answers to the previous question where the choice lay between 'yes' and 'no.'
Additionally, it would seem much easier to make a
clear choice of preference between a free and fee
charging service than to make a judgement about the
possible impact of payment upon the hitherto impar-
tial/independent status of advice. Nevertheless,

183

Table 8.5: Payment and possible adverse effect on
impartiality/independence

	Yes	No	Maybe
	No.	No.	No.
Client Group			
Visits - request and non requested	135	58	57
In-depth work Employers	109	47	48
TUs	54	8	15
Total	298	113	120
Interested Parties Group			
Employers' Associations	9	12	9
National Trade Unions	18	2	9
Management Consultants	2	5	3
Training Institutions	2	4	1
Total	31	23	22

the majority of the client group respondents, 298 of
531 or 56 per cent believe that the impartiality of
advice would be adversely affected by a payment
system. If the 'maybes' are shared equally between
the 'yes' and 'no' responses the 56 per cent
majority rises to 67 per cent. So more than half
certainly and possibly up to two thirds of clients
see dangers to the impartiality and independent
status of advice if fee charging arrangements were
introduced.

A different pattern of response is provided by
the interested parties' group, not surprisingly
perhaps, given their greater distance from the
advisory visit to or project carried out on a
company's premises. Of the 76 respondents 41 per
cent (31) see impartiality being adversely affected
by a required payment. The 41 per cent increases
to 55 per cent if the 'maybes' are again equally
divided between 'yes' and 'no' answers. It is
worth reflecting whether the different emphases
between the two distribution patterns, client group
and interested parties group, are in any way due to
the client companies tacitly accepting that they
would be the ones to pay if fees were charged, and
that impartiality would inevitably shift to some
degree of partiality in the company's favour.

Conceivably for the same reason, a high proportion of trade union respondents involved in in-
depth work see similar dangers to impartiality - 54
of 77, 70 per cent voted to that effect - current
impartiality presumably not being able to withstand
fully the pressure inevitably arising for partial
recommendations where employers paid the bills for
184

advice. By the trade unions at national level the
same misgivings were perhaps entertained but not to
quite the same extent, 62 per cent of that population of respondents voting 'yes' in Table 8.5.
The same level of misgiving was certainly not expressed by the three other interested parties, vide
Table 8.5, but the roles of these institutions are
partly complementary to and partly in competition
with ACAS and they are thus in a very different
position from the employer client and involved
trade union, local or national.
     The institutions constituting the interested
parties group voiced various opinions in Chapter
Six and it therefore seems appropriate to conclude
the present chapter with quotations on the payment
issue from those most likely to be affected by any
fee charging system, ie the clients themselves. A
selection of quotations is necessary because of the
large volume of comment received. Various considerations have influenced the design of the quotations
presentation. The first set of quotations relates
to the question that asked respondents to identify
and evaluate the factors which they considered
contributed most to the use made of the advisory
service. The selected quotations typify the
nature and range of the comments made. Comments
on the group of questions directly concerned with
the payment issue have been separated into two
constituencies, one relating to advisory visits
and the other to in-depth work. In the latter constituency comments are identified as being of
employer or trade union authorship. The comments
in each constituency are sub-divided according to
the three broad reactions of clients to the payment
issue, these being - in favour of payment, ambivalent about the matter, opposed to the idea.

Factors contributing most to the use made of the advisory service

Of the many comments made two could be said to be
critical of the service. Both are given:

> As with all organisations ACAS is only as good
> as the people in it. Some are very poor.
> The particular senior officer used in this case
> is a better than average chap (in my experi-
> ence) and good at this particular subject.

> The calibre of their staff is not comparable to
> consultants. You get what you pay (or don't

pay) for is my view. I would not go back to
ACAS but use a consultancy.

The remainder of the respondents, a much larger number, seemed to fall in the category of broadly satisfied clients. The satisfaction seemed to
be associated with one or more of the following
perceived characteristics of ACAS - accessibility
and speed of response, concern to help, competence,
acceptability, trustworthiness, impartiality.

A competent, friendly source of impartial
information.

We have always found the particular ACAS
representative for our area to be helpful
and available when needed.

I was particularly impressed by the genuine
interest and desire to help.

Readily available for instant answer over the
telephone.

We have found ACAS to be competent, efficient
and painstaking in the quality and calibre of
advice provided.

Main feature being a group acceptable to
unions and management alike. ACAS has this
very important reputation in the (named) area.

Recognised as trustworthy third party -
particularly by the workforce.

I believe it is essential that the service
must be seen as independent and impartial
if it is to succeed. I also believe that it
can only be used in those terms if its
services are free.

Although ACAS is an arm of the Civil Service
and funded by government - nevertheless my
experience has always found them to be impartial.

Impartiality and technical competence carry
considerably greater importance than free and
independence.

The impartiality and objectivity of ACAS is

most attractive to staff and unions who may be
suspicious of consultants chosen and paid for
by management.

Comments were also made relevant to a repeat
order level of satisfaction and the probability of
an untapped advisory market.

Previous involvement with ACAS advisers was
useful and when approached by them on the
availability of a business efficiency survey
we were motivated to use the service.

Worth commenting that this advisory service
provided by ACAS might not be adequately publicised - a number of businessmen seem unaware of
its existence and assume that ACAS is only involved in settling disputes.

The payment issue

Turning to comments made specifically on the payment
issue, the following selection is drawn from advisory visit responses and consists entirely of employers' views. While the divisions between pro,
ambivalent and anti-payment evaluations are to some
extent self-evident, it must be stressed that even
where respondents had claimed, by virtue of a ' No '
answer, that ACAS impartiality would be unaffected by
a fee charging system the 'No' that contributed to
the quantitative evidence of Table 4.10, p.79 , was
often accompanied by qualifying comments which could
justify a number of 'nos' being re-categorised as
'maybes'.

To some degree we believe that a fee paying
service would probably be more professional and
responsible for their advice.

If ACAS were made more self-sufficient it may
help them to become yet more impartial/indepen-
dent. However, organisations paying may come
to expect favourable interpretations.

It might improve the quality and dedication of
the personnel.

If one pays a fee then as a client one would
anticipate a distinct bias to the company
paying for a service ie as a solicitor or audi-
tor is used, albeit objectively.

187

Clients in time would probably only pay for
the advice they want to hear. Consequently
this may affect the impartiality of the
adviser.

How would an aggrieved employee pay for this
service or would the fees be deducted from the
settlement amounts?

(Presumably a reference to unfair dismissal
cases)

There must be no possibility that the quality
of help is dependent on the ability to pay.

Many individuals/small groups might be unable
to afford it or be deterred from approaching
ACAS.

ACAS would be accused of bias towards the
paying party.

Once you pay for something you expect the
service to work for you.

The market is saturated with fee paying
advisory services. ACAS in its present form
is accepted by all as independent/impartial.
Fees paid by employers - would trade unions
pay? would destroy that role.

Well, would trade unions pay? Some quantitative answers to that question have been made earlier,
p.179, and qualitative comment, from the unions,
will now be given in regard to in-depth work.

Provided both sides paid the same (no harm to
impartiality).

Because we are a small independent union we
would never be in a position to pay for this
kind of service.

If payment has to be made by either party for
advisory work then it is assumed that the
service will not be completely impartial as
the adviser may tailor his advice to suit the
customer.

A financial input by either side would affect
our attitude to ACAS's impartiality.

This would identify ACAS as an industrial relations consultancy service, the majority of
which are sympathetic to employers.

I don't think that a commercial consultancy is
ever independent/impartial. It tends to become orientated towards securing the interests
of those who can pay.

As the most likely group of potential paymast-
ers, the employers, from the experience of in-depth
work, present their views.

(Would support payment) but only if the calibre
of the individuals significantly improved.

A fee can increase 'standing' of service and
its appreciation by recipients. However, in
view of the mass of legislation and the desire
to encourage small enterprises, it may be that
a free and accurate service will be most suited
to small businesses.

The professional ability of the service should
not be undermined by the introduction of a fee.
However, the suspicion must arise that the
advice/working relationship is biased towards
the client paying the fee and is therefore not
a true independent/impartial service.

(Partiality) avoided if all parties contributed
equally.

It might be that companies who have need of
expert advice, particularly small companies,
will not have the finance available.

Some firms would not be able to afford ACAS
service so it is important that it is free and
also impartial.

The trade unions have enormous facilities and
would not use ACAS. Thus ACAS would probably
be seen as an organisation paid for by employers and no longer independent.

If management are having to pay the bill then
in the eyes of the union the company can call
the tune.

(By far the most frequent theme and, of course,

Issues of Policy and Payment

a reformulation of the 'piper' evaluation)

> I'm not sure if there is such a status as
> 'paid neutral consultant'.

> After following advice and using consultants
> for time studies, the fact we employed and
> paid them lost the neutrality factor favoured
> by the unions.

> I would find advice hard to accept if its
> provision had been funded by the union - I
> might well go elsewhere.

> You don't pay for what you don't wish to hear.

> Advisory help would be sought on basis that it
> conformed to certain demands, philosophies of
> the organisation. This would eliminate impar-
> tiality.

> To charge for its service the organisation will
> have to sell itself and help the buyer which
> will stop ACAS being impartial if it requires
> repeat business.

> Though it might be more apparent than real
> there would always be fears that 'he who pays
> the piper...'

So the recital about the piper could continue.
Without reproducing data and repeating arguments
and comments that have been presented in this and
earlier chapters, we would contend that what the
total evidence on the payment issue demonstrates,
is that the claimed advantages for a fee charging
ACAS advisory service are greatly outweighed by the
claimed disadvantages of such an arrangement.
Having made that assessment, it seems fitting
to move on to an examination of the role of a free
advisory service in seeking to promote the improvement of industrial relations.

NOTES AND REFERENCES

1. ACAS First Annual Report 1975, HMSO, pp.43-
4.
2. While it is not necessary to catalogue all
ACAS advisory initiatives, mention may be made of
some of the more important among them, eg evidence
for the Royal Commission on the National Health

Issues of Policy and Payment

Service (1978) and for the Royal Commission on the
Press (1975).

Chapter Nine

IMPROVING INDUSTRIAL RELATIONS

Placing a statutory duty on ACAS, as Parliament has
done, to promote the improvement of industrial relations, raises not only the issue of what constitutes improvement but also the issue of what constitutes industrial relations. Although indications
of the content of industrial relations are given
under section 4(1) of the EPA, eg collective bargaining and negotiation machinery, the parameters
of industrial relations have not been defined by
statute. This could reflect uncertainty on the
part of the legislators as to where the parameters
of the subject lie, but whatever the reason for the
absence of a definition, such absence does allow,
intentionally or otherwise, varying interpretations
of the term to be made and thereby assists ACAS to
cope with the inherent dynamism of industrial relations
Industrial relations - a question of definition

For present purposes, it is unnecessary to comb the
highways and by-ways of academic and other industrial relations literature for a definitive definition of industrial relations. A reasonably respect-
able short cut to such an objective can be attempted
from the starting point of what is virtually a
truism, that perhaps every business decision has
some impact, immediate or potential, minor or major,
on the employment relationship. The raising of
capital, the design of a new product, the adoption
of a fresh marketing strategy can all have industrial relations implications. While such items are
unlikely to appear on the agreed bargaining agendas
of employers and trade unions, they may prove to
have far-reaching consequences for the pay, employment and working conditions of managers and managed
alike.

Improving Industrial Relations

There is a sense therefore, in which industrial relations can be defined very broadly to include all activities which affect people's working lives. And yet, no-one would expect an ACAS adviser to advise clients about the operation of the money market, product design or marketing techniques. The expectation would arise not simply from a correctly assumed lack of advisory expertise in such aspects of management but from the prevailing narrower conception of industrial relations as having principally to do with what employers and unions bargain about, which is essentially pay and employment conditions. This conception leaves open the extent to which the bargainers make use of factors such as marketing strategy, product range, deemed to be relevant to the bargaining point at issue. Although the bargaining agenda has expanded appreciably over time, it remains centred on and anchored in the effort-reward relationship and the workplace environment of that relationship.

That governments tend to see industrial relations in this way is evidenced, to some extent, and in the absence of a statutory definition of industrial relations, by the list of matters 'concerned with industrial relations or employment policies' in Section 4(1) of the EPA 1975. This list was introduced by a Labour Government and has been left unchanged by two successive Conservative Governments. From the wording of Section 4(1) it is clear that the list is not meant to be comprehensive, but the fact that it is there at all is indicative of the importance attached by government to the listed matters, as part of its conception of the content of industrial relations. The list is as follows:

(a) the organisation of workers or employers for the purpose of collective bargaining;
(b) the recognition of trade unions by employers;
(c) machinery for the negotiation of terms and conditions of employment, and for joint consultation;
(d) procedures for avoiding and settling disputes and workers' grievances;
(e) questions relating to communication between employers and workers;
(f) facilities for officials of trade unions;
(g) procedures relating to the termination of employment;
(h) disciplinary matters;
(i) manpower planning, labour turnover and

            absenteeism;
    (j) recruitment, retention, promotion and
        vocational training of workers;
    (k) payment systems, including job evaluation
        and equal pay.

    As mentioned above, this list cannot be taken
to constitute any government's view of all the com-
ponent elements of industrial relations. Nevertheless, in addition to being an indication of the
core material of industrial relations, it would seem
to constitute an identification of particular problem areas calling for special attention from ACAS.
That there are other problem areas of industrial
relations can be deduced from the ACAS statistical
tables on subjects of advice. The use of problem area is deliberate, on the reasonable assumption that advice transmission is conditional upon
the prior identification of a problem. People without problems, or who are unaware that they have any,
are not given to seeking advice and not uncommonly
resent advice of an unsolicited nature.
    Reference to the 'subject of advice' statisti-
cal tables in the ACAS annual reports demonstrates
the close similarity that exists between the matters
listed under EPA Section 4(1) (and shown above), and
the topics about which ACAS has given advice. Compared to the statutory list there are some additions
in the ACAS tables, eg 'hours of work, shift working
and "flexi-time"', 'work study', 'job satisfaction',
but as the tables show, these three subjects account
for a modest proportion of advisory work. A greater
amount, on 1983 figures, has been generated by the
recent subject addition, deriving directly from
government interventions in employment matters, of
'self certification and ESSP' (Employers Statutory
Sick Pay). Overall, however, the industrial relations subjects which have been added by ACAS practical experience to the statutory list of examples,
are relatively few and self-evidently closely related to the statutory 'definition' of industrial relations.
    If then the ACAS identified subjects of advice
can be taken to represent the boundary markers of
the ACAS understanding of what constitutes industrial relations, the question may fairly be posed
as to whether, when operating within the limits set
by such markers, ACAS is making its optimum contribution to the improvement of industrial relations.
The question is a fair one because even though essentially reactive in character by supplying advice

194

on request, ACAS has the authority, as previously
indicated, to take advisory initiatives. In addition, if it was thought to be appropriate and
feasible, ACAS could seek to alter clients' and
potential clients' perceptions of what constituted
industrial relations in order to expand the ACAS
range of advisory activities and possibly effectiveness in the direction of improving industrial
relations. These last statements necessitate some
explanation.

Both among industrial relations commentators
and practitioners there is probably a greater tendency than there should be, to regard industrial
relations as the central purpose for which organisations exist. This tendency may well be associated
with the pre-occupation with conflict in our industrial relations system. Suffice it to say, at least
for present purposes, that organisations are not
formed in order to bring about industrial relations.
Organisations are established to produce goods, to
provide services. In essence therefore, industrial
relations are a by-product of the major function/s
for which the organisation exists. Consequently,
troubled industrial relations may have their origins
in the complex of activities through which the organisation seeks to realise its prime objectives of
producing goods or providing services. Accepting
this to be so, a deficient grievance procedure may
be put right by an ACAS adviser, within the conventional boundaries of industrial relations. But industrial unrest and inefficiency might persist because of an obsolete incentive payment scheme and
out of date working practices both of which conditions can be linked to poor production methods, inadequate management organisation and largely poor
quality management staff. To what extent should an
ACAS adviser, assuming he has been asked to assist,
penetrate to the deeper causes of 'bad' industrial
relations in the type of situation just illustrated?

The depth and scale of technical expertise
necessary to extend the range and depth of advisory
work could no doubt be developed if it does not already exist. A strong claim can be made that the
technical, formal authority to advance advisory
work in the way intimated already exists. Section
4(1) of the EPA '75 empowers ACAS to provide advice
'on any matter concerned with industrial relations
or employment policies' (emphasis added). It would
be difficult to maintain that any of the matters in
the illustration of the previous paragraph were un-
connected with industrial relations. Admittedly,

the ACAS authority to give advice is discretionary -
'the Service shall, if it thinks fit...provide...
such advice as it thinks appropriate on any matter
concerned with industrial relations...' (emphasis
added). It could be claimed that it would not be
proper or appropriate for ACAS advisers to start
'meddling' in production control, production
planning, workshop layout, costing systems and bud-
geting arrangements, etc. Such items do not normally appear on the collective bargaining agenda and,
on this view, improvement to such matters would be
best left to specialist consultancy firms.

As just stated, the technical expertise for an
expansion in the depth and range of ACAS advisory
work could most probably be developed. The legal
authority for such an expansion appears to be present in the EPA. A third element necessary for expansion is of much more dubious status, this element being the commitment to an expansionist policy
based on a much more liberal interpretation of industrial relations. Some of the possible objections
to such a policy were voiced in the previous paragraph. To these could be added the sensitivity of
the trade unions about, and probable resistance to,
the idea of the advisory service moving in the direction of management oriented objectives. These
objectives, even if expressed as manpower efficiency or business efficiency, with claimed advantages
for employers and employees, could still add up to
further job losses at a time when unemployment
levels were distressingly high. The clash between
efficiency and job security objectives, as demonstrated in its most bitter form by the miners' strike
1984, would doubtless reinforce defensive trade
union attitudes.

From what has been said, it could be inferred
that ACAS has been unconcerned with manpower efficiency and business efficiency. The opposite, of
course, is the case as a reading of ACAS annual reports, and other ACAS publications, will testify.
A change of policy of the kind intimated above
would be more a matter of change of scale and emphasis to existing policy, accompanied by a larger
measure of publicity than a radical re-think and
fresh direction. For the time being however, it
seems highly unlikely that ACAS will change its
basic approach to advisory work in a manner that
reflects a re-interpretation of the term industrial
relations. But however industrial relations are
defined, there remains a duty on ACAS to improve
those relations. It is to a discussion of that

duty that we now turn.

Improvement - and public policy

Use of the simple phrase 'improving industrial relations ' poses complex considerations. Improvement
would seem to imply the achievement of benefits.
But what sort of benefits and who are to be the
beneficiaries? Improvement would also seem to denote movement, possibly from a state of bad industrial relations to a state of good industrial relations. But good and bad industrial relations are
themselves question begging terms. To a Marxist,
good industrial relations is a contradiction in
terms within a basically capitalist society. From
this perspective industrial conflict in such a
society is inevitable, endemic and symptomatic of
the strains created by the widespread maldistribu-
tion of power and wealth. Although such a conten-
tion can be supported by powerful intellectual
analysis, the detailed nature of the good industrial
relations that should presumably result from an
alternative order of society remains rather unclear
and therefore perhaps of less influence than it
might otherwise be.

But even setting out these rather bald statements suggests that in the prevailing conventional
view bad industrial relations are equated with industrial strife. However, there appears to be less
certainty about what constitutes good industrial
relations, a disclosed or tacit acknowledgement
being made that the absence or low incidence of
strikes, lockouts or other forms of industrial action, does not necessarily add up to good industrial
relations. Industrial peace at any price may be
regarded by managements and governments alike as
too high a price to pay if a mixed economy is to
survive in a fiercely competitive world. Post 1945
governments, both Conservative and Labour, have, on
occasion, and for varying periods of time, placed a
higher value on incomes retraint policies than on
dispute resolution even when the incomes policies
themselves have generated or contributed to the
industrial strife. The miners' strike in 1974
against a Conservative Government's pay policy norm
and strikes by health service and other workers
during the 1979 'winter of discontent' of a Labour
Government, provide examples of this kind.

Although it may be unwise to make an automatic
correlation between industrial action and the 'true'
state of industrial relations, in specific or gener-

al circumstances, strikes, because they are more
readily quantifiable than other forms of industrial
action, remain an important indicator of the relationship between the parties concerned. Whatever
explanations and qualifications of Jesuitical subt-
lety are attached to the definition of a strike and
its measurement on various criteria, and however
much we may be encouraged to believe that the common
cold does far more harm to the economy, strikes of
a particular kind, or on a particular scale, or of
a persistent pattern have moved post-war governments
to intervene regularly in free collective bargaining. Possibly the most notable of such interventions, at least potentially, was the appointment by
a Labour Government in 1965 of the Royal Commission
on Trade Unions and Employers' Associations. The
terms of reference given to the Donovan Commission,
although broadly expressed, were certainly understood to necessitate a close scrutiny of the 'strike
problem' being made. In fact, the central reason
for the appointment of the Commission could be said
to reside in the Labour Government's concern to reduce the level of disorder in the industrial relations system expressed principally through frequent
and widespread unofficial/unconstitutional strikes.
These were held to be damaging to the country's
economic performance, export achievement, balance
of trade and balance of payments.
   The Donovan recommendations of 1968 did not
fully allay the Labour Government's anxieties about
industrial action. In its White Paper of 1969 significantly entitled 'In Place of Strife' it declared
that, 'the growing interdependence of modern industry means that the use of the strike weapon in certain circumstances can inflict disproportionate harm
on the rest of Society'. 1) At intervals since that
time, both Labour and Conservative governments have
had more than one occasion on which to reflect on
how 'strikes against the national interest' might
best be tackled, be they strikes of firemen and
nurses under a Labour Government, or waterworkers
under a Conservative Government. At the time of
writing, (Summer 1984) the issue of how the law
might be used to tackle strikes in essential services remains a live one in certain influential
circles.
   For present purposes however, it is certainly
not necessary to catalogue all the attempts made by
governments since 1968 to use the law and economic
pressures to curb industrial action and its closely
associated activities such as picketing. Latterly,

198

these interventions have emanated exclusively from
Conservative Governments which have also maintained,
if with much reduced emphasis, another major strand
of public policy regarding the reform of industrial
relations. This strand may be described as an en-
deavour, albeit a modest and arguably a narrowly
instrumental one, to tackle the causes as distinct
from the symptoms of industrial unrest. Such initiatives, in recent times, have principally been
made by Labour Governments and have found expression
in such institutions and activities as the ill-
starred Commission on Industrial Relations, the
Committee of Inquiry on Industrial Democracy which
produced the controversial Bullock Report, 2)the
initially successful Social Contract incomes policy
(mid 1970s) and some of the provisions of the EPA
1975.

At the risk of over simplification it can be
said that these latter interventions were motivated,
in part, by a desire to enhance the status and
rights of trade unions, the premise being that by
involving trade unions and their representatives in
management decision making processes, the level of
mutual understanding and trust between management
and the managed - and possibly even between government and the unions - would increase.

In view of what has just been outlined, it can
reasonably be claimed, without going into extensive
illustrative detail, that in a variety of changing,
intricate patterns the strand of public policy on
the handling of industrial strife has been inter-
woven with the policy of trying to promote a more
harmonious social partnership between the interested
parties of industrial relations. That latter policy
has, of course, been given far less weight in terms
of interventions, by the last and present governments but as intimated above, the policy, if not
emphasised, has not been abandoned. Its relevant
expression, for this book, is, of course, to be
found in the EPA 1975, enacted by a Labour Government. The basic duties of ACAS, created as a
statutory body under that Act, incorporate both
strands of public policy mentioned above. The
duties entail assisting with the resolution of disputes and with the promoting of constructive, mutu-
ally beneficial relationships between employers and
their workforces. That is to express the ACAS
duties in very broad, implied terms. But the basic
explicit duties are also expressed very broadly:

The Service shall be charged with the general

> duty of promoting the improvement of
> industrial relations, and in particular of
> encouraging the extension of collective
> bargaining and the development and, where
> necessary, reform of collective bargaining
> machinery. Section 1(2) EPA '75

The particular duty of 'encouraging the extension of collective bargaining' can be seen as fur-
thering the aim of social partnership because a
strong case can be made that well established collective bargaining is the most powerful and effective form of worker participation in management
decision making. That there is nothing new or radical in the encouragement of collective bargaining
by public policy and its associated institutions
can be seen in the Donovan Report:

> Ever since it was established in 1917 it was
> an important part of the Ministry of Labour's
> work to promote good industrial relations;
> and the continuing policy of successive
> Governments has been to support the growth of
> effective voluntary negotiating machinery in
> industry. 3)

However, the growth of negotiating machinery,
and collective bargaining, cannot take place unless
the employer is prepared to recognise the legiti-
macy of the union's, or a particular union's bargaining role. In short, trade union recognition
is a pre-condition of collective bargaining. To
assist unions in their quest for recognition, the
EPA provided, under Sections 11-16, a procedure
whereby employers reluctant to accede to recognition
claims could, in given circumstances, and at later
stages of the procedure, be placed under appreciable
statute derivative pressure to recognise the union/s
invoking the procedure. Within that procedure, a
role was prescribed for ACAS which, in the light of
gathering experience, proved to be damaging to the
reputation of the service. This was because ACAS
was placed, by statute, in the position of appearing
to employers as the advocate of the claimant union's
cause. The appearance may have been false and the
complex procedure imperfectly understood by many
employers concerned, but there can be no doubt that
for a period, and in the perception of too many
employers, ACAS did not behave _impartially_. Essentially for this reason, none of seventy or so ACAS
personnel we interviewed regretted the passing of

'Section 11' and its associated sections. These
were repealed by the Employment Act 1980.
     The above comments on the now defunct statut-
ory recognition procedure have been introduced in
order to emphasise two main points - the dangers to
the impartiality of ACAS, an impartiality much
prized by all involved, that possibly lurk in over
detailed statutory duties, and the fact that despite the repeal of the statutory procedure, the
statutory duty to encourage the extension of collective bargaining remains. Although the last Conservative Government made many far-reaching and
commonly controversial changes to the body of
industrial relations legislation, and the process
seems likely to continue under the present Conservative Government, Section 1 of the EPA, which includes the extension of the collective bargaining duty,
has been left untouched. This is also true for
Sections 2 - 6 of the Act which apply directly to
the service.
     So it now rests with ACAS itself to decide its
own procedures, to establish its own criteria for
handling any trade union recognition issue in which
it becomes involved. That it does become so involved was made known to us by ACAS personnel. In the
absence of public comment to the contrary, the involvement presumably occurs in a non-controversial
way. It also seems reasonable to claim that the
duty to encourage the extension of collective bargaining, with its implied duty to facilitate trade
union recognition, is not carried out in a prosely-
tising manner. Although the balance of CBI and
TUC membership within the Council would almost certainly prevent the development of such a manner,
from our interviews with advisers we gained the
impression that on this issue, as on others, the
advisers were pragmatists rather than crusaders and
would be at pains to avoid accusations of partiality. In the context of encouraging collective bargaining, the encouragement given is likely to be in
the nature of an ACAS adviser explaining the pros
and cons of trade union recognition and of collective bargaining to an uncertain employer who has recently been faced with a recognition claim. Whether
encouragement to recognise the union is actually
given would probably be very much dependent on circumstances because the overriding duty is seen as -
the improvement of industrial relations. The extension of collective bargaining rights to a particular
union could well disrupt stable industrial relations
if, for example, rival unions to the new claimant

union were well established at the location in question. Collective bargaining carried out or attempted by a union which has limited and apathetic support could damage employer/employee relationships.

Despite what has just been said it can be argued that the wording of Section 1(2) is unfortunate. The wording seems to indicate that the improvement of industrial relations and the extension of collective bargaining are automatically connected, even inter-dependent. On some views, that is a dubious even highly contentious proposition. For some employers, so the argument would run, and possibly some among their various workforces, collective bargaining might appear to be the negation of good industrial relations. The automatic compatibility (apparently assumed by the legislators) of the improvement of industrial relations with the extension of collective bargaining can be sharply questioned and recently has been by the influential Institute of Directors. Apparently the letter in question made the following claims.4)

There was much less support for the dogmatic view that the expansion of collective bargaining which must be accompanied by a growth in trade union membership was necessarily the best way forward. Among employers and employees there was altogether a more pragmatic attitude towards collective bargaining and trade union membership. The Institute believed that the terms of reference for ACAS should be deliberately open ended and should aim to promote the improvement of employee relations and encourage mutual respect between employers and employees by means of consultation and cooperation at the place of work.

A number of comments seem to be appropriate to the above claims. The terms of reference of ACAS could hardly be more open ended than they currently are - promoting the improvement of industrial relations. The reference to consultation is specifically covered in Section 4(1) of the EPA:

> (c) machinery for the negotiation of terms and conditions of employment, and for joint consultation;

so arguably is co-operation;

> (e) questions relating to communication between employers and workers; (Workers, it is to be noted, not trade union members or

202

representatives)

The reference to 'pragmatic attitude' towards collective bargaining and trade union membership is interesting. Such an attitude, as we have
several times pointed out, is shared by ACAS advisers. If there is a 'dogmatic view' that the expansion of collective bargaining is 'the best way
forward' we would maintain, from the research experience, that dogmatism is not a characteristic
of ACAS advisory personnel, or of their modus oper-
andi.

The inclusion of 'encouraging the extension of
collective bargaining' among the ACAS statutory
duties can be seen as the logical development of a
public policy adopted in 1917 to promote constructive dialogue between employers and organised workpeople. Such a policy was incorporated in the
various nationalisation acts. It was applied, as
an operational reality, by government through the
Whitley Council system of pay negotiations with
civil service unions. The validity of the policy
has recently been re-affirmed, albeit obliquely, by
the judiciary, the High Court having ruled that
the ban on unions at the Government Communications
Headquarters was unlawful. 5)

Good and bad industrial relations

The centrality of collective bargaining in any discussion of good and bad industrial relations is
very evident. Many quotations, from a wide variety
of sources, could be assembled to support that view.
Two will suffice to illustrate the point.

> ...workers, where they so wish, should have
> the right to negotiate collectively, through
> their trade union or unions, with their
> employer 6)

That might be thought to emanate from a trade
union source but in fact, it constituted one of the
four 'principles that the Government regards as
fundamental'. The Government concerned was the
Conservative Government which enacted the highly
controversial, and as things turned out, largely
strife promoting Industrial Relations Act 1971.

The second quotation is from a trade union
source.

The only effective method of conducting indust-

rial relations in an industrialised and demo-
cratic society is through voluntary collective
bargaining leading to agreements between trade
unions and employers. 7)

Such was the first sentence of - Good Industrial Relations - published by the TUC in 1971. The
term - good industrial relations - is rarely used
in the titles of published material but two academic
authors who have recently and separately used the
phrase in this way are John Purcell 8) and John
Dobson 9). John Purcell's book is a fuller account,
within a discussion of theory, of the CIR's achievements and represents a development from his earlier
work which was commented upon in Chapter Seven.
John Dobson's article poses the question, as its
title - what is good industrial relations? After
reviewing pluralist and Marxist approaches to
industrial relations, Dobson reaches the not unsur-
prising conclusion that, 'even among industrial
relations specialists there is no agreement of what
constitutes good industrial relations'. He main-
tains that compared to the pluralist approach to
industrial relations the radical approach 'is much
more concerned with control, which means that the
adjudicator of good industrial relations must decide whose side he is on - what is good for the
worker may not be good for the employer, and vice
versa.' Further, it can be seen that the work of
ACAS;

is the embodiment of a pluralist approach to
good industrial relations. ...Jim Mortimer,
the recently retired chairman of ACAS, in a
review of the work of ACAS showed his belief
in a pluralist approach when he defined good
industrial relations as 'the achievement by
all concerned of their respective objectives'.
10) Reflecting of course the pluralist assumption that such a course is possible. 11)

Without setting out systematically to test the
validity of the particular perceptions of the ACAS
role just expressed, we thought that there would
nevertheless be point in seeking to obtain the views
of advisers on bad and good industrial relations.
Knowing that ACAS has no institutional, collective
definitions of such terms we were confident that
there could be no pat, party line response to our
question. This proved to be the case.
Each member of the ACAS staff interviewed was

asked whether he would be prepared to write, at a
time convenient to himself, a brief description of
his understanding of the terms ' good industrial
relations'and 'bad industrial relations'. Twenty one
advisers and ACAS managers with advisory experience
set down their thoughts for us. No claim is made
by the respondents, or by us, that these descriptions constitute full accounts of the personal
models of industrial relations systems which advisory staff construct for themselves. What we do
claim is that the definitions provide useful in-
sights into a collection of views and values that
advisers hold to be important in their approach to
the improvement of industrial relations.

As could be expected, the pairs of definitions
vary in length and content. While they are all of
interest, presenting the full collection verbatim
would occupy too much space. A selection has therefore been made by way of paraphrase, partial and
full quotations.

One or two definitions were of a broad, philo-
sophical nature in which the words trust and mistrust were prominent. For example, bad industrial
relations constituted, 'the disregard of human dig-
nity and the need for trust'. By contrast good industrial relations were illustrated by, 'a situation
in which exists a lively appreciation on the part of
employees of what they are doing and why they are
doing it based upon trust and appreciation of the
employer's situation on the one hand, and a demons-
trably compassionate, considerate and trustful attitude to his employees on the part of the employer,
on the other'.

One comment was to the effect that the distinction between good and bad industrial relations was
akin to that between states of happiness and unhap-
piness. The difference could be recognised and experienced readily enough but describing the two
states in an articulate way was much more difficult.

The following pair of definitions is reasonably
typical of a number of others:

> Good industrial relations exist where areas of
> conflict have been reduced to the minimum
> possible with the parties trying to find solu-
> tions which minimise loss for the other - both
> sides concentrating on areas of mutual accom-
> modation. This co-operative state is often,
> although not exclusively, achieved through good
> communications, consultation and a degree of

205

participation.

Ideally a state of good I.R. exists when all parties involved adjudge it to be good, both from their own point of view and the other party's.

Bad industrial relations occur where sectional interests are not sufficiently limited, controlled, channelled or seen as justifiable. Factors normally present are poor communications, inadequate consultation, lack of common purpose, mistrust and resistance to change resulting in apathy or friction.

The above two descriptions use a number of key words eg accommodation, consultation, communications, that appear in many of the definitions. Accommodation may sometimes be formulated as equilibrium eg:

My definition of good industrial relations would be a state of equilibrium. At unit/company level the management would be reasonably satisfied with the productivity/output levels for the cost of the labour force. Employees would be reasonably satisfied with the effort/reward ratio, working conditions and management's use of authority. This state of equilibrium can be affected by external forces or a change in the power balance between the parties due to events in the organisation.

The following is one of the contexts for another of the key words - communications which forms virtually the leitmotiv of the collection of quotations.

Perhaps the most significant features which will help to establish 'good I.R.' are effective and consistent communications (both verbal and written), genuine consultation as a prelude to decision-making and honest rather than tactical negotiations on all matters with a direct bearing on terms and conditions of employment. Mutual understanding and shared perceptions are therefore, in my view, of greater import than 'mechanics' in establishing and maintaining good I.R.

The essential dynamism of industrial relations was brought out in the following definitions:

It seems to me that good IR varies through time and place. There are two essential ingredients, freedom from production-stopping strife and working efficiency. (I see no merit in a regime which buys itself peace at the price of its own viability - or, indeed, at the expense of its customers, if it has a strong position in the market; or at the price of setting a high and unrealistic wage level and thus distorting the labour market in its recruitment area). Throughout, I think there should be desirably a sense of felt fairness and that sense will vary according to the type of industry, its location, the make-up of the labour force, and the time in which the organisation is operating. What was acceptable 30 years ago may no longer be acceptable.

It follows that a balance has to be struck and the art comes in both management and, to some extent, union leaders understanding the needs of the moment. All the needs have to be met, though obviously greater emphasis may be given to one rather than another in the short run. To ignore a facet in the long term must be to court trouble.

The following thoughtful account also includes definitions of industrial relations:

It seems to me that there are many definitions of industrial relations, for example,

1 Regulation - which can take various forms, for example, the regulation of working relationships between an employer and his employees - sometimes represented collectively by trade unions. There is also job regulation, wage regulation etc., but the whole approach of regulation appears to me to imply a degree of control and hence is negative, but it has to be recognised as an element of industrial relations.

2 Techniques - frequently employers seek to evolve their industrial relations policies through the application of techniques (often in isolation), for example they examine

various systems of recruitment, training, work organisation, payment structures, etc. The approach to such evolution of policy is very often by asking questions either of themselves or of someone from ACAS, for example should we have incentives. If so, should they be group or individual incentives. If such an approach is part of a considered strategy, well and good, but if it is fragmented it is attended by considerable danger.

3 <u>Industrial Relations based on non-policies</u> - this is the manifestation of the cult of the great amateur. His method of tackling indust-rial relations is strictly informal and ad hoc. It relies on little more than disjointed chats to individual members of the workforce supple-mented by the so-called 'open door' arrange-ment. In this way the amateur considers he can pick up indications of problems affecting his workforce and deal with them.

4 <u>The TUC</u> - probably claims that solely the establishment of collective bargaining equates precisely with the achievement of good indust-rial relations.

5 I would reject all these approaches and others in isolation as limited, restrictive and lacking a necessary in-built power of review. My broad definition of sound indust-rial relations would be "the establishment followed by the maintenance (through regular, frequent and fundamental review) of a climate of confidence between management and employees within the organisation".

6 I envisage initiatives to achieve such a purpose to be almost invariably taken by man-agement. The initiatives could involve all of the approaches set out above at different times and could involve the use of other skills and techniques for example good communications, consultation, employee involvement and could well include both formal and informal arrange-ments, but the philosophy set out above having been established, the method of achieving the objective of that philosophy would be essen-tially pragmatic. My belief is that this is what ACAS is seeking to do but might not have spelled it out in exactly this way.

This climate of confidence approach also features strongly in the last definitions to be quoted.

I will preface my 'definition' with a fairly short explanation of the considerations and reasoning which it seeks to encapsulate, thus:

1) Industrial relations are the attitudinal aspects of management - employee relations (as distinct from what I would term the administrative aspects, e.g. personnel records, payment of wages, etc.).

2) Industrial relations are an integral factor in business operations, contributing to and affected by the relative success or failure of the business.

3) Businesses are dynamic, as are the relevant social standards (e.g. trade union attitudes, employee expectations, etc.) and the industrial relations 'package' in each business should reflect this factor.

4) Using a form of imagery, I see industrial relations as a chain with 4 main links, namely:

i) basic principles, which might loosely be termed philosophy - the fundamental decisions by the owners and/or senior managers as to where along the "management by coercion" - "management by consent" spectrum an organisation wishes to conduct its industrial relations. This should be a conscious decision based on an understanding of the range of options and the implications of whatever decision is taken.

ii) policies - the operating principles for specific aspects, e.g. recruitment, selection, training, communications, consultation, negotiation, terms and conditions, health and safety, working conditions, etc., which should reflect the 'philosophy' and which, so far as practicable, should be complementary and consistent with one another.

iii) procedures - the systems and arrangements designed to implement policies in the day-to-day conduct of the business, which should therefore reflect those policies and, so far as practicable, be complementary and consistent with one another.

iv) people - that is those employees (management, supervision and employee representatives) who have responsibilities for formulating and/or implementing policies and procedures, whether through communication, consultation or negotiation.

v) the 'chain' will be weakened either by omission, inadequacy or inconsistency at any stage in any particular aspect (e.g. if communications policies are not matched by effective procedural arrangements and/or adequate training in communications skills of the people concerned) and industrial relations will be less good in consequence.

In the context of the above description, I would broadly define good industrial relations as a climate in which management and employees effectively contribute to the achievement of their objectives through the development of policies which

i)   are consistent with and contribute to the overall objectives of the business

ii) are consistent and compatible with one another

iii) are supported by effective procedures, practices and people

iv)   take account of the dynamics of business operations and social standards

v)   are founded on mutual respect and trust, recognizing the special role and importance of good communications, and

vi) are effective in resolving disputes and differences in a constructive manner without recourse to compulsion, coercion or other sanctions.

From the sample of quotations given, it is evident that advisers do not hold simplistic views

about what constitutes good and bad industrial
relations or about the methods by which bad industrial relations might become good industrial relations. Those views have been formed from extensive
practical experience in a wide variety of industrial relations situations. The extent to which
those views, in conjunction with other factors,
can bring about an observable improvement in the
total industrial relations system naturally remains
problematic. (It will have been noted that all the
definitions relate to micro, single organisation
situations and not to the macro level of industrial
relations activity). ACAS advisers are under no
illusion that they can effect radical improvements
to the general state of industrial relations in
Britain. Operating in its conciliation mode, and
less frequently in its arbitration mode, ACAS can
sometimes resolve industrial disputes and thereby
assist conflict reduction. But many of the more
serious disputes of recent years have arisen in
the public sector and as a consequence of a particular government's stance on a particular payment
or efficiency issue. In such circumstances, it is
difficult to see what role ACAS advisers could play.
   The role they can play, as the evidence has
demonstrated, is a useful and appreciated one,
among the myriad locations of industrial relations
which lie outside the realm of highly publicised
set-piece battles in which the hand of government
is obvious or barely concealed. The total actual
good achieved among the myriad locations may be
modest in relation to what needs to be done in the
total industrial relations system. More could be
done if more resources were made available, advisers being convinced that the untapped, potential
demand for advice is large scale. But even so, to
expect major reforms to be achieved via the advisory activity is unrealistic and may reflect a
fundamental misunderstanding of the precise statutory duty placed on ACAS. That duty has been carefully worded under Section 1(2) of the EPA 75 not
as - improving industrial relations - but as 'the
general duty of promoting the improvement of industrial relations'. (emphasis added)
   The main burden of improving industrial relations must rest with the direct participants, with
employers, trade unions - and government in its
various roles of employer, law maker, economic
manager etc. The burden may be eased by independent conciliation, arbitration - and advisory work
but cannot be transferred to ACAS. Advisory work

itself will only have a favourable impact so long
as those to whom the advice is given find it acceptable. That the advice is widely acceptable, and
the reasons for this state of affairs, have been
demonstrated in this book. It seems fitting therefore, to leave the last words of our study to those
whose opinions should matter most - the clients.

The phrase used above - widely acceptable -
was chosen because, as we have pointed out, advice
is not invariably accepted. Criticisms are sometimes made that advice is insufficiently positive
or imaginative or as stated here limited in character:

> There are restrictions on the practical
> things ACAS can do, eg work study.

However, frequent reference has been made to
ACAS advisory competence in the procedural and wage
payment systems areas:

> Disciplinary disputes which were a major source
> of industrial relations irritation reduced to
> a trickle and now dealt with quickly and
> sensibly.

> The adviser's contribution both in training
> and 'uniting' the joint (job evaluation) panel
> was excellent. His advice inevitably led to a
> greater understanding of the principles of
> job evaluation and the adviser's was a major
> contribution to the successful conclusion of
> the exercise.

> Pay anomalies have almost been eradicated -
> work practice is more open - management are
> now aware that members cannot be switched from
> job to job without considering the effect on
> the members. Jobs advertised now carry job
> grading and salary for the job. (Union)

Some advisory interventions have averted possible disputes, restored economic viability and
saved jobs:

> If the company had not sought advice and acted
> on it, it is quite likely that at some time in
> the future a quite serious dispute would have
> arisen.

> Company was heading for possible bankruptcy

due to lack of work and work we did have being done at a loss - now much healthier financially and workforce much happier.

The entire organisation would have been disbanded and all 55 operatives, at this branch, out of work.

Some small companies which have been helped, believe much remains to be done:

I think if the service was made more generally known especially to managers of small companies disputes of this type I had would not arise.

The services of ACAS are not used to anything like the degree demanded by the need, particularly in the many thousands of medium to small firms.

Large companies (the quotation is not an isolated one) also value advice:

Contact with ACAS is generally to keep abreast of a variety of matters and for general discussion. We value the contact and service very much. (Co with 14,000 employees)

Impartiality remains central to acceptability:

ACAS were viewed by our own employees as totally unbiased - hence the reason for their involvement. (a company)

Management were able to accept and understand the advice given as the neutral point of view. (a union)

Union involvement is new to us - they (ACAS advisers) were able to 'cool' the situation and explain the union position factually and impartially. (a company)

It did improve the relationship with staff locally by giving them an opportunity to talk together with an independent body. (a company)

The fact that it (ACAS) is impartial helps tremendously with the shop floor. (a company)

Perhaps the very last words should be those
with which we began:

How far that little candle throws his beams!
So shines a good deed in a naughty world.

NOTES AND REFERENCES

1. In Place of Strife - a Policy for Industrial Relations, Cmnd. 3888, HMSO, (1969),p.8.
2. Department of Trade Report of the Committee
of Inquiry on Industrial Democracy, Chairman Lord
Bullock, Cmnd. 6706, HMSO, (1977).
3. Report of Royal Commission on Trade Unions
and Employers' Associations 1965-1968, Cmnd. 3623,
HMSO, (1968), para 433, p.115.
4. The Times, 11 June 1984. Guardian, 21
June 1984.
5. Regina v Secretary of State for the Foreign
and Commonwealth Office and Another, ex parte
Council of Civil Service Unions and Others Law
Report, The Times, 17 July 1984.
6. Industrial Relations Bill Consultative
Document, Department of Employment and Productivity,
(1970), p.2.
7. Good Industrial Relations, A guide for
negotiators, Trades Union Congress, (1971), p.5.
8. Purcell, Good Industrial Relations : Theory
and Practice.
9. John R. Dobson, 'What is Good Industrial
Relations?' Employee Relations, 4,2 (1982), pp.5 -
10.
10. J. Mortimer, 'ACAS in a Changing Climate:
A force for good IR?',Personnel Management, vol.13,
no.2 (February 1981), p.22.
11. Dobson, 'What is Good Industrial Relations?'
p.7.

Appendix A

RESEARCH RATIONALE AND METHODOLOGY

Apart from ACAS's own explanatory material very
little had been published about the advisory function when ideas about research into that function
were being considered in 1981. This lack of information and independent commentary about advisory
work added weight to the two main reasons for undertaking the research.

By 1981 ACAS had gained appreciable industrial
relations experience and remained sufficiently
different from its predecessor institutions to justify its advisory work being examined and discussed
in some detail. The second and major reason was to
form some assessment, inevitably on a sample basis,
of the effectiveness of advisory work. This seemed
an especially justified reason in respect of an
organisation required by law to promote the improvement of industrial relations. It was thought that
the evaluation part of the enquiry would obviously
make more sense if it was preceded by a brief account of how ACAS came to be established and by an
adequate description and discussion of the ways in
which ACAS organised and carried out its advisory
duties. That account, description and discussion
became the first three chapters of the book.

Certain features of the discussion are examined
in greater depth in later chapters after the analysis of the evaluative evidence from ACAS clients and
interested parties such as employers' associations,
has been completed. By presenting the material in
this sequence, it was thought that a more informed
judgement about the ACAS advisory role could be made.
For example, to have launched, in the early part of
the book, into the debate about whether the advisory
service should remain free or become fee charging,
would have been ill-conceived because an adequate
context for that debate, as well as for various
other issues, first needed to be established.

To return to the origins of the research, sufficient funds were made available by the SSRC (now
ESRC) for a pilot study to be undertaken during
1982 and 1983 into the advisory role of ACAS. The
research grant enabled one full-time research assistant to be employed on the project. Pilot study
implies something of an exploratory nature requiring
samples of relevant phenomena to be observed with a
view to further and more detailed work being carried
out. Given the essential transactional nature of

advisory work, and the volume of such work, it
seemed plain that information and opinions would
need to be gathered from <u>samples</u> of those engaged
in the transaction of advice giving and advice
receiving.

Access to the advice givers was rightly pre-
sumed to be easier to obtain than access to the
advice receivers, the clients. ACAS is a public
institution, publicly funded and publicly accountable and therefore pre-disposed to be receptive to
requests for information. By contrast, the trans-
actions between the ACAS advisers and their client
companies/trade unions are private and confidential.
Unless companies and trade unions could recognise
this to be the case, very little could be achieved
by way of advisory or conciliation and arbitration work. Their consent is necessary, for example, before publication of advisory case studies in
ACAS annual reports can be made. A means had therefore to be sought for obtaining the consent of a
sample of ACAS clients to answer questions the
researchers might put to them.

As could be expected, only ACAS has a list of
institutions with which it has had dealings. Because of the confidentiality bond between ACAS and
its clients, and the confidential status of the
records kept on all advisory work carried out, it
was both proper and the only feasible effective
means, for ACAS itself to invite a sample of clients
to co-operate in the research. ACAS generously
agreed to send out such invitations to samples of
their clients, both in relation to advisory visits
and to in-depth work. With access to advisers and
to clients assured in principle, it became necessary to make the final decisions about the questions
to be put and about the size and characteristics of
the sample populations of clients and advisers to
be approached.

The question of samples raised a number of interesting issues. A sensible starting point in regard to clients seemed to be the linking of any
samples chosen to the operational and statistical
methods employed by ACAS itself. It will be seen
from Chapter Two that in its annual reports ACAS
presents statistics for in-depth work and advisory
visits separately and in relation to four main criteria - subject matter of advice, industry group,
size of organisation and ACAS region. Could representative samples of clients based on one or more
of these criteria be constructed and approached?

In theory representatives samples of <u>potential</u>

respondents could be constructed, at least on some of the criteria. It would be possible, for instance, to take some proportion of companies in particular size bands in particular industries as a sample. To add the dimension of subject-matter would be more difficult because advice about more than one subject is commonly given at a visit and during in-depth work. To design a sample on one or more of the criteria mentioned would entail a detailed and probably lengthy examination of ACAS records (they are not computerised), something which ACAS itself could not do because of limited resources and something which it is unlikely to allow others to do because of the confidentiality bond between the service and its clients. In any event, the benefits of trying to construct a sample in this way are not self-evident, not least because of the unknown nature and level of any response on any particular criterion such as size of organisation or type of industry.

There were two other complications to consider. While frequency of mention of a particular subject, of a particular size of organisation, gives some indication of the importance of those subjects and sizes for the work of advisers, the frequencies in themselves can tell us nothing about whether advisory work is thought to be more effective in organisation size A than in organisation size B. To omit organisation size B or industry group X from the enquiry because of infrequency of mention of B and X might be to omit from the evaluation processes instances of where the best or worst work was done. Furthermore, as is pointed out in Chapter Two, the published ACAS statistics on which some sort of sample would have to be based, treat all pieces of work as equal in terms of notional time consumed. The relevant tables present a simple numerical count of activities, by type, carried out and give no indication of the actual time spent on them. Yet it is known that the man-days taken up by projects, for example, can vary extensively. A better approach to constructing a representative sample could perhaps be made if ranges of man-days, by type of advisory activity, were available from the statistics, on the reasonable assumption that the amount of advisory time consumed is a good initial measure of the significance of the advisory intervention in question.

Even if the difficulties mentioned above could be overcome, the problem would remain of deciding whether the client's evaluation of advisory work

should be sought in one or more regions. It is
difficult to conceive that any single region in
terms of its industrial and employment structure
could serve as a fully representative sample of the
nation. Alternatively, it would be possible, for
example, to select two possibly contrasting English
regions for study. Experience in the highly industrialised North West could be compared to that in
the far less industrialised South West. To extend
the range of comparisons perhaps one non-English
region should be included but on what rational let
alone national grounds should the choice be made
between Scotland and Wales?
     Having thought about these various complica-
tions it was decided to consider a different sampling approach by concentrating on the central purpose of the enquiry, that being the search for a
more accurate gauge than had existed hitherto, of
advisory effectiveness. In seeking the client's
evaluation of advisory work the critical factor was
time - the time for which the memories of busy
managers and workers' representatives would remain
fresh about the advisory work in which they themselves had been involved. Not only would memories
fade but the longer the intervals between the completion of a visit or project and our enquiry, the
greater the risk would be that some of the managers
and trade unionists concerned would have moved
elsewhere. Furthermore, the longer the period between the advisory intervention and our enquiry the
greater would be the probability of the assessment
of the impact of the advice being obscured by new
factors entering a particular industrial relations
situation. Careful estimates had therefore to be
made about the time intervals in question, ie between advisory recommendations being made to a client
and our evaluation request.
     That consideration in turn strengthened the
view that the focus of sampling concern should shift
from, for example, subject or industry group to
time - the time periods being long enough for the
type of work undertaken. If requests for co-operation with our research could be sent to ALL clients
for decided periods, the sampling difficulties
associated with industry, size of firm, etc. might
well be avoided. Advisory visits, with their attendant paper work, usually occupy a day's work and
it was thought that a time sample of a complete
month's visits might, given sufficient client response, provide a reasonably sized sample and that
this might reflect a reasonable distribution of

218

replies by, size of firm, industry, etc. Pieces of
in-depth work take far more time than visits. The
work may be carried out in stages over a longish
period. A time sample of a year seemed appropriate
for this form of work.

Because of limited resources, it had already
been decided that clients signifying their readiness to volunteer information to us would do so by
completing a questionnaire and not by personal interviews which would have entailed substantial trav-
elling and subsistence costs. The possibility of
personal follow-up discussions,in a limited number of
instances, was allowed for by asking questionnaire
respondents if they would be prepared to talk to the
researchers. Most indicated that they were so prepared.

A questionnaire was first designed for advisory
visits and a pilot study was undertaken of visits
carried out during two consecutive months in one
English region. An account of the nature and findings of the study was subsequently published. As a
result of this initial experience, slight modifications were made to the questionnaire design, separate questionnaires were devised for in-depth work
and the decision was taken to seek client evaluation
of advisory visits and in-depth work in all nine regions. As mentioned above, the time samples were to
be one month for visits and one year for in-depth
work and ALL clients, including involved trade unions who are particularly prominent in in-depth work,
were to be invited to co-operate in the research.
As described in Chapters Four and Five, in terms of
the period of the year/s in which they were undertaken, the time-samples were not identical for each
region but were staggered in order to provide not
a single but a series of snapshots of advisory activity and evaluative comment. It is the analysis
of the 548 returned questionnaires, none of which
has been seen by any member of the ACAS staff, that
constitutes the core of the research. It is fair to
claim that no systematic evidence about ACAS advisory work has previously been gathered on this scale
by independent research.

In contrast to the complexities leading up to
the receipt of 548 completed questionnaires from
ACAS clients, it was a relatively simple matter to
make arrangements to visit each regional office of
ACAS and to interview a sample of advisers. More
information about the nature of the samples is given
in Chapter Three and the advisers' views on a range
of matters appear in that chapter and in Chapters

Seven, Eight and Nine. Each adviser was interviewed privately, usually with both researchers
present, and the interview followed a set pattern
which was flexibly applied. Interviews tended to
last for two to three hours but some were much
longer dependent on the status and associated experience of the person interviewed. As could be
expected from the nature of their work, the
advisers gave considered and articulate responses
to questions.

The methodology employed to question the interested parties, ie employers' associations, trade
unions in their formal institutional role, management consultants and training bodies, is described
in Chapter Six. Most of the written sources of
information pertinent to the research consist of
published and unpublished ACAS documents. Wherever
possible the source has been referenced.

Sample bias?

When considering the total evidence supplied by the
548 clients of ACAS in the research sample, it is
obvious that such clients constitute managers and
trade union representatives who, for the most part,
have been well pleased with the advisory service
received. The comment may therefore be made that
having only heard from satisfied clients our sample
is biased, the assumption being that dissatisfied
clients exist but, for whatever reasons, they have
chosen not to express their dissatisfaction to the
researchers. A number of observations may be made
on that comment.

As stated previously, the invitation from ACAS
to co-operate in our research was sent to the total
populations of clients for the periods of time concerned. Assuming their existence, dissatisfied
clients therefore had the same opportunity as other
clients to express their opinions and on the same
understanding as other respondents, that information
and comment would go directly to the researchers and
not to ACAS. It would be a simple enough tactic for
a critical client to indicate his readiness to co-
operate in the research in order to receive a questionnaire which he could 'complete' by perhaps a
page of comment sharply critical of ACAS, and then
return, even possibly anonymously, to the researchers. We can only say that we received no questionnaire of that kind. We should also point out that
the postal cost of returning a questionnaire was
borne by the research budget in order to encourage

a high response rate from client populations - whatever their views.

Critics of public bodies, especially if they
are aggrieved and articulate critics, are not
usually slow to come forward but we have had no
client evaluation that fell into that category. In
fact, the evidence pointed the other way, letters
and phone calls being received to the effect that
although the questionnaire was not appropriate to
the circumstances in question, such clients valued
ACAS assistance. Some clients in this category
went to appreciable trouble to record their experiences and assessments and the latter can be fairly
summarised by the opinion of one client who had
'always found ACAS staff very helpful'.

The ACAS invitation to its clients to co-operate in our research asked the client to indicate
'yes', or 'no' to co-operation. Eighty six 'nos' were
returned in respect of in-depth work. The corresponding negative response for visits was 104. Inquiries were made of each of the 190 clients who
actually signified that they did not wish to take
part in the research. While the major purpose of
the enquiries was to determine the reasons for this
reaction, the possibility of dissatisfaction with
ACAS remained a factor to be borne in mind. As
ignoring the invitation to co-operate in the research could also be interpreted as saying   no, was
a formal recorded ' no ' indicative simply of
politeness or of other factors   possibly bearing on
the effectiveness of ACAS advice?

In 105 of the 190 instances no reason was given
for declining the invitation to co-operate. To
speculate why this should be so seems less profitable than concentrating on the other responses. The
remaining 85 answers proved to be mundane rather
than indirectly indicative of the client's evaluation of advice. In 28 cases either the individuals
concerned had left or retired from their companies
or the organisations concerned had ceased trading.
Twenty tree respondents claimed that the ACAS involvement in their organisations had been insufficient to warrant assessment. Fourteen respondents
stated that they had insufficient time to spare to
co-operate with the research project. It is tempting to think that if pressed further, a fair number
of those who had given no reason for declining to
take part in our inquiry might have opted for the
insufficient time to spare response. The remaining
20 of the 85 answers were scattered across a variety
of explanations, each insufficient in itself to seem

particularly important, eg understaffed, invitation
already received at head office.

Taking the total population of 190 negative responses to the research co-operation invitation,
and the dozen or so types of reason they embraced,
there is no hint, let alone a clear indication, that
such responses were due to dissatisfaction with ACAS
advisory help, or with ACAS work more generally, or
to disquiet about the research undertaking itself.
The one response possibly reflecting misgivings of
that sort was expressed cryptically as 'ACAS help
inappropriate to research'.

So much then for what we were able to glean
about reasons for non co-operation in the research.
Another and related line of enquiry concerned the
possible reasons why a proportion of those clients
who had agreed to co-operate in the research had
subsequently failed to return questionnaires.
There seemed to be more scope for profitable speculation on this matter. A client might regard the
questionnaire as too long, too complicated, inappropriate for his specific circumstances. He might
have had second thoughts about the value of the advice received or about the wisdom of venturing an
evaluation. It was decided to transform such lines
of thought into a systematic enquiry which, for
in-depth work, was carried out in five regions.
At the time in question, 76 clients were telephoned,
sometimes more than once, to establish how matters
stood in regard to the return of questionnaires.
Fourteen of the 76 questionnaires were eventually
returned but it is not possible to say whether this
was in any way due to what clients may have perceived as a form of progress chasing on our part.

In the event, three main reasons were advanced
to explain the non-return of questionnaires -
'technical' difficulties; staff turnover; pressure
of work. In a small number of cases the questionnaire had been thought too long, or had been mislaid
in transmission between the hierarchical levels of
an organisation. More frequent reference was
made to changes in personnel to account for the non
completion of questionnaires. In other words, key
individuals who had been closely involved in the
in-depth work had moved elsewhere. This turnover
factor applied to trade union officers as well as
to managers. But pressure of work on the individuals concerned appeared to be the principal reason
for not having returned questionnaires. In the
course of telephone conversations with those concerned, evaluative comments on ACAS were made by these

representatives of ACAS clients. Most, not all, of
such comments were appreciative - typical examples
being, from separate instances, - 'can't speak too
highly'; 'delighted with everything they've done';
'found them extremely helpful'; 'fairly useful -
has usually resulted in an improvement.' The diss-
enters, two, expressed their measures of dissatisfaction as disappointment following the outcome
of an unfair dismissal case, and a non committal
evaluation containing a suggestion that ACAS had not
looked at things thoroughly enough and had perhaps
reached certain conclusions too quickly.

A similar programme of enquiries was carried
out regarding the non-return of questionnaires on
visits. Fifty five clients in four regions were
approached by telephone and a similar pattern of
responses, if with notably different emphases, to
that of in-depth work, emerged. In a higher and
largest single proportion of instances, the questionnaire was thought inappropriate to the circumstances
- as, for example, 'the chap from ACAS had just
dropped in for a chat' this being a client's summary
of a non-requested visit. Similar instances were
described as 'have a man who calls in every 6
months, find it most valuable'; 'a new ACAS man
called to introduce himself - I therefore can't
answer most of the questions'. Staff turnover
hardly featured as an explanation for non-completion
of questionnaires but pressure of work was mentioned
several times. In 30 instances it proved impossible
to ascertain the reason for the non-return of the
questionnaire or to discuss the general ACAS role
with a client to whom a visit had been paid. But
on the evidence of the conversations where explanations were offered, we have no reason to suppose
that silence should be equated with hostility to
ACAS. Experience gained from this telephone follow-
up enquiry suggested that silence probably had much
more to do with the difficulties associated with
ensuring that appropriate messages reached potential
respondents it had been impossible to talk to directly and with a widespread disinclination to
fill out more forms than are thought to be essential.
Whatever may be thought about over-egging the
pudding, it seems only fair, from the volume and
nature of the evidence we have from the various
telephone conversations, to re-affirm the satisfaction expressed by ACAS clients with ACAS advisory
assistance. One quotation will suffice - 'very
useful - they do a very effective job'. As far as
the follow-up sampling of visits described above was

Appendix A

concerned, no client expressed dissatisfaction with
ACAS in the telephone conversations that occurred.
   From what has been described in the past few
pages, it will be seen that serious attempts were
made to encourage higher response rates of returned
questionnaires and that within such attempts there
resided the possibility of a wider range of assessments of advisory visits and in-depth work emerging
than had been expressed in the returned questionnaires. We may have had some success in improving
response rates but overall the additional evidence
does not alter the general evaluation by clients
of ACAS advice as well pleased. Thus within the
limited means at our disposal we did go some way to
seeking an answer to the question of whether our
sample of evaluations by clients constituted a
sample biased in the direction of satisfied clients.
We have reported on what we found from our additional enquiries and conclude with the claim that whatever views are held on the nature of the sample, the
value of the evidence gathered from 548 clients
should greatly outweigh the value of conjecture
based on an assumption of a biased sample.

Appendix B

ACAS REPORTS AND PUBLICATIONS

This is ACAS
Advice on Personnel Management and Industrial
Relations Practice
Conciliation between Individuals and Employers
Assistance with Industrial Relations Problems
Improving Industrial Relations - A Joint
Responsibility
Conciliation, Arbitration, Mediation in Trade
Disputes
Industrial Relations Handbook (available from
HMSO price £5)

Booklets

Advisory Booklet No 1 Job evaluation
Advisory Booklet No 2 Introduction to payment
systems
Advisory Booklet No 3 Personnel records
Advisory Booklet No 4 Labour turnover
Advisory Booklet No 5 Absence
Advisory Booklet No 6 Recruitment and selection
Advisory Booklet No 7 Induction of new employees
Advisory Booklet No 8 Workplace communications
Advisory Booklet No 9 The company handbook
The ACAS Role in Conciliation, Arbitration and
Mediation
An Industrial Relations Advisory Service - The
ACAS Role
Conciliation by ACAS in complaints by indivi-
duals to Industrial Tribunals

Discussion papers

1 Developments in harmonisation
2 Collective bargaining in Britain : its extent and level

Codes of Practice

1 Disciplinary practice and procedures in
employment
2 Disclosure of information to trade unions
for collective bargaining purposes
3 Time off for trade union duties and activities (Codes of Practice are available from HMSO
price 15p each)

225

Appendix B

Annual Reports

First Annual Report 1975 (available from HMSO
price £1.20)
Annual Reports 1976-1982 are available from
ACAS
(Unless otherwise stated all ACAS publications
are free and are available from any ACAS office)

INDEX

ACAS
- Council 4, 37, 43-5, 50, 112, 148, 150-2, 165, 168-9, 201
- formation 3
- head office 40-5, 46, 49-50, 147, 163, 166
- independence 3-5, 147, 151
  - see also impartiality
- region 34-41
- statutory duties 5, 8-10, 192, 199-200, 211
  - see also Employment Protection Act
- terms of reference 8-10, 147, 202-3

advisers
- background etc. 51-6, 96-7
- generalist 37-8, 141-7
- grades 38
- numbers of 40
- period appointment 39, 54, 143-5
- self management 34, 47-9
- specialist 3, 9, 37-8, 141-7

advisory work
- advisory booklets 153
- advisory leaflets 153-4

Codes of Practice 148, 149-53, 166
demand related 15, 27, 30, 36, 43, 45, 167
development visits 13, 15, 43, 47, 64, 73, 79, 80, 153, 167
discussion papers 152
enquiry points 13, 39, 56, 154-7
evaluation of 12, 46-7, 49, 51, 212-14
- see also perceptions
follow-up visits 49, 64-5, 79
impartiality 3, 55-6, 69, 77, 79-80, 93, 96, 104-9, 119-26, 128-33, 134-7, 138-40, 174, 177, 178, 180, 181, 182, 190, 200-1
- see also ACAS independence and - payment issue
inquiry work 157-64
measurement of 6-7
operational guidelines 44-5, 48, 50, 169-73
- see also policy